To Marshall Wernick in friendship Al Mellman

A RADICAL
APPROACH
TO
JEWISH HISTORY

AL MELLMAN

ISBN #1-889534-64-1

Published by
Jay Street Publishers
155 West 72nd Street
New York, NY 10023

To contact author:
e-mail: amellman@lausd.k12.ca.us

To my children,
Jay and Martha,
Jeri and Ken,
and Kenny
who together are my future

CONTENTS

INTRODUCTION

No book begins *ab initio.* This one begins with great respect and affection for my father, Jacob Mellman, born in 1890 to very poor parents in Dureshova, Podolia, region of Czarist Russia, now a part of the Ukraine. He came to America in 1906, with little formal education, but great faith, enormous love for his extended family, and with a searching mind. Orthodox until he died, he still respected Jews of any stripe, except those who hid their Jewish roots.

He was beloved in St. Louis, Missouri by people of all races and creeds. His funeral cortege was one of the largest in the city's history, yet he never earned more than a subsistence income. Still, he was always charitable–so much so that he borrowed money so that those who came to his home or office would never be turned away empty-handed.

After siring his first son in 1916, Jake Mellman decided that he could not bring his son up to be a Jew unless he stopped working on Shabbos. He decided to become a lawyer, because he found that courts were closed on Saturday. With no formal education, but a tremendous love of learning and full of a determination not uncommon to the Jewish immigrants at that time, he completed his law degree at Washington University in 1921. He was the first of a distinguished line in the extended Mellman family to complete a college degree program.

From the moment he graduated until he died in 1963, he was true to his religious values, kept the Shabbos, and used it for learning, so that in a few years he had become expert in Talmud. From that time on he used his Shabbos to teach a group at the synagogue. His students adored him and one of their last acts, prior to his death, was the presentation of a new tallis to their teacher, Yankel Mellman. He was buried in that tallis.

It is almost irreverent to dedicate this book to my father; he not only understood my radicalism inside the Jewish community, he rejoiced in it. Jake Mellman was a constant writer of letters to the papers in which he took on those who did not live up to their public trust. It offended his moral fiber that elected or appointed officials misused their positions.

He was equally appalled by rabbis and synagogue leaders who oppressed their members. I learned righteous indignation from a master, and I also learned that there was a time and need for conciliation and consolation. I owe so much to my father that this book belongs to him. Some of my radicalism is a response to the unwillingness of leaders of the Jewish community to come to terms with modernity and scientific thought. Another part of my position stems from the relative illiteracy of most Jews. Jewish Education has failed them by leaving them without the underpinnings of knowledge and culture to be able to handle Jewish situations in a critical way. In America we need sharply different means of Jewish communication. To that end this book is written.

Others, too, have to be praised and thanked for their additions to my understanding of Jewish History and to some of the unusual theories that I suggest.

First, Rabbi Robert P. Jacobs, of St. Louis, Hillel Director at Washington University, in 1946, found me attending the university and searching for ideas. He fed me a good diet of books and discussions. Had it not been for Bob, who sent me to Brandeis Camp Institute the following year, I would probably still be working in the area of atomic physics and barely on the periphery of the Jewish Community.

At Brandeis Camp, I experienced for the first time a positive Jewish environment and I responded to that so emphatically that the rest of my life has been spent involved professionally in Jewish communal life. I even considered for several years becoming a rabbi. At Hebrew Union College in Cincinnati, I met the next major figure who influenced my thinking.

In 1950, Dr. Ellis Rivkin, professor of history, gave me the first taste of a critical approach to Jewish History. He is one of the seminal teachers and writers in the whole field of Jewish thought. It was he who taught me to use sources, and it was also Rivkin who demonstrated the efficacy of experimenting with new ideas and theories. He taught me to take every historian, including myself, with more than a grain of salt. In addition, his lectures opened the field of historiography to me. I wrote two unpublished, but graded, papers for him, which I still treasure. Some of the ideas in this book are built on those papers. The first was called, *The Rise and Fall of the Hasmonean Dynasty*, the other, *Amos Never Lived*. Dr. Rivkin, I still sit at your feet.

Also at Hebrew Union College, another giant affected my thinking and my life. Dr. Leo Baeck, the head of the Berlin Jewish Community under Hitler, and himself a survivor of a concentration camp, was brought to America as a visiting professor by President Nelson Glueck, the president of Hebrew Union College-Jewish Institute of Religion, and he gave an occasional lecture to the students.

One still sticks in my memory, although more than fifty years have passed. The title was *The Impact of the Printing Press on Judaism*. With immense erudition and noble humility, Dr. Baeck traced the story of the movable type press and the Gutenberg Revolution on Jewish life. He demonstrated the effect that universal availability of books had on the thought and structure of the Jewish community. He spoke about the German Jewish experience as it enfolded under the impact of modernism. Dr. Baeck helped me to begin the process of looking for causes of change and movements.

Finally, but certainly not the least, I must express at this late moment my gratitude and love for the man who first encouraged me to begin teaching. Sam Kaminker, a saint and educational genius, asked me in 1961 to teach at the College of Jewish Studies of the Union of American Hebrew Congregations in Los Angeles, where he was the dean. At the time, I needed the additional earnings, and agreed to teach persons who were working towards a certificate as a religious school teacher. I was shocked to find that I loved not only the act of teaching, but also the search for answers to historical problems. Sam responded, as I suppose he did to all of his teachers, by constantly challenging me to a new course and new ideas. I know of no other dean, who would call at 2 AM and say, "Al, I have an idea for your course, could you come over?"

No one could say "no" to Sam and neither did I. So I learned from this gentle son of a Chassidic rabbi, not only history, but also how to share a love for our people.

Let me add only one more, not an historian, but whose personality still affects every moment when I teach or lecture. Through Brandeis Camp, I met and eventually spent a whole summer with Max Helfman, one of the greatest American-Jewish musician and composer, and the Camp's Director of Music. I watched, and like every person who ever met and heard him, fell in love with him and Judaism. Max had the ability to communicate as only an artist can. He was able to have musically illiterate people sing with gusto and well. Beyond that he was the focus for a total cultural revolution on the American Jewish scene. There is hardly an American Jewish institution where his music is not used. Jewish music at camps was his milieu. No one who spent an hour in his class or at his table, will ever forget his charisma. Thousands of Jews are creative Jews simply because they allowed Max to affect them. More than twenty-five years after his death, I still hear people speaking of Max Helfman. Max, you are missed by me, too.

So, this book is to a large extent a reflection of my Dad, Rabbi Jacobs, Ellis Rivkin, Dr. Leo Baeck, Sam Kaminker and Max Helfman. If it succeeds in its purpose, it is a fitting tribute to them.

It would be only natural, but certainly fitting, that I pay my respects, love and thanks to my wife, Jan, who for the past more than forty years, has borne with me through so many professional trials and so many evenings alone at home, as I went out to deliver this lecture or that course. She understood how much this course and book has meant in my own spiritual development and the confirmation of my values. *Now on to Jewish History.*

PROLOGUE

This book is an attempt to develop an approach which will enable the reader to do several things with added knowledge and understanding. First of all, you will be able to avoid the pitfalls of relying on myths, which have been created in more primitive times to explain the past. Next, you will acquire a simple means of placing events on a timeline, and therefore begin the process of seeing the relationship between general world history and Jewish history. Finally, I hope that the understanding will help make you a more active and involved Jew, one who realizes that history can teach without involving mythology.

Jewish history has only been written in a usable form for about 175 years. Prior to that time whatever history writing, recorded by Jews, was encomious, with the sole purpose of idealizing the past heroes and for the establishment of Jewish pride. Only under the impact of modern science and historiography have Jewish historians begun the process of writing about the Jewish past critically and without chauvinism.

Today most Jewish history books are still written for the purpose of playing to Jewish ethnocentrism. "I am so proud to be a Jew" comes out on every page. Jews are the best thinkers and every good idea must be tied to a Jewish source.

In the early nineteenth century, particularly in Germany, scholars began to look at the past in order to understand it, rather than to glorify it; however, it was certainly evident that the writers and scholars were concerned that Judaism be placed in a proper and positive light. As a result, one school of thought that came about, which will be discussed in the context of this book, proposed that everything good was Jewish and everything Jewish was good.

Other schools of Jewish History were also developed in this same period. Some placed their themes in the light of the concomitant histories being written, which had a particular bias reflecting nationalistic approaches or religious attitudes. Much depended on which were the predominant scholars of the time or place or the prevailing political mood of the times.

For example, in Germany, where to be a Jew meant that you were identified by religion, Jewish historians were impelled by the milieu to stress completely the religious background of the Jew in the absence of the nationalistic threads that are a part of Jewish existence.

On the other hand, those Jewish writers who lived in Czarist Russia, where Jews were considered one of the many national groups, fostered a de-religionizing of Jewish life and played up the peoplehood of the Jews.

I pay great respect to those who have preceded me in the attempt in one or more volumes to capture the Jewish past. Nevertheless, it has become more and more obvious that there is a need for a new approach to Jewish History that is critical, as scientific as possible and one that doesn't tax the credibility of modern American Jews.

It is simply not enough to say that something has happened. Modern thinking Jews need to know why things happen as they did. Explanations by the use of miracles are passé. One cannot trust a history that relies on miracles, for then the reader becomes a passive part of the history. We live in a time when Jews have begun to play a vital part in the affairs of mankind. It is our contention that with a greater understanding of what has created the present day Jew, he can develop methods of making Judaism a more meaningful part of his life. Also, those who are involved in the Jewish community, as it is organized, will be able to operate in a more cognitive and responsible way, for the facts of Jewish existence will be shared from a common intellectual base.

I have been a teacher of Adult Education for more than a quarter century during which I have conducted this course almost 50 times as well as having given hundreds of lectures on parts of that history. During that time, I have developed a number of theories about events and movements in Jewish history, which will be presented in the text. Of course, I will take responsibility for my ideas and therefore may claim credit for any validation that readers may find useful.

The purpose of developing these theories was simply to make sense of events which puzzled me and other modern Jews alike.

For example, one of the strangest arrivals on the Jewish scene is Hillel. Jewish tradition has always insisted on making Hillel the counterpart of Jesus. He was kind, gentle, quoted lovely homilies and proposed changes in Jewish Law. In addition, like Jesus, later followers proclaimed him to be a direct descendant of King David, the precursor of the Messiah. He is at least a saint, and, of course, his opponent is a boor. Hillel's quotes are still uttered today, and some even put into song, while Shamai, his political opponent, has only one statement credited to him, in a long line of apothegms.

Somewhere, there is a need for a more rational approach to who Hillel was, what his philosophical and political approaches were, and how he came to represent the power of the Jewish Establishment during the Roman period, one of the most disastrous in our history.

That is only one of the subjects requiring a new approach. Throughout this book numerous theories are proposed which are meant to explain some of the inexplicable events and movements. It is obvious that there will be readers who will not accept the theories at all or in part, but having proposed them, I challenge those who reject them to come up with better explanations.

One final note, this book is written primarily for American Jews. The focus is on helping them to understand their roots. Too few American Jews have any sense about what is in their background beyond their own generation.

The usual response to the question, "Where did your parents or grandparents come from?" is "Russia." If the questioner asks the responder as to where in Russia, the answer comes forth as a shrug, which means, "How should I know?" It is precisely germane, because the site of origin of the ancestor is one of the determinants of the culture and religious values of the descendants. We will attempt to show the differences between Northern, Central and Southern Russia-Poland and each area's impact on Modern Jewry.

Similarly, there is a substantive difference between the milieu of Northern Germany and Southern Germany, or between Austria and Hungary. Therefore, it is important that those who are searching for their roots– and we can assume that it would be one of the reasons for reading a Jewish History–learn a great deal of the geography of Europe, as well as the political and social context of places where Jews lived prior to America.

Let me add a more personal note. When I was beginning to search my own roots, I read as much about the Jews in Eastern Europe as possible. The books were excellent, but when I checked the facts with members of my own family, their experiences were quite different. I was not able to confirm the history, even though the books were obviously correct, as were the observations of my relatives.

How can this divergence be explained? I began to do research on these writers who had discoursed on Eastern European Jewry. With almost no exception, it was found that all the historians were from the general area between Warsaw and Wilno in Lithuania, northeast of Warsaw. The area was more than a thousand miles from where my ancestors came from, and, in many ways, a million light years away culturally. My family was the poorest of the poor from a very small family in Podolia, called Dureshova, on the border of present Moldavia and Rumania, now called Moldava. It is no longer in existence. There must be thousands who wanting to know their own background, can not find what they need in books. Having tested this in classes, I was able to develop a differential history for what I call Litvak Jews and those who lived in Southern Russia.

Following this line of thinking, I have created a didactic tool for getting across to my students the four basic areas of Jewish life in Europe. This theory I have called the *Mellman Quadratic Theory of European Jewish History.* Let me confess that this sounds somewhat egotistical, but it reflects more than thirty years of study and questioning on my part. Again, I leave the reader to pick arguments, to find fault. I would welcome that, as I have in my classes and lectures.

I hope to accomplish a number of achievements in this book. The first is to develop a consistent history of the Jews with reliance not on myths, but on a search for truth.

Secondly, the personages upon whom Judaism has grown must be explained as humans, with foibles, political positions and errors and not as superhuman angels.

Finally, I would hope that any Jew reading this book, including converts, is able to fit themselves into the context of history. In my courses I have stressed that the ordinary Jew in Oshkosh, Wisconsin is as much a part of Jewish history as the head of a major Jewish organization. More than that, a comprehensive history should be able to explain the differences that separate Jews as well as those that bind them together.

My challenge is to make the 4,000 year odyssey of the Hebrew people, who eventually became the Jews, as comprehensive as possible. If the average Jew reading this comes away with a better understanding of his past and thus his commitment is made more meaningful to him or his community, I have fulfilled my role as a teacher. Further, if I have been able to stimulate study by those more qualified to delve into and write about some of the areas that I have stressed, this book will have been worth the effort.

1 ✡ IN THE BEGINNING

Here istory begins simplistically with the creation of writing. This is such a banal, elementary statement that it may pass over the ordinary reader. Jews are so used to thinking of the present Jewish calendar of some 5800 years, that thinking beyond this time frame becomes difficult. Jewish history must begin with the first evidence of the people who became the Jews in a later period. To begin our journey we must come to that era in which the antecedents of the people called Hebrews first appear.

As best as I can determine, it is the time of the development of the Fertile Crescent along the Tigris and Euphrates. The first writing that has been deciphered is dated by the archaeologists at about the year 2000 BCE, *(Before the Common Era)*. There is little possibility of any Hebrew history prior to that writing. The first stage of importance for this book is the rise of the Mesopotamia Empire, which attained its peak about the year 1750 BCE. In the Fertile Crescent, the people developed means of creating more food and other agricultural products than the indigenous could consume through the invention of terraced farms. This method of farming saved the already scarce water supply that the Middle East has become accustomed to, and produced a food surplus.

In such an environment, means were devised to trade this surplus for products in other communities, which needed the excess agriculture for their own sustenance. And a result of bartering, the leaders of Mesopotamia were able to produce excess capital, which represented a sign of an expanding economy.

At this point an historical axiom will be introduced, which will be repeated over and over in the book. This axiom will be the means of exploring the fate of the Jews in any area, country or region as history progresses.

Axiom I – Whenever a society, family or person produces excess capital, that entity can and usually will expend the excess on non-material and conspicuous items. It is in the period of having excess capital that such entities patronize the arts, build monuments to themselves and support elements of creativity that typify the values expounded by the leadership of the group.

Corollary 1– Whenever a society is expanding, that society has little need for scapegoats.

Corollary 2 – We should expect, if this is true, whenever a society is expanding its economy, that the situation of the inhabitants would be improved. Conversely, if the situation of the Jews and other inhabitants is good in a particular region or country, we should be able to observe that the area is expanding its economic base.

The Fertile Crescent became the World Trade Center, which is typified by the Biblical story of the Tower of Babel, where all the tongues of the world were spoken. If *Axiom I* is true, the fact that the Bible describes the architecture as a tower indicates that there was excess wealth in the Empire. Archaeological discoveries beginning almost a century ago have produced evidence that the Middle East at the time of the rise of the Babylonian-Mesopotamia Society was a beehive of economic activity. This activity was not only immense, but also geographically wide-spread. There is evidence that trade was integrated from Egypt to Eastern Persia and from Armenia in northern Turkey to the tip of the Arabian Peninsula.

It is from this period that the Biblical stories seem to arise. What the tale of Abraham leaving Ur Kasdim (Ur of the Chaldees) reinforces is the fact that there had been a good economy there, but when a drought occurs, Abram (as he is known early in the book of Genesis) leaves the home of his father. He moves up the trade route of the Euphrates River and then has a number of adventures with the local people, with God and also with angels or messengers of God.

What becomes more evident is that Abraham never owns land, and moves around the whole area rather easily. He visits with kings, high priests and other wealthy land owners, yet is never permitted to buy property. A poignant story is his request to buy a piece of land for the burial of his beloved Sarah. In reality, he is allowed to lease the spot for her and his own burial. The story makes little sense on the face of it, especially the quaint answer given by the editor of the Bible about his name. Abraham, the writer maintains, is a Hebrew, because he came from the other side of the river.

The explanation has never sat well with scholars for three reasons. First, Abraham could have easily been identified by his tribe or his country of origin. Secondly, the river is never identified and so far as we know, all rivers in the Bible are identified. Finally, people at that time knew very well what *Ivri,* translated in the Greek to "Hebrew" meant. Hebrew obviously designated much more than what the editor put forth. It was not until the past century that archaeologists found references in Tel Amarna that a similar word appears that parallels the Abraham saga.

That word, *Habiru,* has changed the recounting of the early history of the Jews. The word means, in general, a member of a group of landless mercenaries, day laborers, who lived as tolerated non-citizens in many areas of the Middle East. The Habiru seemed to have organized or designated themselves around either a leader or by a remembered clansman of the past.

In the Hebrew texts, these groups were either called Ben–something or Shevet–meaning to be someone. It should be noted that Ben in Hebrew means *son;* it also has other meanings. B'nai Brith does not mean Sons of the Covenant, but, rather, *Members of the Covenant.*

If someone is asked how old he is, his response would be "Ani ben––" (whatever age he is), meaning he has the attribute of that age. In much the same way, it is our contention that when the Bible describes a group as *"B'nai––,"* it means that the people are followers of a particular leader.

Shevet means *tribe,* but not necessarily direct descendants or extended family.

It makes more sense to think of the biblical designations of tribes and "sons of—," as marks of affiliation rather than genealogy. Considering this so allows for the extraordinary increases in numbers and affluence of Abraham in a very short time and without any obvious means for creating such wealth.

The time-line for the period of Abraham must be approximately the middle of the 18th century BCE. It is about the time of Hammurabi, whose laws seem to be one of the very first written and are still extant.

It is at this point, circa 1750 BCE, that we begin the history of the Hebrews; and this book will cover about 3700 years of history.

If this theory is true, we can assume that the period of Abraham, Isaac and Jacob takes approximately 250 years. We can trace the movements of the Habiru into Egypt at about 1500 BCE. We must also assume that human life spans have not changed radically in those 37 centuries, so more credence is given to the idea that the Patriarchs are actually prototypical for the writers of the Bible.

There is no historical evidence of the Hebrews in that time frame. Historiography requires that there must be substantiating evidence before we can assume the relative truth of the stories of that period. Other than in the Bible, there is no evidence of an Abraham, Isaac or Jacob. Thus far, with all the archaeological work done in Israel, not one discovery of the Patriarchs has been uncovered. This omission confirms the earlier conclusion that they are examples out of the past for the tellers and writers of that period.

For that matter there is no historical record of any of the people mentioned in the Five Books of Moses, nor of any of the people in the early pages of the historical books of the Prophets, the second section of the Jewish Bible. Actually, the first personality out of Jewish tradition who can be separately identified is David, for in other sources statements are found referring to King David.

Therefore, it is only possible to recreate what may make sense out of the ancient oral traditions which were combined into that which we call the Bible. To make that sense is one of the tasks for this book.

The Habiru spread over the Middle East, at first as individuals, but later into groups in order to provide greater strength and security. The groups identified themselves with names of prominent leaders of the past. Additionally, each Habiru group also accepted cult beliefs, based on gods indigenous to the areas where they operated. The probability is that some groups were more comfortable in Syria, some in Northern Canaan, and others along the coast or in the desert areas. It may be assumed that the Habiru tended to accept the native gods of the area and the leadership of the people they were serving.

We make the assumption that there were many more Habiru than those who eventually became the Israelites that left Egypt. Accepting this, we may assume also that each group selected as its personal god, or gods, such local deities as Baal, Moloch, Astarte, Marduk, El, in all its variations, and the four letter god who traditional Jews do not name except with euphemisms, but who later scholars called Jahveh *(pronounced Yahveh)*.

These gods, plus many more, seem to be related to certain areas, mountains, or as in the latter case, a desert god, who is movable. What we can determine is that the El god seems to be a mountain god, whose people worship by going to the top of the mountain. There were many Els in the primitive Canaanistic society, such as Eli Tziyon, El Elyon, El Shadai. There is an additional assumption that Elohim is a syncretic word to include all or most of the Elim, the simple plural of El.

Jahveh precedes Moses even in the Bible. Jethro, who is to become Moses' father-in law, is already described as a priest of Jahveh. It is also while Moses is on his forced escape to the desert for killing an Egyptian that he meets Jahveh in the famous story of the Burning Bush, where he makes the covenant with the desert god. He then returns to Egypt and prepares to lead various Habiru out of Egypt, having brought their previous gods here when they came to Egypt.

Here the scenario follows the Exodus, except for the miracles, which are the product of primitive minds. The Habiru are merged by Moses and are projected into the same desert to which Moses had escaped earlier. This disparate group becomes a motley band. There are 12, 13, 14, 15 and even 16 tribes at various times. What we learn from the narrative is that Moses is given words to utter on the mountain in the desert. Its locale is no accident. He utters the famous Sh'ma, which through history has taken on a number of meanings for Jews.

This is the play: the groups of tribes are obviously, in part, groups which serve El, while others were those who accepted Jahveh. The Sh'ma in this case must be read in different terms.

Sh'ma	–	*Pay Attention*
Yisrael	–	*Your name is now Israel*
Jahveh	–	*The Desert god is*
Elohenu	–	*Our Elohim*
Jahveh	–	*That god is*
Echad	–	*Not many, but one.*

In a sense, the Sh'ma became what is now a common term in today's society, the logo of a merger. It becomes the symbol for the conglomeration of basically two different cultural and geographical forces, those from the mountainous north and the others from the southern desert areas. It is in this context that one is able to understand the Jacob's Ladder fable, which ends with Jacob receiving a northern name, Israel. It is an attempt to include Jacob-Yaakov, a southern derivation into the fact of the Sh'ma. How else could the people have been called Israel? The merger was accomplished in the Moses tale through giving the united people the northern name while still retaining the southern god, Jahveh.

EL. Names and Places

The geography of Palestine is such that the mountains are all in the north and the relatively low lands are in the south. It seems possible that each northern mountain had its own cult dedicated to an El. One should only take note of the names of people and places in the scriptures which include the word, El, such as Elisha, Elimelech, Eli and Shmuel. They are just a few of the proper names. Bethel and Carmel are two examples of geographical names of northern sanctuaries.

On the other hand, those names which represent the southern traditions have some variations on Jahveh, such as Ja, Hu or Jahu. Yaakov, Yirmiyahu, Yeraboam, Yehoshua and Yehuda are variations of that inclination. Of course there are combinations of both traditions, such as Jael and Eliyahu, which may indicate some syncretism of the two.

Now return to the Moses story. What is proposed is that the Israelites, as they are henceforth called, are never known as Hebrews after that time. They are called B'nai Yisrael, or Adat B'nai Yisrael *(the Congregation of the Children of Israel)*, and with the period of the Exodus, another historical scale of life is entered. The former Habiru, upon entering the area of Canaan, become landed people and shift from being considered itinerant and alien into a strong, for the time, nation on land which Jahveh gave them.

Readers should understand that at this time that there was nothing written down which was considered Holy Writ. Traditions were essentially oral. It appeared that those who maintained the individual cult sites were the ones who maintained the justifying traditions. Stories were told honoring the past heroes and, in turn, honoring those who benefited from the cult, usually the priests. Since there must have been contact from one high place to another, one can be certain that there were oral plagiarisms from one group to another. Rituals were modeled after one another, with some differentiation to separate one from another.

At About the Year 1250 BCE

The exodus can be dated at approximately 1250 BCE, due to events that were taking place in Egypt that parallel the time and events described in the Moses story and of Joshua, Moses' successor. We have left the period which may be described as Pentateuchal, or within the five books of Moses, and entered the period of Israelite history found in the Books of Joshua, Samuel and Kings I, the years of 1250–1000 BCE. If we are to accept these books as somewhat valid, they become the core of the argument that Moses never wrote the Five Books credited to him.

In particular, the Book of Joshua and the following Book of Judges, detail some of the most primitive ideas which the Israelite put into practice. It is in these books that we are able to read of Jephtha's daughter, whose tale is very close to the story of Midas, but more gory. There is the strange tale of Samson and his love affair with the Philistine, Delilah, and his vow to keep his hair which, like the Sikhs of India, is considered the core of strength and must never be cut.

During this period of 250 years, the Book of Judges reveals all sorts of pagan behavior, and also all manners of pre-temple activities, prohibited by the Book of Deuteronomy, supposedly accepted by the Israelites earlier. Everyone had the right to sacrifice wherever he pleased. Levites became priests. What makes this all believable is the fact that the stories in the Book of Judges are not written for public relations, but rather to detail past history as it seemed to happen. The writing is sanguinary and quite specific.

2 ✡ THE RISE OF THE MONARCHY

It is only with the rise of the most prominent judge, Samuel, that we begin to sense a change of the society from primitive agricultural one to a more variegated country. Prior to this time, tribal interests basically protected their boundaries; with Samuel we begin to see a more inter-tribal figure. As the Philistine threat wore heavy on individual tribes, Samuel tried very early on to bring more cooperation among the northern tribes.

The very birth of Samuel to the barren Hannah evokes the most primitive part of the Israelite religion. She could not have children, and her husband prays annually at the sanctuary, Shiloh. In her anguish, she visits the priest, Eli, at his place in Shiloh. She prayed and subsequently became pregnant and delivered her son, Samuel. He had been dedicated to the priesthood, and became Eli's successor and the judge "from Dan to Beer Sheva." This ranged from the very north to as far south as the hegemony of the Israelites extended.

Up to that time, priests and judges were dynastically appointed. The sons of the leader became priests and judges. But when it became obvious that Samuel's sons were incapable of succession, Samuel appointed Saul, a Benjaminite, a northerner, to the position of King of Israel. It is probable that Saul became ruler of only a part of the area of the twelve tribes, because not all the tribes accepted him. If one reads between the lines about the struggles between Saul and David, it becomes clear that there was no love lost between them. Besides, at the time that Saul is killed in battle with the Philistines, David is already king of Judah.

Then came all the tribes of Israel to David unto Hebron, and spoke, saying, "Behold, we are thy bone and flesh. In times past, when Saul was king over us, it was thou that didst lead out and bring in Israel and the Lord said to thee: 'Thou shalt feed My people Israel and thou shalt be prince over Israel.' " So all the elders of Israel came to the king to Hebron; and king David made a covenant with them in Hebron before the Lord; and they appointed David king over Israel.

David was thirty years old when he began his reign and he reigned forty years. In Hebron he reigned over Judah seven years and six months; and in Jerusalem he reigned thirty three years over all Israel and Judah.

And the king and his men went to Jerusalem against the Jebusites, the inhabitants of the land, who spoke unto David, saying: Except thou take away the blind and the lame, thou shalt not come in hither, thinking: David cannot come in hither. Nevertheless, David took the stronghold of Zion; the same is the city of David. And David said on that day: 'Whoever smiteth the Jebusites and getteth up to the gutter, and [taketh away] the lame and the blind, that are hated of David's soul—.' Wherefore they say: 'There are the blind and the lame; he cannot come into the house.' And David dwelt in the stronghold, and called it the city of David. And David built round about from Millo and inward. And David waxed greater and greater; for the Lord, the God of hosts, was with him.

And Hiram king of Tyre sent messengers to David, and cedar-trees, and carpenters, and masons; and they built David a house. And David perceived that the Lord

*had established him king over Israel and
that He had exalted his kingdom for His
people Israel's sake.*

*And David took him more concubines
and wives out of Jerusalem after he was come
from Hebron; and there were yet sons and
daughters born to David. And these are the
names of those that were born unto him in
Jerusalem: Shammua and Shobab and
Nathan and Solomon; and Ibhar, and
Elishua, and Nepheg, and Japhia; and
Elishama, and Eliada and Eliphelet.*

This segment of Samuel is one of the most significant passages in the Prophets, for it makes clear that David
was a southern king years before Saul's death, and that
his god was Jahveh, and Jerusalem was never part of the
territory until some 250 years after the death of Moses.
It is at this time, about 1000 BCE, that we can begin to
speak of a United Kingdom of Judah and Israel.

To return to an earlier theme, Judah represented
the Jahvist idea. The very name in transliterated Hebrew
is Ya-hudah. Israel, on the other hand, signified the Elohist
tradition, with names beginning or else ending with either El, and with every mountain being the residence of
El. Whenever the English Bible uses the term Lord, it is
a translation of Jahveh, and when it says God, it refers to
Elohim; Lord God is Jahveh Elohim, and O Lord Our God
is Jahveh Elohenu

When David becomes king of the United Kingdom,
it is possible for the first time to speak of Judaism, the religion of Judah. This takes place about the year 1000 BCE,
when he exercises through his leadership, military might
and presence, control over the Holy Land, and insisted that
his subjects, North and South, should show deference to
him, his city and his Jahvist cult of priests, those who claim
their descent directly from Aaron. His High Priest, Zadok,
continues in that position after David's death and especially
after the construction of the First Temple. We know little of
Zadok, but we know for certain that the name, when trans-

literated into the Greek Bible, appears as Saduc. So for some 70 years until 930 BCE the kingdom was not only united under David's dynasty, but the priesthood of the Saducite dynasty had been in place in Jerusalem, in what was certainly the most glorious habitat to any god up to that time.

We now recall the idea of Axiom I – expanding economies. Because of David and Solomon's expansion of the original kingdom and the requisite of tribute from all sorts of neighboring areas, the economy of Judah and Israel grew enormously, encouraging the Judah people to spend some of the excess on buildings, temples, art and other artifacts of culture, such as poetry, chronicles and literature. Consider a person in the American society who had begun saving more than his absolute necessities. He will use the savings for purchasing or developing objects which are non-capital creating. For example, he might buy art, improve his home or contribute to an organization which is classified as philanthropic or artistic. In our society, in order to create the milieu for expansion of arts, religion or other parts of culture, the community must provide for expansion of the economy.

On the other hand, in a society, group or family, where there is little excess capital, all of the moneys and energies are expanded for human consumption and needs. There is little left for what may be called pleasures. This is a corollary to Axiom I.

Axiom I and its corollaries, expressed so simply, reflect my view that this theory is one of the *Truths of History*. Wherever we can find evidences of an expanding economy, we should be able to find those facets of literature, art and architecture. The reverse would also be true: where we find a society with a defined set of artifacts representing that culture, we should expect to find an expanding economy. The greater the expansion, the freer the society, since each person is helpful in creating the good things of that society. There should be less need for the leadership to depend on scapegoats to control that society, since in such a case, the thrust is to broaden the base of producers.

In Jewish history, this is a recurring theme – that wherever a society or a country is expanding its economy, it may be expected that the fate of Jews is relatively good. On the contrary, if the area is in decline, then Jews within that society would be in trouble. This is a very simplistic approach, and yet, if true, would go a long way towards developing an approach to understanding what brings about the rise of anti-semitism in the history of the Jews.

In many respects this defines a part of the radical approach of this book. Even today, in the nineties, there are writers who try to determine anti-semitism on the basis of rejection of Judaism. Nothing could be further from the truth. It would not explain how the same society could at one time totally welcome the Jews and, at another, perpetrate cruel and fatal acts against them.

But let the story continue. David and Solomon extended the boundaries of the United Kingdom far beyond what had been prescribed in the promises made to Moses in the desert, according to the Torah. This brought tremendous riches to the Judahites. The fact that David and Solomon were able to exact tributes from distant countries and royalty is one proof, but also the descriptions in the Books of Kings of the enormous wealth of Solomon, and the number of his wives and concubines make him the epitome of the oriental potentate.

It is really from Solomon's time that Axiom I begins to assert itself. There must have been tremendous capital to inspire and subsidize a magnificent temple. An additional premise is that a group of writers or story tellers are developed, whose sole function is to create tales about the wisdom of David and Solomon, and especially that Jahveh had blessed the seed of David for all time. The dynasty could be enshrined forever and backed up by the priesthood in the temple in Jerusalem, with rituals meant to indicate that Jahveh was the Most High God, over all other gods, whose people must now bring their tribute to Jahveh's temple and to David and his heirs.

It was not unusual in that region for kings to have

chroniclers. Indeed, a number of times, the stories of the kings are supposed to be detailed in the "Chronicles of the Kings." Scribes were normally used for keeping the records of the events of moment for the king, but also to spread the glory of the regent. There must have been a number of professional writers in the courts of both David and Solomon, who felt called upon to pay their highest respects to their lord and king.

By the time of Solomon's reign, which began about the year 970 BCE, the demand by the Jerusalem government and priesthood for tribute, especially from the Northern Elohist group, must have become more and more unbearable. Solomon's showpiece to Jahveh and his own appetites for objects of wealth must have been ill reviewed by the Israelite groups. Where other tribal leaders should have been sharing in the power and glory, only the Judahites seem to prosper. It was only the military strength of Solomon that prevented a revolt from breaking out.

When Solomon died, the force was no longer faithful to the court, and when there was an attempt to have a National Unity vote by the leadership, Rehaboam, Solomon's son, refused to reduce the tax load, but, indeed, increased the burden on the North. Ten and a half tribes, all loyal to Elohim, seceded from the United Kingdom, and immediately established their temple at Bethel, dedicated to the service of Elohim, whose symbol at the entrance of his temple was a golden calf.

The Shepherd of the South

It is at this point in history that the literary tradition, which has been posited as having begun during the Davidic and Solomonic period, started to play its tune. Almost immediately, after the split in the Kingdom, we find the story of the Book of Amos, the shepherd of the southern area, describing an almost unbelievable scene.

This uneducated farmer proceeds to the temple in the North and berates the leadership of the northern tribes in the name of Jahveh, the dynasty of David and the city of Jerusalem. Here is the great theme of the early prophets, which in beautiful Oriental poetry declaims three themes in so many ways. It is the contention of this book, that the thread of the prophets is to the three part chain, or in Hebrew, Kesher Hamshuleshet, which have become the unique voice of the Prophets. They are:

- *the uniqueness of David and his genes,*
- *the unbelievable role of the city of Jerusalem, the city of David,*
- *the preciousness of the people of Judah and Jerusalem, soon to be called Jews.*

These three concepts run through the Prophets as a mighty stream, setting the stage for the Messianic idea to blossom under the two Isaiahs.

Essentially, what is proposed is the following: the prophetic writings were simply that, writings which were used to elevate the Davidic period into what can be called the "End of Days." No period of history has been extolled so gloriously and magnificently, and Jews will return to that period by returning to Jahveh through repentance and to his law. When the Jews will do so as a people, then Jahveh will restore the monarchy under the descendants of David, would redeem Jerusalem and recreate the Jewish people to their rightful role at the center of the universe. *"For out of Zion would come forth the Torah and the word of Jahveh from Jerusalem."*

The early prophets articulated or wrote their words in Judaic dialects in honor of the Davidic dynasty, even to pointing their fangs against the North, saying, in effect, "You who have broken away from Jerusalem, have gone astray by once again returning to your ancient mountain god, El, and rejecting, not only Jahveh, but also his chosen monarch, the direct descendant of the first Messiah, David. If you continue in your ways, then Jahveh, at his own time, will bring down destruction on Israel, the Northern Kingdom." This is the essential message of the early prophets.

The messages of the prophets are in poetry. It is no accident that the whole of the prophets were placed later to musical notations, which can be easily chanted by every Bar or Bat Mitzvah. The orations are essentially metered poetry which usually have three or four beats in each half sentence. ////:/// is a usual sentence, with each / coming at the accent of each word. Each sentence has two parallels at the colon. That is, the first may say something like, *"O sing out, you mountains,"* and *"cry forth, you hills"* ends the parallelism.

It is with this hypothesis that we have created a historical fiction. There is a problem in that we have no idea how the Books of Prophets were transmitted and eventually written down. There seems to be no group or person described in the Bible or otherwise, who have been labeled as having this responsibility. The only scribes mentioned are priests, and the philosophy of the prophets was the antithesis to their concern. If anything, the prophets were overwhelmingly anti-clerical.

Therefore, the proposal at this point is that a group of literati, possibly maintained by the Davidic dynasty and who had become the encomium writers of Judah and Jerusalem, created and developed the orations of the prophets for that purpose. It is they who created and developed the three-fold Davidic crown of Jahveh, Jerusalem and the Jews. Three has always been a magical number among Jews. (Three patriarchs, three crowns of the Torah, three levels of a Jew, Cohen, Levi, and Israel, and the famous saying, *"Al sh'losha devarim haolam omed"*– on three things does the world stand.) It was this group of writers who were able to magnify leaders in the past, with wholly fictional fables, such as Amos and Hosea. It is very possible that they never existed. There are no supporting pieces of evidence that would indicate that they were historical figures. They existed in the memories of the past. In the long run, it makes little difference. What is more important is the fact that these personages became symbols for the Jewish people.

Our contention is that these writers helped to transmit the prophets to encompass the ideology of the Davidic line, in contrast to two possibilities – first, that there might be legitimacy to the secession of the Northern tribes, and the second, to forestall any possibility that a person other than from the Davidic line might take over the kingdom. By tying those ideas to Jahveh and Jerusalem, they gave a religious tone to a nationalistic idea. I have called this group of writers the Judaic Literary Society, whose main function was to maintain these three-fold ideas.

From 930 BCE, at the breakup of the United Kingdom, until the rise of Assyria as a major power in the eighth century BCE (700's), the prophets or their writers spoke only about Jahveh and that he would descend on the Northern tribes for leaving their brothers and their God for El. With the appearance of the Assyrian neighbors, they made the claim that the Assyrians were selected by Jahveh to deliver judgment on Israel. In 721 BCE, the Assyrians defeated the northern 10½ tribes, which marked the first time that any Israelite tribes had been conquered.

At this point I must introduce the concept of imperialism and its effect on the Judahites.

The Assyrian concept of imperialism was a simple one – destroy the power of the indigenous leadership by moving it to many different locales in the empire. This would create a sort of assimilation which would prevent the possibility of revolution against the Assyrian monarchy. This is precisely what happened to the tribes of the North. Not every person, but a sufficient number, and of course the most important, were evacuated in order to deprive the Northern Kingdom of any power. Couple this with the primitive idea that when a people is conquered, it is because the god of the victor is better than the local god – i.e. El. It did not take long for the general disappearance of the milieu of the north as the bailiwick of the Elohist god.

It is now possible to state with some authority that from 721 BCE, the only tradition left of the Davidic and Solomonic period was captured by those writers who molded the prophets. Prior to 721, they were writing that Jahveh would punish the North for the departure from the Davidic traditions. After 721, the prophets speak in a different tone to the Judah and Jerusalem group since their prophecies had come true. Now, if the Southern group did not return to those three-hundred-year old ideas, then they too would be destroyed.

The thread holding the Prophets together through the Judean Literary Society and its leadership, becomes the tradition, which lays the ground work for the different religion from the previous ones. The Books of Kings in the Bible are framed in stories about the Judean kings. They are considered good kings only if they follow David and Jahveh's laws. They are evil, if they do not. Idol worship seems to be the main criteria of whether a king is good or not.

At this point, it is appropriate to add the second Axiom:

Axiom II – Whenever a society is near destruction, the leaders of the group or society, fearing the loss of the values of the community, begin the process of codifying the past. This is equally true for countries, societies, families and individuals who, faced with an impending trauma, start the process of saving the products of the past and placing them in such a way that the future will know what to carry on. The suggestion is that whenever a family suffers the death of a patriarch or matriarch, there is an attempt to save all the pictures, the artifacts, to write a history of the family and to trace the genealogy.

Corollary to Axiom II – Whenever one finds a codification in history, it is a symbol of the near-end of the period of that society. The leaders now attempt to save the important values of the Old Regime, whatever transpired. This corollary becomes extremely important in Jewish History, for we shall find many evidences of codification, and each one will be explained against this corollary.

Between 721 and about 650 BCE, the Assyrian Empire began to decline, and under pressure from the Egyptian Empire in the West and other forces at the eastern end of the Empire, they were slowly taken over by the adjacent eastern empire, the Babylonians. In a sense, I could indicate the change from Damascus to Baghdad, or from present Syria to Iraq. The Judah king at this time was a very young Josiah, who came to the throne at the age of 8 and in a remarkable story, as told in *II Kings, Chapter 22,* laid the groundwork for a most unusual change in Jewish History.

The story begins with the idea that the temple of David needed repair. Josiah orders the repairs under the leadership of the priesthood of Jahveh. To the best of our knowledge this reconstruction was taking place about 621 BCE, just four years after the fall of Assyria to Babylon. As the tale unfolds, a book or a scroll is miraculously found in the temple. When the scroll is brought to the king, he asks that it be read to him. When this is done, he shows his anguish by tearing his clothes for not having kept the laws as laid down in the scroll.

Josiah orders his administration to consult with Huldah, the prophetess, who predicts that the kingdom would suffer all sort of indignities and shame because the Judahites have not kept those laws found in the book. Josiah then convenes all of the people to hear the book read and they accept it and agree to a covenant, a "brit." Josiah, with the support of the leaders, begins a puritanical revolution, in which he orders the destruction of all idol worship, phallic worship, gods of the sun, moon and stars, and crushed the services of the male prostitutes, all of which take place right in the temple of Solomon. He also razes the holy places of the groups which offered sacrifices to the Moloch. He burns the Chariots of the Sun God, and destroys as well the pillars that Solomon had placed inside the Temple.

Josiah then orders the Passover to be celebrated in Jerusalem. The story makes very clear that Passover had not been celebrated since the time of the Judges, 1250 BCE. Recall that this is over 600 years later. It is extremely important, that this event, which is described in *II Kings Chapter 23, Verse 21,* be noted. Subsequently, we will analyze this passage against others as we try to determine the development of the writing of the Bible as we know it.

Most critical Biblical scholars see this scroll as the beginning of the written Torah. By comparing what is described in the Josiah story and parts of the Pentateuch, the five books of Moses, it becomes fairly clear that there is a very sharp connection between what is drawn there and what is detailed in the fifth book, Deuteronomy in Greek and D'varim in Hebrew. The philosophy is almost precisely what the Josiah story spells out.

The basic theme is that all idolatry must be ruthlessly wiped out of the country, and the temple must be purified again, so that "only at the place which Jahveh has chosen to cause his name to dwell therein" may sacrifices be brought to Him, our Elohim. This phrase appears more than fifty times and only in the book of Deuteronomy. The usual term that is applied to this phrase is "centralization of the cult," precisely what the Josiah story is professing.

What we may assume at this point is that the book that was "found" was at least a portion of what eventually became Deuteronomy. In 621 BCE this is the only written Torah, as far as is known. This concept is quite a radical departure from the idea that Moses, himself, wrote the five books from the mouth of the Lord. This idea is repeated in every synagogue when the Torah is removed from the ark, even though the rabbis know full well that this action was not possible. It is precisely this Josiah story which should enable modern Jews to begin to understand the creation of the Bible. It is the story of Josiah that contains the germ of the idea of human creation of the Bible. For, if as most modern historians agree, the Bible was created by Man, then it is incumbent that modern men and women try to figure out, as best as they can, how it came into existence.

3 ✡ HOW THE BIBLE WAS CREATED

For some four centuries scholars have been attempt ing in this "Age of Analysis" to decipher the author ship of the Bible. It is not necessary to plod through all the layers of this scholarship. Rather, it is necessary to introduce the reader to the form of Biblical Criticism, which is popularly known as the JEDP theory. In the JEDP theory it is generally considered that there are at least four layers of authorship in the Five Books of Moses.

They include the Jahvist (J), a southern writer or writers, whose main thrust is based on Jahveh as God. "J" has an essential southern philosophy, tied to the old desert god, who moves with his people. "E" is the Elohist, who is involved with the worship in the high places. E's milieu is in the north of Israel. "D", the Deuteronomist, is the product of the writers of the fifth book of the Torah – involved with the centralization of the cult, with a pro phetic approach to ethics and morals, and uses the com bination name, Jahveh Elohenu. "P" is the priestly writer's area. He is the one who keeps the genealogy lines and is concerned with the Temple, the correctness of the priestly service, what the priests wear, the sacrifices and the proper time for such services. "P" occupies about 60% of the five books. Thus we have the JEDP Theory.

Most Biblical scholars add an editor, and because most of the early Biblical Critics were German, they used the term, Redactor, which in German means *editor.* Some writers use the expression, JEDPR. Much has been writ ten about which code came first or last, but for our pur poses, it should suffice to note, that there are a number of traditions which were incorporated into the written Bible.

Turn back to the King Josiah story, about the year

621 BCE, from which an assumption can be made that either Josiah or some of his followers wrote or had the book of Deuteronomy compiled to justify the centralization of the religion in Jerusalem, and the elimination of the many cults which had been introduced into the Temple by Solomon and others. At this time there was an immense attack on the "false" religion of the North, which had been captured by Assyria approximately 100 years earlier.

In addition, Deuteronomy affirms, or reaffirms, that the priests of the sons of Zadok, a direct descendant of Aaron and the High Priest at the Temple when it was constructed, were the only valid High Priest family. This will become more obvious later in history.

After 621 BCE, so far as we now know, the only written law was Deuteronomy. Earlier, in Axiom II, it had been stated that whenever a society is in decline, one might expect that society's leaders would attempt to codify the past. This is precisely what Deuteronomy appears to reflect.

About 700 BCE, the Assyrian government, which had earlier conquered the North (Israel, the Elohist society) was itself conquered by a new power to the East, Babylonia (Iraq). Josiah must have assumed that the new power, which now controlled the territory almost within 14 miles of Jerusalem, would turn its might against Jerusalem and Judah.

Under such pressure from Babylonia, Josiah certainly wished to unite his weak country. Deuteronomy was his method. By 621, almost all of the prophets had been written, including Amos, Hosea and the other early prophets, which would account for the prophetic tone of Deuteronomy. Also, the Judean Literary Society was concerned with David's line, including Josiah, as well as the centralization of Temple worship in Jerusalem.

Deuteronomy becomes the written constitution of the two and a half tribes of the South. Kings II, Chapters 22 and 23 detail this covenant.

Josiah was eight years old when he began to reign; and he reigned thirty and one years in Jerusa-

lem; and his mother's name was Jedidah, the daughter of Adaiah of Bozkath. And he did that which was right in the eyes of the Lord, and walked in all the ways of David, his father, and turned not aside to the right hand or to the left.

And it came to pass in the eighteenth year of King Josiah that the king sent Shaphan the son of Azaliah, the son of Meshullam, the scribe, to the house of the Lord, saying: Go up to Hilkiah, the high priest, that he may sum the money which is brought into the house of the Lord, which the keepers of the door have gathered of the people; and let them deliver it into the hand of the workmen that have the oversight of the house of the Lord; to repair the breaches of the house; unto the carpenters, and to the builders and to the masons; and for buying the timber and hewn stone to repair the house. How be it there was no reckoning made with them of the money that was delivered into their hand; for they dealt faithfully.

And Hilkiah, the high priest, said to Shaphan the scribe: 'I have found a book of the Law in the house of the Lord.' And Hilkiah delivered the book to Shaphan and he read it. And Shaphan the scribe came to the king and said: 'Thy servants have poured out the money that was found in the house and have delivered it into the hand of the workmen that have the oversight of the house of the Lord.' And Shaphan the scribe told the king, saying:'Hilkiah the priest hath delivered me a book.' and Shaphan read it before the king. And it came to pass when the king had heard the words of the book of the Law, that he rent his clothes. And the king commanded Hilkiah the priest, and Ahikam the son of Shaphan, and Achbor the son of Micaiah, and Shaphan the scribe and Asaiah the king's servant, saying: 'Go ye, inquire of the Lord for me, and for the people, and for all Judah, concerning the words of this book that is found; for great is the wrath of the Lord kindled against us, because our *fathers have not hearkened unto the words of this book, to do according unto all that is written concerning us.'*

So Hilkiah the priest, and Ahikam, and Achbor, and Shaphan, and Asaiah, went unto Huldah the prophetess, the wife of Shallum, the son of Tikvah, the son of Harhas, keeper of the wardrobe – now she dwelt in Jerusalem in the second quarter – and they spoke with her. And she said unto them: 'Thus saith the Lord, the God of Israel: Tell ye the man that sent you unto me: Thus saith the Lord: Behold, I will bring evil upon this place, and upon the inhabitants thereof, even all the words of the book which the king of Judah hath read; because they have forsaken Me and have offered unto other gods, that they might provoke Me with all the work of their hands: therefore My wrath shall be kindled against this place and it shall be quenched. But unto the king of Judah, who sent you to inquire of the Lord, thus shall you say to him: Thus saith the Lord, the God of Israel: As touching the words which thou hast heard, because thy heart was tender, and thou didst humble thyself before the Lord, when thou heardest what I spoke against this place, and against the inhabitants thereof, that they should become an astonishment and a curse, and hast rent thy clothes, and wept before Me, I also have heard thee, saith the Lord. Therefore, behold, I will gather thee to thy fathers, and thou shalt be gathered to thy grave in peace, neither shall thine eyes see all the evil which I will bring upon this place.' And they brought back word unto the king.

And the king sent and they gathered unto him all the elders of Judah and Jerusalem. And the king went up to the house of the Lord, and all the men of Judah and all the inhabitants of Jerusalem with him, and the priests, and the prophets, and all the people, both small and great; and he read in their ears all the words of the book of the covenant which was found in the house of the Lord. And the king

*stood on the platform, and made a covenant before
the Lord, to walk after the Lord, and to keep his
commandments, and his testimonies and his statutes, with all his heart, and all his soul, to confirm
the words of this covenant that were written in the
book; and all the people stood to the covenant.*

*And the king commanded Hilkiah the high
priest and the priests of the second order, and the
keepers of the door, to bring forth out of the temple of
the Lord all the vessels that were made for Baal and
for the Asherah, and for all the host of heaven; and
he burned them without Jerusalem in the fields of
Kidron, and carried them unto Beth-el. And he put
down the idolatrous priests, whom the kings of Judah
had ordained to offer in the high places in the cities
of Judah, and in the high places around about
Jerusalem; them also that offered unto Baal, to the
sun, and to the moon, and to the constellations, and
to all the host of heaven. And he brought out the
Asherah (Phallic symbol) from the house of the Lord,
without Jerusalem, unto the brook Kidron, and
burned it at the brook Kidron, and stamped it small
to powder and cast the powder thereof upon the
graves of the common people. And he broke down
the houses of the sodomites (male prostitutes) that
were in the house of the Lord, where the women wove
coverings for the Asherah. And he brought all the
priests out of the cities of Judah and defiled the high
places where the priests had made offerings, from
Geba to Beer-sheba; and he broke down the high
places of the gates that were at the entrance of the
gate of Joshua the governor of the city, which were
on a man's left hand as he entered the gate of the
city. Nevertheless the priests of the high places came
not up to the altar of the Lord in Jerusalem, but they
did eat unleavened bread among their brethren. And
he defiled Tophet, which is in the valley of the son of
Hinnom, that no man might make his son or his
daughter to pass through the fire to Molech. And he
took away the horses that the kings of Judah had*

given to the sun, at the entrance of the house of the
Lord, by the chamber of Nathan-melech the officer,
which was in the precincts; and he burned the chariots of the sun with fire. And the altars that were on
the roof of the upper chamber of Ahaz, which the
kings of Judah had made and the altars which
Manasseh had made in the two courts of the house
of the Lord, did the king break down from thence,
and cast the dust of them into the brook Kidron.
And the high places that were before Jerusalem,
which were on the right hand of the mount of corruption, which Solomon the king of Israel had
builded for Ashtoreth, the detestation of the
Zidonians, and for Chemosh, the detestation of
Moab, and for Milcom, the abomination of the children of Ammon, did the king defile. And he broke
in pieces, and cut down the Asherim and filled their
places with the bones of men.

Moreover the altar that was at Beth-el, and the
high places which Jeroboam, the son of Nebat (that
is, the first king of the North) who made Israel sin,
had made, even that altar and the high place he
broke down; and he burned the high place and
stamped it small to powder and buried the Asherah.
And as Josiah turned himself, he spied the sepul-
chres that were in the mount; and he sent, and took
the bones out of the sepulchre and burned them upon
the altar, and defiled it, according to the word of the
Lord which the man of God proclaimed, who proclaimed these things. Then he said: What monu-
ment is that which I see? And the men of the city
told him: ' It is the sepulchre of the man of God, who
came from Judah, and proclaimed these things that
thou hast done against the altar of Beth-el". And he
said: "Let him be; let no man move his bones'. So
they let the bones of the prophet that came out of
Samaria. And all the houses also the high places
that were in the city of Samaria, which the kings of
Israel had made to provoke (the Lord), Josiah took
away and did to them according to all the acts that

he had done in Beth-el. And he slew all the priests of the high places that were there, upon the altars, and burned men's bones upon them; and he returned to Jerusalem.

Obviously there was much idolatry in the area even in the Temple of Solomon. The extra-long details listed here were simply to show the state of the life in and around Jerusalem. But the sentences which follow this puritanical revolution are necessary for the unfolding of this story.

And the king commanded all the people, saying: 'Keep the passover unto the Lord your God, as it written in the book of the covenant.' For there was not kept such a passover from the days of the judges that judges Israel, nor of the kings of Judah; but in the eighteenth year of King Josiah was this passover kept to the Lord in Jerusalem. Moreover them that devined by a ghost or a familiar spirit, and by the teraphim, and idols and all the detestable things that were spied in the land of Judah and in Jerusalem, did Josiah put away, that he might confirm the words of the law which were written in the book that Hilkiah the priest found in the house of the Lord. And like unto him was there no king before him, that turned to the Lord with all his heart, and with all his soul and with all his might, according to all the law of Moses; neither after him arose there any like him.

It appears from the Hebrew text that until the year 621 BCE, the Judah people had never celebrated Passover before. Rather, if we understand the text, it reveals that for the first time in over 600 years (the Exodus was about 1250 BCE) Passover had been celebrated. This story reveals one possible explanation for the construction of the Bible. But what about the other four books? At least for the present, the assumption is that "D" was the first written documentation. Of course, there were certainly other oral traditions, some much older than Deuteronomy.

With this first Torah as the hypothesis, the major holiday is the Spring festival in the month of Aviv.

The Babylonian Exile

It was not more than a generation later, in the year 586 BCE, that the country of Judah and Jerusalem was under siege by the forces of Nebuchadnezzar of Babylonia. Jerusalem was laid waste, the temple destroyed, and the regal leadership and its entourage were taken as slaves to Babylonia. This period begins the Babylonian Exile. It is imperative that a discussion begin here about the style of imperialism practiced by the Babylonians. The Assyrians, after capturing Israel, used a premise in their empire whereby those conquered were dispersed or assimilated, whereas the Babylonians had a different method.

For whatever reasons, the Babylonians were a much more heterogeneous group than the Assyrians; they allowed their captives to maintain their own communities and culture. Shortly after the year 586 BCE, we find descriptions of Jewish communities and educational programs. Indeed, several of the prophetic books and psalms were written and used in Babylonia.

It is just that distinction between the two invasions of Israel on the one hand and Judah on the other, which permitted the growth of the Judaic tradition to be saved, and to this date almost nothing of the Israelite tradition of the North to be kept. What we have after 586 BCE are essentially the traditions which the prophets maintained, as well as the that of the Judaic priests, who kept their own laws and culture. Whatever we call Judaism today stems from that group who went into exile in that year, and what they created there. Certainly, the structure for the community allowed and encouraged this continuity.

A new concept of Jahveh developed in exile. We find it in what scholars call Isaiah II (Chapter 40 and on), in which a change in the role of Jahveh is evident. Up to the Exile, the belief was that Jahveh resided in Jerusalem. What Isaiah II proposed in his orations is that Jahveh went into exile with his people and at the proper moment, He would, through a direct descendant of David, bring back the Judahites to Jerusalem, and that city would be the capital of a new world. For the same God who had brought them out of slavery would redeem the exiles. It is likely that the royal family was in control of the Judah communities which were spread around the Tigris and Euphrates Rivers, particularly around Babel, the capital of the empire.

In about 540 BCE, the empire to the east of Babylonia conquered that power and made it a part of the Persian Hegemony. The Babylonian Exile lasted about 50 years, and since the memories of Judah and Jerusalem were so recent, they played a major role in the future thought. For it was here, prior to the capture by the Persians, that the exiled writings were absorbed into the Psalms, and the Prophets becoming a treasure of the Judaic people. These writings continued the program of the Judah Literary Society and its adulation of the three-fold ideas. Until this time, the priests seem to have had little role in the body politic of the Exiles, for they were devoted to the tradition which emphasized the role of Aaron and his direct descendants.

When Cyrus the Great took over the Persian Empire, including the Exiles, a totally different style of imperialism was adopted. The Persians saw their ruler as a priest, or possibly the reverse was true. It is phenomenal that even today the Persians have as their leader an Ayatollah, a priest. Nationalism was far less important than the cultic worship led by priests.

Upon request by the Judah community to return to Jerusalem, Cyrus allowed a contingent of them to return. They were led by two heads of the community: Zerubabel, a direct descendant of David, and Joshua, the next in line in the Aaronide link to the High Priesthood. From this point on, and for a number of centuries following, the clash between these two dynasties, the sons of Zadok and the sons of David, played a major role in the creation of what we call Judaism, that is, the religion of Judah.

It appears from the book of Ezra, that those who lived in Jerusalem and the environs neither wanted a king or a priest, nor did they want a temple which they would have to support. The first deputation of Zerubabel arrived in Jerusalem and tried to recreate the Davidic kingdom; however, as stated in Ezra IV, the move failed. The story continues with the return of the Exiles to Babylonia. We know very little of the life of the Babylonian Judah community, except that the life was better than we have been led to believe.

The group that followed Zerubabel came with innumerable gifts of gold and silver for the temple, and also with many slaves. This fact alone would indicate that the Jews were hardly in degradation and poverty. Quite the contrary, it appears that the Judahites were held in great esteem by the Babylonians and, as a result, the group was allowed to return in order to establish a representative economic base for the empire in Jerusalem.

This particular venture failed and must simply be reported, for soon afterwards in a very dramatic scene in Nehemiah VIII, Ezra assembled the returnees to read to them the law.

And when the seventh month was come and the children of Israel were in their cities, all the people gathered themselves together as one man into the broad place that was before the water gate; and they spoke unto Ezra the scribe to bring the book of the Law of Moses, which the Lord had commanded to Israel. And Ezra the priest brought the Law before the congregation, both men and women, and all that could hear with understanding, upon the first day of the seventh month. And he read therein before the broad place that was before the water gate from early morning until midday, in the presence of the men and women, and of those who could understand; and the ears of all the people were attentive unto the book of the Law. And Ezra the scribe stood upon a pulpit of wood, which they had made for the purpose, and beside him stood Mattithiah and Shema and Anaiah and Uriah and Hilkiah and Maaseiah, on his right hand; and on his left hand, Pedaiah, and Mishael, and Malchijah, and Hashum, and Hashbaddanah, Zechariah and Meshulam. And Ezra opened the book in the sight of all the people- for he was above all the people- and when he opened it, all the people stood up. And Ezra blessed the Lord, the great God. And all the people answered, 'Amen, Amen", with the lifting up of their hands; and they bowed their heads and fell down before the Lord with their faces to the ground. Also Jeshua and Bani, and Sherebiah, Jamin, Akkub, Shabbetai, Hodiah, Maaseiah, Kelita, Azariah, Jozabad, Hanan, Pelaiah, even the Levites, caused the people to understand the Law; and the people stood in their place. And they read in the book, in the Law of God, distinctly; and they gave the sense, and caused them to understand the reading.

And Nehemiah, who was the Tirshata, and Ezra the priest the scribe, and the Levites that taught the people, said unto all the people: 'This day is holy unto the Lord your God; mourn not, nor weep.' For all the people wept when they heard the words of the Law. Then he said to them: Go your way, eat the fat and drink the sweet, and send portions unto him for whom nothing is prepared; for this day is holy unto our Lord; neither be ye grieved; for the joy of the Lord is your strength.

So the Levites stilled all the people, saying: 'Hold your peace, for the day is holy; neither be ye grieved.' And all the people went their way to eat, and to drink, and to send portions, and to make great mirth, because they had understood the words that were declared to them.

And on the second day were gathered together the heads of fathers' houses of all the people, the priests, and the Levites, unto Ezra the scribe, even to give attention to the words of the Law. And they found that the Lord had commanded by Moses, that the children of Israel should dwell in booths in the feast of the seventh month; and that they should publish and proclaim in all their cities, and in Jerusalem, saying: 'Go forth unto the mount, and fetch olive branches, and the branches of wild olive and myrtle branches, and palm branches and branches of thick trees, to make booths, as it is written.' So the people went forth, and brought them, and made themselves booths, every one upon the roof of his house, and in their courts, and in the courts of the house of God, and in the broad place of the water gate and in the broad place of the gate of Ephraim. And all the congregation of them that were come back out of the captivity made booths, and dwelt in the booths; for since the days of Joshua the son of Nun unto that day had not the children of Israel done so. And there was very great gladness. Also day by day, from the first day unto the last day, he read the book of the Law of God. And they kept the feast seven days; and on the eighth day was a solemn assembly, according unto the ordinance.

(Chapter IX continues) *Now in the twenty and fourth day of this month the children were assembled with fasting and with sackcloth, and earth upon them. And the seed of Israel separated themselves from all foreigners and stood and confessed their sins, and the iniquities of their fathers. And they stood up in their place, and read in the book of the Law of the Lord their God a fourth part of the day; and another fourth part they confessed, and prostrated themselves before the Lord their God.*

From the text, Ezra assembled the Judahites on the first day of the seventh month to read the law to them. One might not be certain of which month this was, except that the later part of the story shows it to be, what we call today, Tishre, the month of the New Year, Rosh Hashonah. On the second day, Ezra again calls everyone together to expound the Law. In the reading he finds that the Judahites must in this month celebrate the holiday of Booths

(Sukkot), which takes place on the fifteenth day of the month. Therefore, it is fair to say that the invocation of the law by Ezra took place on the first two days of Tishre, or the two days of Rosh Hashonah, of today.

A strange problem is presented in this chapter. Rosh Hashonah takes place on the first day of the month, and Sukkot on the fifteenth day. Today Jews celebrate the tenth day of that month with Yom Kippur, the holiest day of the year. It is not even mentioned by Ezra, a priest, when wisdom would state that a priest would certainly have recognized that day rather than Sukkot, which is much more of a national holiday, commemorating the Exodus. This would be especially evident, since Yom Kippur is the day of the High Priest, when he, at the high point of the day's service, was permitted to utter the name of Jahveh in the Holy of Holies. From this, it can be assumed that the holiday of Yom Kippur was created later than 450 BCE. The story gives further evidence, since it states that Sukkot had not been celebrated since the time of Joshua, who lived about 1250 BCE, some 800 years prior.

To review: In 621 BCE, Josiah established Passover, which Kings II, 23, expounds had not been celebrated since the time of the Judges (about 1250 BCE). Sukkot had also not been celebrated since Joshua's time and now we find that in 450 BCE Yom Kippur, the High Holy Day for the priests, is not mentioned nor, for that matter, is the first day of the month called Rosh Hashonah. *Very Strange!*

It therefore becomes evident that one must try to develop a theory of how books of the Bible came to be what they are and who wrote and edited these books. Without becoming too technical, it is from the sources which have been mentioned here, that Biblical Historiography takes shape. For a person who is orthodox or traditional, such thoughts border on the heretical, but for those who have been brought up in the modern age of analysis and research, in which the scientific method was created, the whole process of looking critically at the Bible should be fairly natural. Of course, one must take the words of serious thinkers in this process and not the apologetic and sermonic methods of simplistic rabbis and teachers whose sole purpose is to defend the Bible and the past interpretations.

The task of finding the Truth is a particularly charged religious value, far more intense and valuable than reflecting on the past. In a sense, it is a matter of choosing to utilize those who are doing archaeological digging in Israel over those whose major activities seem to be protecting the Tradition. What is hoped is that this section will open your mind and propose to Jews today a pathway to see Jewish tradition in a more meaningful light.

So, now, an attempt to explain the construction of the Bible.

To begin, we start with the finding or writing of the "D" book, the scroll found in the Temple about the year 621 BCE. Shortly after the Ezra period, we find that we can place the other four parts of the Law of Moses into the canon. The Theocracy of Ezra came into existence about 450 BCE, with the formal written constitution, the Torah, basically as written today.

For those who are not familiar with the Torah, it should be stated that the hero of the five books is not Moses, but rather his brother Aaron. Sixty per cent of the books are devoted to the role of the High Priest, his sons, and their place in the temple. Their clothes are described in great length, as well as the acts of slaughtering to take place during the sacrifices. Included is the fact that the High Priest is the only one who may enter the Holy of Holies, and utter the magic four letter word, which is the name Jahveh. Also, it is the High Priest who takes upon himself the sins of the community and transfers them to God on Yom Kippur, which was not in existence at the time of Aaron.

Moses dies, leaving no dynasty, but even today there are descendants of Aaron, the Cohanim, including those whose names are Cohen, Kahn, Kagan, Aaronson, Katz and other variations . A studied reading of the Torah will indicate the extent of the impact of the priesthood upon the books.

Scholars who have studied these books have posed the following: there are at least four different strands that exist in the Torah. The first called "J", represents a writer or writers who follow the Jahvist tradition. They are essentially southern in outlook, representing a nomadic viewpoint of a movable God, with no special cult spot, but rather moving with his people. Later J becomes involved with the move to Jerusalem, but only by implication. Of course J uses in his narratives the term Jahveh as a representation of God.

The second is "E". This writer or writers use the words El and Elohim to represent the Northern idea of deity. What can be developed from scholars is that in primitive Canaan or earlier, each mountain or high place had its own El. As conquests and amalgamations took place, the Els were joined into a Godhead, called Elohim. This can be better understood if one remembers that the northern tribes who broke off from the 12, after Solomon's death, called themselves Isra-el, whereas the southern two plus tribes were called Ya-hudah, Judah. Another ideological difference can be seen when one understands that only Elohim had angels. All angels have names which end in El, such as Gabriel, Michael, Uriel and Uzziel. Jahveh has no angels, whereas the mountainous Els seem to have their messengers from the top of the mountains.

Another of the sources was already mentioned is "D". If, as assumed, it represents the attempt to centralize the weakening power of the Southern government, then D fully carries out that purpose. So many times in D, we see the phrase, *"at the place at which Jahveh Elohenu shall cause his name to rest there."* This can only refer to the acts of Josiah, in Kings II, 22, in which he destroys the false altars, and all that was described above in the long quote. By placing similar words in the Deuteronomic orations of Moses, substantiation is given. The morals and ethics of "D" are at a much higher level than those in the prior two sources, causing most scholars to date "D" at a somewhat later time in Judah history. Finally, the accent of D is totally southern, which would also give it a later date.

The fourth major source is thoroughly involved with the priesthood cult, and particularly that of the family of Aaron. It is by far the largest part of the Torah. It is designated by the letter "P" for Priestly Code. "P" is primarily concerned with the proper genealogy, proper procedures of handling sacrifices, and the counting of numbers and generations. This source is not involved with the necessity of the secular rulers, but rather with the ritual purity of acts and the actors, the appropriate dress, that one sits in the correct order, and laws to exclude those who are not able to abide by ritual cleanliness.

These are the main sources out of which the written text comes together in the Torah. Because most of the text scholars able and willing to analyze in such a manner were German academicians, they referred to the final editorial sources as "R", redactor, which simply means editor in German.

There is what scholars have referred to as the JEDPR Documentary Theory. It is these scholars who have attempted to understand and analyze the inconsistencies and dichotomies that appear in the text. Those who have been unable or unwilling to explore these theories have no truck with the creative thinking which has gone into these developments.

It is sad that liberal Jews, by and large, have not been involved with even touching these theories and simply have no feel for the ideas. In fact, those Jews who are liberal tend to avoid the Bible, contending *"it is all a bunch of myths."* However, it is the search for our history and the truth that makes the critical study of the Bible a beautiful task.

Cogent Reasoning

Having at least spread out these ideas. an attempt must be made to develop a cogent purpose for developing our historical narrative. Dismissing the very early stories of the Patriarchs as primitive legends of heroes of the past, means that the period of the Patriarchs must be put into some perspective. It is not important for this purpose to claim historicity to an Abraham or Jacob. Rather, what can we develop out of the newest archaeology and critical study?

First, Abraham's story makes sense in the context of the Mesopotamian period, when there was great wealth and household gods. If Abraham's time is about 1750 BCE, his move parallels others who travelled from the Persian Gulf to the Nile with stopovers in Canaan. In this period, there was a group of Habiru, landless people, who under the leadership of one or another, act as migratory mercenary forces for the landed gentry of the times. This would explain why Abraham is able to meet with the kings of Egypt and Salem, and never owns land, but becomes increasingly wealthy in movable stock. The roots of the group around Abraham are from Mesopotamia.

Some of the Habiru end up in Egypt, Some of these are northern based, and therefore involved with the El gods. Others are from the south, and are dedicated to the Jahveh deity. The Joseph story in this chronology fits the period around 1500 BCE. However, the four generations – Abraham, Isaac, Jacob and Joseph – must fill 250 years. Either the Bible narrative or the ages of these leaders is true, or a conclusion must be drawn that the stories are historically untrue.

There must have been many Habiru groups at that time. A number of these came together in eastern Egypt and were subsequently converted from mercenaries to slaves. They maintained their identification with leaders of the distant past, calling themselves by the name Ben—. (It should be noted that the word "Ben" has many other meanings besides "son'. It also has the connotation of being a follower or one having the attribute. For example, B'nai Brith does not mean "sons of the covenant', but rather "followers of the covenant'. If a person is asked how old one is in Hebrew, the question is asked, ben kama atah?', meaning not, "the son of how much are you?', but rather' how old are you?', or 'what attribute of age are you?') So, the tribes of Israel must not have been genetic sons, but rather groups organized around revered leaders.

These Habiru tribes seem to have lived in fairly close proximity, with the accompanying accretion of the ideas and cults of the El and Jahveh ideas of the past.

Whether there was a Moses is also not necessary for the history of the next period. Somehow these Habirus left

Egypt for what has been called the Exodus. The descriptions of this period reflect a time about the year 1250 BCE – again 250 years. What can be surmised is that some 12-15 Habiru tribes of the North and South joined to leave Egypt, resulting in quarrels over leadership.

A possible scenario is that the major Habiru groups were the B'nai Yaakov, representing the Southern Jahveh theology, and the B'nai Yisrael, the El group. If so, then this would explain the folk story developing that both were one and the same person, since the Jacob's ladder story indicates that it was the angel of Elohim, who changed Yaakov's name to Yisrael. Thus, through one statement, we have a synergism of the two major divisions of the Habiru. It is the Sh'ma, put into the mouth of Moses, that solidifies this amalgam. The Sh'ma becomes, not a symbol of monotheism, as our rabbis are inclined to say, but rather a Logo for the new corporate venture of the Exodus.

The Sh'ma, as a symbol, gives the people the Elohim name, but the God is the southern Jahveh. It is on that premise that the literary history of the Israelites is based. Certainly, history has changed the meaning of the Sh'ma since its original purpose. The fact that the Sh'ma entered the prayer book in every service gave it an interpretation far different than what was intended in the original.

At this point in the history narrative, approximate dates are listed for the Biblical period.

Abraham	about 1750 BCE
Joseph	about 1500BCE
The Exodus	1250 BCE
The Judges	1250–1000 BCE
King David	1000 BCE
First Temple	970 BCE
Split of the Kingdom	930 BCE
Period of Literary Prophets	from 900 BCE
Defeat of Israel by Assyria	721 BCE
King Josiah and Book D	621 BCE
Capture of Jerusalem by Babylonia	586 BCE
First Deputation from Persia	540 BCE
Ezra establishes the Theocracy	450 BCE

AL MELLMAN

4 ✡ THE UNKNOWN PERIOD
THE PLATONIC TIME

If one accepts the premise in the preceding chapter, the
Five Books of Moses, or Torah, were completed about
450 BCE and were the foundation of the theocracy, established by Ezra, the priest, the scribe. It is therefore no
accident that the hero of his writing is Aaron, and that the
leader of the government would be a High Priest of the
Aaronide group. More specifically, the High Priest-gov-
ernor must also be the first son of each generation, and
therefore the son of Zadok, the High Priest during the
building of the first temple of David and Solomon.

The next period to be studied will be a totally new
and revolutionary era, quite different from the Habiru,
the Judges and certainly that of the Kings of Judah. Even
more significant is that we can not turn to the Bible for
sources of this later period, after 450 BCE.

That fact is evident because the last historical
event in the Hebrew Bible occurs with Ezra in his last
chapter, with the description of the forcible separation of
the intermarried Judahites from their foreign wives. *As
an aside, it is evident that prior to Ezra, intermarriages
were totally acceptable among the Judahites.*

Certainly, men were entitled to take for wives from
any group, and at that time it was probably true that the
children followed the lineage of their fathers, for why else
would they have brought their children with them from
Babylonia.

This next period is the most difficult one in Jewish history to construct and reconstruct. The sources are
very limited. Yet one must attempt, in spite of that limita-
tion, to build a sensible history. An additional problem re-

56

lates to the many myths that have been passed on about this gray era. Even in later books of the complete Bible, there is very little that can be used as a source for historical purposes.

The one writer who can give us insights into the Ezra period, better known as the Second Commonwealth, is the most misunderstood Jew of his time, Joseph, the son of Matthius, usually called by his Roman literary name, Flavius Josephus.

It is mostly from Josephus that we learn anything about the period between 450 BCE to 70 CE, the date of the destruction of the Temple and government. We can hardly turn to rabbinical sources, for rabbis are seldom interested in detailing events or movements. But by a peculiar and unusual set of circumstances, Josephus actually wrote a *History of the Jews* up to his time, as well as a very detailed account of the *War Against the Romans,* in which he was a first-hand observer as well as participant in some of the major battles. Beyond this documentation, he wrote an autobiography and several marvelous essays on problems faced by Jews, such as Anti-Semitism, and life after death as viewed by religious Jews.

Josephus will be the source for much of the following history. There is some question about what sources Josephus relied on, but it should be indicated that he places Ezra immediately before the Queen Esther story. He then devotes two paragraphs on the next 117 years, something so out of character for Josephus, for he is long-winded and precise every where else.

Josephus, in Book XI, describes these four generations in the following:

> *When Elishab the high priest was dead. his son Judas succeeded in the high priesthood; and when he was dead, his son John took that dignity; on whose account it was also that Bagoses, the general of another Artexerxes army polluted the temple, and imposed tributes on the Jews, that out of the public stock, before they offered the daily sacrifices, they should pay for every lamb fifty shekels. Now Jesus was the*

brother of John, and was a friend of Bagoses, who had promised him the high priesthood. In confidence of whose support, Jesus quarreled with John in the temple, and so provoked his brother, that in his anger his brother slew him. Now it was a horrible thing for John, when he was high priest, to perpetrate so great a crime, and so much the more horrible, that there never was so cruel and impious a thing done neither by the Greeks nor Barbarians. However God did not neglect its punishment, but the people were on that very account enslaved and the temple polluted by the Persians. Now when Bagoses, the general of Artexerxes's army knew that John, the high priest of the Jews, had slain his own brother Jesus in the temple, he came upon the Jews immediately, and began in anger to say to them, "Have you had the impudence to perpetrate a murder in the temple? And as he was aiming to go into the temple, they forbade him to do so; but he said to them, 'Am I not purer than he that was slain in the temple?' And when he said these words, he went into the temple. Accordingly, Bagoses made use of this pretense and punished the Jews seven years for the murder of Jesus.

Now when John had departed this life, his son Jaddua succeeded in the high priesthood. He had a brother, whose name was Manasseh. Now there was one Sanballat, who was sent by Darius, the last king (of Persia) into Samaria. He was a Cuthian by birth; of which stock were the Samaritans. This man knew that the city Jerusalem was a famous city, and that their kings had given a great deal of trouble to the Assyrians, and the people of Celsyria; so that he willingly gave his daughter, whose name was Nicaso, in marriage to Manasseh, as thinking this alliance by marriage would be a pledge and security that the nation of the Jews should continue their good will to him.

Josephus does not hesitate to spend pages on pages on the most excruciating details about the ancestry of some inconsequential personage, the dimensions of the temple or the imagined letter from one official to another. But he seems to have had no other sources for the period and is forced to condense this more-than-a-century to some 600 words.

A few words about Josephus. In his autobiography, he explains that he was a descendant of the first of the 24 courses of Priests, and that makes him of royal blood of the Hasmoneans. His father had been of the nobility, but was also considered well by the people for his righteousness. Like Jesus, Josephus, at about fourteen, was considered so bright that the priests and other leaders came to him for his opinion of the Law.

At sixteen, he decided to try out several of the known sects. Since he was of the priesthood, he was originally a Saducee. It is Josephus who first alerted us that the three major sects are the Pharisees, Saducees and the Essenes. He detailed that he finally, after spending time with them all, as well as one called Banus (probably a Baptist, and may even be John), joins the Pharisees. He later became a general in the war against the Romans, about the year 68 CE, but not being sympathetic with the war or its objectives, he deserted to the Roman general, Vespasian. He predicted that Vespasian would become the Emperor of Rome. At this point, Vespasian took Josephus under his wing and made him his ward.

After the war, when the Jews were defeated, Josephus went to Rome, where he moved into Vespasian's home. There he was asked to write a *History of the Jews* and other materials, particularly the *War Against the Romans.* Parenthetically, he has been denied as an historian by many Jews, because they deemed he was a traitor to the revolution. Subsequently, we shall show that many of the leaders of the Judah community, for their own purposes, did precisely what Josephus had done, but their story would be told in time.

Josephus must be read as any other source, to be analyzed, to be accepted or rejected, where good historical sense is appropriate, and to be evaluated when Josephus' own conclusions or fables are too far-fetched for modern man. Other sources may turn up which would have to be evaluated and weighed in some balance; however, after 1900 years, most of what he tells us bears good evidence of what occurred.

To return to those two paragraphs of Josephus, it must become obvious that the high priesthood had at that time become fairly dissolute and subject to the political vagaries of the Syrian satrapies or provincial leaders. As depicted by Josephus, the high priests are no more than oriental potentates.

A figure whose presence is still being felt by Jews and Judaism today entered the scene at this point – Alexander the Great, son of Philip of Macedonia, who rose out of Greece and conquered much of the Near East from the Persians. Students of ancient history know much of the Golden Age of Greece and Alexander's contribution to its spread around the known world. Jews today generally have difficulty placing him into context of Jewish History. It is impossible to understand Jewish History without grasping the significance of Alexander.

He is known for having conquered all the Middle East up to the Ganges, including much of North Africa, Turkey, Persia and, of course, very easily, Judah. (Until this time, the country is known as *Judah*, but with the capture by the Greeks, the transliteration into Greek became *Judea*. During this Greek period the name Judea will be used.)

The Greek's move into Judea took place approximately 333 BCE, when Alexander is welcomed as a conqueror by the priest-governors of the period. Judea becomes subject to the Greeks, who are very benevolent conquerors. They offer to their subjects protection and the right to participate fully in the Greek Empire. The process necessary for that participation is called Hellenization, the ideology, now called Hellenism, after the Greek word for Greece, *Hellas*. Since much is talked about the clash between Judaism and Hellenism during Chanukah, considerable space will be devoted in exploring this phenomenon, for Hellenism is probably one of the most misunderstood words in history.

When Alexander the Great conquered the greater part of his known world, he arrived, not as the usual conqueror, but rather with a unique baggage. This consisted of the greatest period of intellectual life that had ever developed, the Golden Age of Greece. The person who had the most impact in this constellation of stars of this period was Plato, who always is called *The Philosopher,* as Shakespeare is called *The Bard.*

Unfortunately for most American Jews, the Greek period is unknown, and the three greatest philosophers of this time must be set in some context.

The first of the three, Socrates, early in the fourth century BCE, developed the system to which he lent his name, the Socratic Method. His search for "Truth" led him to create this method, by using what is called dialogue, in which one person makes a statement, and the response is aiming for a truthful answer. Or to reverse it, a statement is made, followed by a question aimed at eliminating what is not true. In a sort of negative approach, Truth is arrived at by eliminating what is not valid. This method is most evident if one watches court trials. The assignment for the court is the truth. The lawyers may only ask questions of witnesses. Should a lawyer ask a question which may not be appropriate, the judge may rule that the question is irrelevant to the basic charge of the court. With this method, Socrates stimulated the advance of Greek philosophy.

One of his students, Plato, began to seek out the truth in many specific areas and facets of the world. His concerns were the ways to study Man, Art, Politics, Love, Government, Ideals, Values and about every other part of the universe of his time. He literally taught under a tree in a part of Athens called *Academe,* from which the term, *"Groves of Academia,"* arises for university life. Plato came to the conclusion that all systems of the universe are doubled, that is that there is a dualism implicit in the very existence of the world. For this reason, Plato is also dubbed *The Dualist.*

Plato, in developing the idea of dualism, felt that there were two parts to whatever he observed – the ideal and the real. If not totally ideal, then the division was more ideal as against the less ideal. He postulated that there are essentially two worlds. The one, occupied by the God or Gods, was above and beyond this world and therefore labeled Supernatural. The Gods of the Pantheon were governed by supernatural law, otherwise known as the occult. We humans and all matter in this world are bound by those rules which are commonly called Natural Law.

One may picture the Pantheon placed in its own sphere, distant from the world of Nature. Between this world and the natural world, Plato hypothesized a void or jumble, which he labeled Chaos. There was no direct connection between the two worlds. It is absolutely impossible for a human in the natural world ever to reach up to God, however the Gods could and usually did reach down over the Chaos to distort Natural Law. We call that reaching down across the Chaos by the Gods or God, *Grace*. It is through Grace that a miracle occurs. In Hebrew, the word is *Chen*. Parenthetically, Sephardic women who have the Hebrew name of *Chana*, usually have the Spanish name, *Gracia*, or are called *Grace* in English.

Whenever a god or gods use grace to undo Natural Law, we humans call this a miracle. (There but for the grace of God go I.) In fact within the Platonic system proof that there is a god relies on the appearance of miracles. No miracle – no god.

Plato went further in this dualism by insisting that all ideas and matter are essentially dual, for example:

God	Devil
God	Man
Man	Woman
Body	Soul
Good	Evil
White	Black
No Sex	Sex
Homosexual Love	Heterosexual Love
Philosopher	Slave

It is obvious that the list could be carried on in-definitely. It suffices that in the Platonic mode the first of each of these was considered better than the latter. (One should also recall that Platonic friendship is one between a man and a woman who are able to eliminate the sexual needs between them.)

The important facet of this is that God or gods are not in this world, but live in an ethereal cosmos, not bound by natural law. Occasionally, the deity decides to inter-vene in the normal currents of the real world, which takes place only at the instance of God. In general, in this Platonic mode, the deity moves in miraculous and strange ways, and the only time one takes note of it, is when a traumatic experience takes place, either for good or bad.

To conclude this brief exposition of Plato, Socrates laid the groundwork for Plato. Plato's student was Aristotle, for whom we are in debt for preserving much of Plato's ideas and words. To add to the continuum, Aristotle was the mentor of Alexander, who absorbed the Platonic thinking into his actions in the development of his empire. The contention is that the Greek Empire was essentially built on the values and directions of Plato. Hellenism, as it developed, was the logical extension of Plato's world.

Hellenism was the method of imperialism which the Greeks imposed on their subjects, from the Ganges to North Africa. It consisted, practically, of the following five dimensions:

1) The empire is to be built on the structure of a united group of city-states, developed around the main city, which would be a Polis, to be governed by the Elite, namely philosophers, who would rule through a Boulé.

2) To become a member of the Boulé, one had to be a student in the Academy, be knowledgeable in phi-losophy – precisely the philosophy of Plato. Anyone could be admitted into the academy, but, normally, pref-erence was given to those who had been in power, prior to the Greek arrival.

3) The Greek language and culture was to be learned.

4) The men who were eligible to be a part of the Boulé had to participate in the athletic events of the gymnasium. These activities were to take place in the nude. It can be assumed that some of the corollary activities were homosexual acts.

5. Sacrifices were to be brought to the Greek gods and goddesses. These sacrifices were not thought as religious acts, but more as ethnic acts of solidarity.

These five parts were the concomitant elements of Hellenism. These facets were the requirements of those who wished to have political and economic power in the Greek empire. The Empire was constructed upon the development of trade between one Polis and another, and therefore, those who were in the Boulé were the ones who might benefit most from their participation. Further, it makes sense that those who felt a part of this program were, by nature, city-folk. On the contrary, those who worked the land and lived in small towns were not able and often unwilling to join an academy to become a member of the Elite.

When Alexander arrived in Jerusalem, according to Josephus, he was welcomed by the HighPriest-Governor, and thus they became his subjects. *Judah* became *Judea*, which was as close as the Greeks could spell and pronounce Judah. Soon after that, Alexander died at the age of 33, and the Empire was split into four parts. One was Macedonia, which Cassander ruled, another was Hellespont, the area now called Turkey, headed by Lysimachus. More important to this history is the fact that Egypt's king was Ptolemy, and the ruler of Syria and Babylonia was Antigonus. If one looks at the map of the divided Greek Empire, one will quickly notice that Judea rests almost directly on the boundary line between the latter two.

This geopolitical oddity was the determining factor for the Judeans for more than a century. The High Priest became a bargaining position for whichever of the two powers was in control. Josephus in Book XII, Chapter 4, details the role of tax farming, which was the authority given by the king to someone to collect the taxes for a fee.

The ruler of the Syrian group was Antiochus, after the city of Antioch, his capital.

After this Antiochus made a friendship and a league with Ptolemy and gave him his daughter Cleopatra to wife, and yielded up to him CeleSyria, and Samaria, and Judea and Phoenicia, by way of dowry. And upon the division of the taxes between the two kings, all the principal men farmed the taxes of their several countries, and collecting the sum that was settled for them, paid the same to the kings. Now at this time the Samaritans were in a flourishing condition and much distressed the Jews, cutting off parts of their land and carrying off slaves. This happened when Onias was high priest; for after Eleazar's death, his uncle took the priesthood, and after he had ended his life, Onias received that dignity. He was the son of Simon, who was called "The Just": which Simon was the brother of Eleazar, as I said before. This Onias was one of a little soul, and a great lover of money; and for that reason, because he did not pay the tax of twenty talents of silver, which his forefathers paid to these kings out of their own estates, he provoked king Prolemy Euergertes to anger, who was the father of Philopater. Euergetes sent an ambassador to Jerusalem, and complained that Onias did not pay his taxes, and threatened, that if he did not receive them, he would seize upon their land, and send soldiers to live upon it.

The story continues with a long drawn out tale of how Onias lost the rights to tax farming. It is obvious from the text that purchasing the right was something that the High Priest handled in Jerusalem for the king.

The story in Josephus continues in Chapter 5 of Book XII:

About this time, upon the death of Onias (the

*grandson of the previous Onias) the high priest,
they gave the high priesthood to Jesus, his brother;
for that son which Onias left (or Onias IV) was yet
but an infant, and its proper place we will inform
the reader of all the circumstances that befell this
child. But this Jesus, who was the brother of Onias,
was deprived of the high priesthood by the king,
who was angry with him, and gave it to his younger
brother, whose name also was Onias; for Simon had
three sons, to each of which the priesthood came,
as have already informed the reader. This Jesus
changed his name to Jason, but Onias was called
Menelaus. Now as the former high priest, Jesus,
raised a sedition against Menelaus, who was ordained after him, the multitude were divided between them both. And the sons of Tobias took the
part of Menelaus, but the greater part of the people
assisted Jason; and by that means Menelaus and
the sons of Tobias were distressed and retired to
Antiochus, and informed him that they were desirous to leave the laws of their country and the Jewish way of living according to them, and to follow
the king's way of living. Wherefore they desired to
build them a Gymnasium at Jerusalem. And when
he had given them leave, they also hid the circumcision of their genitals, that even when they were
naked, they might appear to be Greeks. Accordingly, they left off all the customs of their own country and imitated the practices of the other nations.*

This paragraph is one of the most penetrating of
Josephus' writing, for he makes very clear that there had
been much conniving by the rich and the high priests, so
that even one who aspired to be a high priest could convert to total Greek practices, including the actions in the
gymnasium. In this context, they could be called radical
Hellenists.

The next paragraph tells how Antiochus, the vil-
lain of Chanukah, decided to wage war on Egypt in about
the year 168 BCE. After some preliminary excursions,

he is soundly defeated when the Romans enter into the war on the side of the Egyptians. This is the first time that the Romans enter the scene in the Middle East.

Upon returning from his defeat, Antiochus decided to make Judea pay for his loss. On the 25th day of Kislev, Antiochus came up to Jerusalem, raped the temple of its wealth, forbade the bringing of the traditional sacrifices, took many slaves, burnt many buildings and built a citadel there. According to Josephus, he ordered another altar built on the altar of the temple, upon which he ordered pigs slaughtered. He forbade the rite of circumcision, and destroyed any Torahs found. It should be recalled at this time that the Torah consisted of only the five books of Moses.

It is important to understand that Hellenism was not always the evil concept that is portrayed in Jewish History. Ptolemy, in order to increase a famous library in Egypt, ordered that the Torah be translated into Greek. The apocryphal story is that seventy Jewish leaders were each placed in separate rooms with instructions to convert the Hebrew into Greek. By a miracle, the result was an exact word for word translation. This Septuagint, meaning the seventy, has been one of the most useful tools for scholars in comparing the Greek and the Hebrew. More important for the purposes here is the fact that the number chosen is 70, which will come up again later.

Antiochus took out his vengeance on the Judeans for having lost so badly in his battles with the Egyptian-Greek forces. He precipitated the amalgamation of some parts of the Judean people around the Maccabeean party, which led to the revolution against the Syrian Greeks and their cohorts among the Judeans.

What is proposed at this point is a radical view of what has been taught for centuries about the Revolution and the holiday Chanukah that commemorates the victory. Again Josephus provides us with the clues in Book XII, Chapter VI, where he begins the story of the revolution.

Now at this time there was one whose name was Mattathias, who dwelt at Modin, the son of Simon, the son of Asmoneus, a priest of the order of Joarib, and a citizen of Jerusalem. He had five sons; John, who was called Gaddis, and Simon, who was called Matthes, and Judas, who was called Maccabeus, and Eleazar, who was called Auran, and Jonathan, who was called Apphus. Now this Mattathias lamented to his children the sad state of their affairs, and the ravage made in the city, and the plundering of the temple, and the calamities the multitude were under; and he told them that it was better for them to die for the laws of their country, than to live so ingloriously as they then did.

But when those that were appointed by the king came to Modin, that they might compel the Jews to do what they were commanded, and to enjoin those that were there to offer sacrifice, as the king had commanded, they desired that Mattathias, a person of the greatest character among them, both on other accounts, and particularly on account of such a numerous and so deserving a family of children, would begin the sacrifice, because his fellow citizens would follow his example, and because such a procedure would make him honoured by the king.

But Mattathias said that he would not do it; and that if all the other nations would obey the commands of Antiochus, either out of fear, or to please him, yet would not he nor his sons leave the religious worship of their country. But as soon as he had ended his speech, there came one of the Jews into the midst of them and sacrificed, as Antiochus had demanded. At which Mattathias had great indignation, and ran upon him violently, with his sons, who had swords with them, and Apelles the King's general, who compelled them to sacrifice, with a few of his soldiers. He also overthrew the idol altar, and cried out, " If," said he, " anyone be zealous for the laws of his country, and for the worship of God, let him follow me." And when he had said this, he made haste into the desert with his sons, and left all his substance in the village. Many others did the same also, and fled with

*their children and wives into the desert, and dwelt
in caves.*

*But when the king's generals heard this, they
took all the forces they then had in the citadel at
Jerusalem, and pursued the Jews into the desert; and
when they had overtaken them, they in the first place
endeavored to persuade them to repent, and to choose
what was most for their advantage, and not put them
to the necessity of using them according to the law of
war. But when they would not comply with their per-
suasions, but continued to be of a different mind,
they fought against them on the sabbath day and
burnt them as they were in the caves, without resis-
tance, and without so much as stopping up the entrances of the caves. And they avoided to defend themselves on that day, because they were not willing to
break in upon the honour they owed the sabbath,
even in such distresses; for the law requires that we
rest upon that day. There were about a thousand,
with their wives and children, who were smothered
and died in these caves; but many who escaped joined
themselves to Mattathias and appointed him to be
their ruler, who taught them to fight, even on the
sabbath day; and told them that unless they would
do so, they would become their own enemies, by observing the law (so rigorously). while their adver-
saries would still assault on this day, and nothing
could then hinder but that they must all perish without fighting. This speech persuaded them.*

*And this rule continues among us to this day,
that if there be a necessity, we may fight on sabbath
days. So Mattathias got a great army about him
and overthrew idol altars, and slew those that broke
the laws, even all that broke the laws, even all that
he could get under his power; for many of them that
were dispersed among the nations round about them
for fear of him, He also commanded that those boys
which were not yet circumcised should be circumcised now; and he drove those away that were appointed to hinder such their circumcision.*

But when he had ruled one year, and was fallen into a distemper, he called for his sons, and set them around about him, and said, "O my sons, I am going the way of all the earth; and I recommend to you my resolution, and beseech you not to be negligent in keeping it, but to be mindful of the desires of him who begat you, and brought you up, and to preserve the customs of your country, and to recover your ancient form of government, which is in danger of being overturned, and not to be carried away with those that, either by their own inclination, or out of necessity, betray it, but to become such sons as are worthy of me; to be above all force and necessity, and so to dispose your souls, as to be ready, when it shall be necessary, to die for your laws; as sensible of this, by just reasoning, that if God see that you are so disposed he will not overlook you, but will have a great value for your virtue, and will restore to you again what you have lost, and will return to you that freedom in which you will live quietly, and enjoy your own customs. Your bodies are mortal and subject to fate; but they receive a sort of immortality, by the remembrance of what actions they have done. And I would have you so in love with this immortality, that you may pursue after glory, and that , when you have undergone the greatest difficulties, you may not scruple, for such things, to lose your lives. I exhort you, especially to agree one with another; and in what excellency any one of you exceeds another, to yield to him so far, and by that means to reap the advantage of everyone's own virtues. Do you then esteem Simon as your father, because he is a man of extraordinary prudence, and be governed by him in what counsels he gives you. Take Maccabeus for the general of your army, because of his courage and strength, for he will avenge your nation and will bring vengeance on your enemies. Admit among you the righteous and religious, and augment their power"

Josephus continues with the death of Mattathias

and Judas taking over administration of public affairs, and then details the war against Antiochus. With the victory of forces, Judas orders on the 25th of Kislev of 165 BCE that the temple be rededicated. Josephus ends this story in Book XII, Chapter II, with the following:

Now Judas celebrated the festival of the restora-
tions of the temple for eight days and omitted no
sort of pleasures thereon; but he feasted them upon
very rich and splendid sacrifices; and he honoured
God, and delighted them by hymns and psalms. Nay,
they were so very glad at the revival of their cus-
toms, when after a long time of intermission, they
unexpectedly had regained the freedom of their wor-
ship, that they made it a law for their posterity, that
they should keep a festival, on account of the resto-
ration of their temple worship, for eight days. And
from that time to this we celebrate this festival, and
call it Lights. I suppose the reason was, because this
liberty beyond our hopes appeared to us; and that
thence was the name given to that festival. Judas
also rebuilt the walls around the city, and reared
towers of great height against the incursions of en-
emies, and set guards therein. He also fortified the
city Bethsura, that it might serve as a citadel against
any distresses that might come from our enemies.

To recapitulate this chapter of Josephus, Mattathias had five sons, each of which had two names, one Hebrew, the other Greek. Maccabeus was Judas' Greek name, in much the same way that many Jews today have both an English name and a Hebrew name. Mattathias, on his own, according to Josephus, declares a new law, although the Torah quite specifically states that on the Sabbath you shall do no work, and that is the law which enables the enemy to kill so many. In addition, he suggested that the sons welcome others into the group. Finally, we have the story of the first Chanukah in 165 BCE, which was called Lights, and was declared an eight day festival, an old custom for festivals.

*Consider: no miracles, no jar of oil that lasts
eight days, when it was only supposed to have one
day's worth of light in it. This was not a Menorah
holiday, but rather a religio-national celebration.*

What is posited here is that the Maccabean Revolution was not a war against Hellenism, but rather a civil
war against those in the country, who were radical Hellenists. Mattathias gives every indication that he was no
fanatic about his religious past, he called his sons with
two names, he broke the law in order to live, and as will
be seen later, he adopted several of the Platonic ideas
and incorporated them into a later movement.

There were, at this time, at least three major
groups. The first were the Elite, made up mostly of the
high priests and their followers, who were amenable to
gross accommodation with the Syrian Greeks. The second group, led by the Hasmoneans, were the moderate
Hellenists, who were willing to accept parts of the Greek
program, except for two matters – the sacrifices to the
Greek Gods and Goddesses, and the   Gymnasium, with
its athletic programs in the nude, which probably led to
homosexual activities. What they did accept was the
Greek language, Platonic philosophy with its dualism,
and the Boulé style of government.

The third group, which was called the Chassidim,
were absolutely opposed to any acceptance of Hellenistic
ideas. They were Jewish Puritans who wished to return
to some past vision of Judaic life, built on old traditions,
many of which were in the Torah. However, reading in
that passage in Josephus, they were destined to be destroyed because they would not fight on the Sabbath. Some
of them, when the Revolution began, joined Mattathias
who told them that they were permitted to fight on Shabat.
*"And this rule continues among us to this day, that if there
be a necessity, we may fight on sabbath days."*

By what authority did Mattathias operate and how
is it that this is still Jewish Law? Somehow, the question
has not been answered or possibly never been asked. Prior
to this period, only the elite priests could interpret the

Law. Now,this priest, Mattathias, from a small town, Modin, and not from the highest order, the sons of Zadok, was capable of changing the law and making it stand forever. That is one of the first questions that has to be phrased about this period. When the other pieces are put together, an understanding of this new world, the Hasmonean Dynasty, may be felt.

As Mattathias was dying, he called his sons together, as Josephus states, and designates Simon as the father-leader of the group, and Judas as the General of the Armies.

Turn now to the story of Chanukah. Mention has already been made of the fact that no cruse of oil was in this story, and that there was nothing unusual that the holiday was celebrated for eight days. But why should it be called Lights? It is here where we must turn to Plato for clarification, for in his system, light is the symbol of the divine, and all ideals are embodied in Light. Light is also symbolic of Truth and the very Godhead. There is no connection between this holiday and the present traditions of lighting the Menorah of eight parts. This deviation is obviously a later tradition.

The story continues with more victories for Judas, and the eventual establishment of a Judaic state, with Simon elected as the High Priest by the people, as well as being the Ethnarch, that is, the national head. Here we have the joining of the cultic and the secular leadership although that person was not a member of the High Priest family, the family of Zadok. A revolution had taken place. The Zadokites were displaced, even though the Torah specifically says that the High Priest must be the first son of the first son, etc. of Aaron. If the Five Books of Moses were meant to be a priestly document, the Maccabean Revolution was a terrible defeat for the Zadokite priests. In fact Josephus states that Onias went with his followers to a Ptolemaic city, Heliopolis (City of the Sun), and built a Jewish Temple, like the one in Jerusalem, quite in contradiction to Deuteronomy.

Immediately after describing this event, Josephus introduces us for the first time to the three sects among the Jews. Simon has died and was succeeded by his son, Hyrcanus, not a very Jewish name. Hyrcanus expanded the kingdom, and the story continues in Josephus, Book XIII, Chapter X, 5.

However, the prosperous state of affairs moved the Jews to envy Hyrcanus; but they that were the worst were the Pharisees, who were one of the sects of the Jews, as we have informed you already. These have so great a power over the multitude, that when they say any thing against the king or against the high priest, they are presently believed. Now Hyrcanus was a disciple of theirs and greatly beloved by them. And when he once invited them to a feast, and entertained them very kindly, when he saw them in a good humor, he began to say to them, that they knew he was desirous to be a righteous man and to do all things whereby he might please God, which was the profession of the Pharisees also.

However, he desired that if they observed him offending in any point, and going out of the right way, they would call him back and correct him. On which occasion they attested to his being entirely virtuous; with which commendation he was well pleased. But still there was one of his guests there, whose name was Eleazar, a man of ill temper, and delighting in seditious practices. This man said, "Since thou desirest to know the truth, if thou wilt be righteous in earnest, lay down the high priesthood, and content thyself with the civil government of the people." And when he desired to know for what cause he ought to lay down the high priesthood, the other replied. "We have heard it from old men, that thy mother had been a captive under the reign of Antiochus Epiphanes." This story was false, and Hyrcanus was provoked against him; and all the Pharisees had a very great indignation against him.

Now there was one Jonathan, a very great friend

of Hyrcanus, but of the sect of Saducees, whose notions are quite contrary to those of the Pharisees. He told Hyrcanus that Eleazar had cast such a reproach upon him according to the common sentiments of the Pharisees, and that this would be made manifest if he would but ask them the question. What punishment they thought this man deserved? for that he might depend upon it, that the reproach was not laid on him with their approbation, if they were punishing him as his crime deserved. So the Pharisees made answer, that he deserved stripes and bonds, but that it did not seem right to punish reproaches with death.

And indeed the Pharisees, even upon other occasion, are not apt to be severe in punishments. At this gentle sentence, Hyrcanus was very angry, and thought that this man reproached him by their approbation. It was this Jonathan who chiefly irritated him, and influenced him so far, that he made him leave the party of the Pharisees and abolish the decrees they had imposed on the people, and to punish those that observed them. From this source arose that hatred which he and his sons met with from the multitude: but of these matters we shall speak hereafter.

What I would now explain is this, that the Pharisees have delivered to the people a great many observances by succession from their fathers, which are not written in the laws of Moses; and for that reason it is that the Saducees reject them, and say that we are to esteem those observances to be obligatory which are in the written word, but not to observe what are derived from the tradition of our forefathers. And concerning these things it is that great disputes and differences have arisen among them, while the Saducees are able to persuade none but the rich, and have not the populace obsequious to them, but the Pharisees have the multitude on their side. But about these two sects and that of the Essens, I have treated accurately in the second book of Jewish Affairs.

For the first time, the basic difference between the Pharisees and Saducees is explained. It has to do with two kind of laws. The Saducees followed only the written Law, which at this time was the Torah, whereas the Pharisees had an additional set of laws which were claimed to be passed on from their forefathers. In addition, the Pharisees were the popular religion, whereas the Torah was basically the law for the rich. (More of this later, for the story continues.)

Hyrcanus is succeeded by his eldest son, Aristobulus, who destroyed his brothers, and seemed to run a reign of terror in Judea. When he died, his wife, Salome, made her son, Alexander Janneus, king, who by hiring mercenaries, expanded the kingdom of Judea immensely, but was not liked by the populace. With his death, the rule of the country was turned over to his wife, Alexandra, who became the regent of Judea. Her first act was to make peace with the Pharisees by giving them control of internal affairs, while she retains power over foreign matters. She appointed one of her sons, Hyrcanus, to be High Priest.

At this time, the Romans, who had been active in capturing much of the Greek empire and Northern Europe, began to have some impact on the country of Judea.

It is my contention that the Pharisees created in this period several major ideas and developments that are still having an impact today. First, they created the idea of an Oral Law, which they traced back to Moses through their forefathers. This followed the Platonic system that there are two parts to everything. In this case, the written Law belongs to God, and therefore must not be tampered with. Coupled with the Written Law is the Oral Law, which is human, flexible and meant to refer directly to the needs of the common man.

In parallel, they created an additional or possibly a contending legislative and judicial body, consisting of 71 members who did not receive their positions *genetically* as the priests normally did, but rather was *granted,* based on merit. This, too, would follow the Greek style of elitism, that anyone versed in philosophy could become a member of the Boulé. This Boulé becomes, even in name, a Greek institution, the Sanhedrin, led by a Nasi, the one and seventy ordinary elite members. They constituted the bearers and interpreters of the Oral Law. The two-part Law had a major rule. Anything which was written down must never be memorized, and the Oral Law must never be written down.

The next accomplishment of the Pharisees was the changing of the Written Torah. Until 165 BCE, the Torah consisted of the five books for which Moses was the author. The Pharisees decided on their own that with only these books, the Zadokite priests were the major dynasty of the Judeans. For the Pharisees, it became necessary to undercut the priesthood according to the Torah. They then turned to the collections of the Judah Literary Society whose hero was David. They added the Books of the Prophets to the Canon and ruled that whenever the five books were read in worship, that one was obligated to also read from the prophetic books as well.

The Pharisees then created an institution that has had a major influence, even today. In an attempt to deny to the Jerusalem temple and its Zadokite priests the sole means of reaching God, they made it possible for the individual to participate at home in Judea. The concept, which created places of worship called *Maamadot,* were placed in various parts of Judea. In one respect these maamadot are similar to the division of France into departments. There were 24 Maamadots; each Maamad was led by a family of priests, a family of Levites and a family of Israelites. Whenever a service occurred in the Jerusalem Temple, a parallel service was held in the major town of the Maamad, with one exception: In Jerusalem, services plus animal sacrifices took place, but in the Maamad, only the songs and words were used. Undoubtedly, the priests in the hinterland read the rules of the sacrifices in lieu of actually performing the acts. The area residents came to these services, and were relieved of coming to the Temple. The synagogue as we know it today, undoubtedly, arose from these Maamadot, and the services developed out of this program.

Due to the Maamodot, as well as the philosophy of the Pharisees, there was a change in the concept of God. Earlier, God had been pictured as a monarch, and to some extent tyrannical, omnipotent and arbitrary, whereas the new concept became more a personal deity for each Jew. If God resided only in Jerusalem, then one had to go there, mediate with the priests, and bring physical offerings in tribute. But if God spoke to the normal individual, he could be visualized differently. It was the Pharisees who introduced the idea of Father-God, who can and must be addressed personally. God became the Av, and in worship, Avinu- our father.

Out of these contributions, the Pharisees basically created a Judaism, not too distant from that which we possess today. If so, then traditional Judaism is primarily a Platonic variation of Jewish Law and practices, with the underlying theme, the dualism of Plato. There is the two-fold law, the two worlds, God in his heaven, Man in his world, the duality of man with the body and soul, the soul being permanent and belonging to God, and the body, a temporary vessel of that soul: All themes existent in modern Judaism.

In terms of time we are about 100 years after the Hasmonean Revolution or about the year 63 BCE, as we enter the Roman period of Jewish history.

Once again in review:

The Babylonian Exile	586 BCE
Ezra and the Theocracy	450 BCE
Alexander the Great	333 BCE
The Maccabean Revolt	165 BCE
Roman Capture of Judea	63 BCE

5 ✡ THE ROMAN PERIOD
AND THE CLOSING OF THE BIBLE

This was the legacy of the Hasmoneans, as the Roman armies entered Judea and Jerusalem in 63 BCE. It is necessary at this point to indicate the differences in the imperialistic policies of the Romans and the Greeks. Basically, the phrase, "Divisum et Imperium," carries out the method of Roman empire rule. Their goal was *Pax Romana,* usually translated as *Roman Peace.* More correctly, it means a total Roman Empire, completely dominated by Rome, and that all roads lead to Rome. Just as Gaul was divided into three parts, in order to prevent any merging of forces who might consider revolt, Judea was divided into four parts, each led by a tetrarch. The major tenet of the Romans was that those who are conquered are to be divided, families split, enslaved and oppressed by the overwhelming strength of the minions of the conquerors.

When the Romans defeated the Antiochans with the help of the Judeans, Caesar designated Hyrcanus as the High Priest, and Antipater to be the procurator of Judea, that is, the official agent of the emperor, and, mainly, his financial advisor. Antipater was the father of Herod, who was to become more well known in World History.

Herod was appointed Governor of Galilee at the age of fifteen. He became notorious very early in his career for his part in the murder of a Hezekiah, described as a robber. Josephus often uses this same term to label revolutionaries against Rome and Roman supporters. It may very well be his way to cover the fact that there were Judeans who were actively fighting Rome. Still later, the writers of the Gospels calls Barrabas a robber, and have the Jewish crowd choose him over Jesus to be released by the authorities.

Herod is accused of having Hezekiah murdered before he was even condemned to death by the Sanhedrin. There is an overlong story of Herod's devious behavior. Its conclusion is that Herod made an alliance with Mark Anthony, and in exchange for a large sum of money, Herod would become King of Judea.

Herod, now a complete subject-king of the Romans, took over all of the Judean institutions, including the Sanhedrin. This was in the year, 30 BCE. A most interesting development soon takes place after his ascension to the throne. We know from the Talmud, that a Babylonian Jew is made Nasi in that same year. This is the famous Hillel, who becomes a saint in Jewish lore. Eisenstein, the author of an encyclopedic book on the Talmud, *Otser Yisrael* (Treasure of Israel), suggests that Hillel was a friend of Herod (Herodias), and according to the custom of the day, prophesied that Herod would become King. As an after thought Eisenstein said that it was possible that Herod made Hillel the Nasi, the head of the Sanhedrin. One must puzzle as to why the Sanhedrin, this locally based institution in Judea, would have an outsider become its president. More importantly, why would Herod want such an outsider as the leader of the Boulé, the Hellenistic-style assembly?

One possible explanation is there had developed in Judea, within the Pharisees, two separate and disparate political parties and ideas. One group of Pharisees saw Judaism as one of the *religio licta*, a permitted religion, of the Roman Empire. For them Judaism was a series of rituals, philosophy and good deeds, modified by Pharisaic worship, not a national culture, dominated by religion. The other group maintained a strong nationalistic base, with their strength coming out of the Prophets and the Messianic idea of Jerusalem and the Judeans. Herod, by seeking out a foreigner who could not claim Judean nationalism for his ideas, hoped to support this side of this argument.

The other group, also Pharisaic,was intensely nationalistic, anti-Roman, and was more concerned with restricting the group to those who were born Jews. Thus, we might infer that they were opposed to divorce, inter-marriage, conversion and any radical changes with the past. This group eventually split into a number of groups, some terroristic, others less so.

If Herod appointed Hillel, and there is no reason to think otherwise, it seems obvious that he represented that school of thought that meant accommodation with Rome and Herod. His opponent was Shamai. Hillel is called by the Talmud, a Maykil, a liberal, while Shamai is known as Machmir, a conservative, which would fit the analysis here.

We have little evidence of the clash between Hillel and Shamai from Josephus, although he uses what must be their Roman names of Pollio and Sameas, when he refers to them. The Mishna, the first written Oral Law, compiled in about 200 CE, speaks of many differences of opinions between Hillel and Shamai. Incidentally, whenever there was a conflict, the decision was always according to Hillel. As an aside at this point, we know today that the Menorah for Chanukah has eight lights and one Shamas for lighting the other eight.

The question was put: How do we light the candles on Chanukah? Hillel stated that we light one candle the first night, adding one each succeeding night, while Shamai took the position that on the first night, we should light all eight, and diminish them by one, with only the one on the last evening. Hillel's theory was that Freedom, since Chanukah, represented by Lights, was increasing day by day, whereas Shamai felt otherwise.

As previously stated, the Pharisees, according to Josephus, believed in some freedom of action, and they also taught that Moses had given an oral tradition at the same time that he gave the Torah on Mount Sinai. It is necessary to mention the first paragraph of the Pirkey Avot, the Ethics of the Fathers.

> *Moses received the Law from Sinai and com-*
> *mitted it over to Joshua, and Joshua to the elders,*

*and the elders to the Prophets, and the Prophets to
the men of the Great Synagogue.*

This is the line of Masorah, which is the tradition
or Oral Law. It is important to note that nowhere do the
priests enter into this chain, but rather the tradition em-
phasizes that the line was non-genealogical. Even Moses
does not pass it to his son, but rather to his military successor.

Thus did the Pharisees undercut the authority of
the Aaronide leadership of the priests – those who followed the idea that the direct descendants of Zadoc were
the proper monarchs. They therefore took the name of
Zadukim, or as we know from the Greek Bible, and the
Christian writings, Saducees. *Saduc* in Greek is close to
Tsadok of the Hebrew. There is no Ts in the Greek language.

When it comes to the meaning of the name
Pharisees, or Paroshim, every historian translates it from
a Hebrew word, Parash, meaning to separate, deeming
them to be Separators, or Protestants.

*(I have never been satisfied with that explanation.
Whenever dissenting groups select names for themselves, one
of the opposing group chooses a name of a leader, then the
other group selects the name of someone who represents an
opposite point of view. For example, in the United States, the
Democratic party had two divisions – one called (Thomas)
Jeffersonian and the other, (Andrew) Jacksonian. Each group
thought that these two men best represented the ideals of the
party. In the Republican Party there were the (Robert) Taft
Republicans, the other, (Dwight) Eisenhower Republicans.
If the premise is correct, the Pharisees also selected someone
in the past who represented their ideal.*

*It is my contention that there was someone in the
not-too-distant-past with whom the Anti-Saducees chose to
identify. His name must have been so important that the
party could, through him, visualize its goal. The problem is
to determine who this Pharis might be. After some search,
the following is a conjecture which appeals to me.*

His name first appears in the story of the first return from Babylonia with Zerubabel. There is a listing of the families of Priests, Levites and Israelites who returned (Nehemiah VII,6.) The first family of the Israelites is called B'nai Parosh.

The fact that the family was listed first indicates that it was pre-eminent among the Israelites. Later, in the Talmud there is a discussion of the Maamadot, the 24 courses, which became the synagogue, there are 24 priestly families, who are accompanied by 24 Levite families, and 23 Israelite families. A strange arrangement. The Talmud then continues that the B'nai Parosh family, the same group, were given two portions of the Maamadot.

It would appear that the B'nai Parosh were highly considered by the founders of the Maamadot. A later explanation evolves that this family was a direct descendant of King David. Remember that the Pharisees placed great trust in the Prophets and the Davidic line.

There is a linguistic problem, for wherever it appears, Parosh is spelled with an Ayin – that is pay, resh, ayin, vav and shin. The Ayin letter is very gutteral, pronounced in the past almost like a "G". For example, Gaza, the town, is spelled with its first letter an Ayin, yet it is always called Gaza. Amorah, the most evil city, is always written as Gamorrah today.

Nevertheless, there is other evidence that some people in the area pronounced the Ayins like Alefs –unsounded – and Alefs as Ayins. This could easily be done when the Ayin appears in the middle of a word. We also know that sometimes an Alef may fall out of words as a silent letter. If so, it may be possible that in this case the Ayin either was silent or dropped. In that case, Parosh was a symbol of the Messiah idea, with its return to greatness of the nation.

Calling a party after David might have been too revolutionary and possibly too monarchical, and therefore they selected the descendant, well known as the direct descendant of David. Such explanation makes more sense to the writer, much more than the one which makes of the Pharisees a Lutherian religious group. In fact, it is almost impossible to explain the war against the Romans which ended with

*Masada without some major nationalist group as the insti-
gating force for the revolt. It is the contention of the writer
that the Pharisees originally were religio-nationalists, which
later split into two groups.)*

Herod's arrival on the scene and his Romanophile
attitude, as well as his harsh treatment towards his opponents, could easily have led to the splintering of the Pharisee party. There were those who, for either political or
personal economic reasons, saw benefit in accommodating the Romans. They would have had financial or religious imperatives with the status quo. Others, less affluent and more conservative, saw themselves as defend-
ers of the status quo ante, that is prior to the Roman influences and power.

The first of these would be Hillel, a non-Judean by
birth, and selected by another non-Judean, Herod, to head
the Sanhedrin. Hillel saw Judaism as a series of acts, philosophies and beliefs which made it a religion in Roman
terms. It is possible that Hillel, responding to the power
of the Roman Empire, foresaw that the hope of Judaism
was in tying the tail of the Sanhedrin to the Emperor.
Reject the stories of Hillel and his poverty as told in every Jewish school book. His grandson, Gamaliel, the
Rabban, or the head of the Sanhedrin, is described in the
Talmud as the wealthiest Jew in the Roman Empire.

Shamai, his opposite, on the other hand, was opposed to any changes in the legal system which might
undermine the nationalistic approach of the Pharisees.
He was opposed to intermarriage, conversions, and business accommodations with the Romans. It is Hillel, who
created the Prosbul to permit business to continue through
loans which were forbidden in the Torah.

The problem that we have in the sources is that
all of them are written by followers of Hillel, so that Shamai
is always portrayed in the worst light. Zionists should
identify with Shamai, if the premise is correct. What is
certainly true is that our Jewish tradition today is Hillelite
in conception, and the fact that there are Hillel Foundations, Hillel Academies, and other institutions named for

Hillel and not one for Shamai, proves the point.

To prove further that Hillel favored the rich and the Romans, one should read one of his famous sayings, often quoted by members of peace organizations.

"Be of the disciples of Aaron, loving peace, and pursuing peace, loving mankind, and bringing them nigh to the Torah."

This is not a pacifist speaking, but, rather, it must be put into context of the times. Hillel, in the midst of Roman occupation state, says:

"Be like the Saducees, (the Priestly party of Aaron), who are not creating problems with the Romans, but rather make peace with them."

More importantly, try to have them convert to Judaism; in other words, this is an attack on those who demonstrate the wide difference between the two in philosophy.

In another case, the story is about Hillel and Shamai, which definitely demonstrates their split in ideas. The parable goes that a Roman soldier comes to Shamai to ask him to teach him all about Judaism, *"Al regel Achat"* (on one foot), a Hebrew idiom meaning *quickly.* Shamai orders him out of his home, and is pictured as a boor for telling the man that that was impossible because he was not born a Jew. So the centurion goes to Hillel, who talks to him in a Jesus-like phrase, *"Love thy neighbor as thyself. Now go and study."* In other words, in order to become a Jew, Hillel maintains that one need only act and think properly and then one can convert to Judaism. It is the Hillelite philosophy that enabled Judaism to expand so rapidly in the Roman Empire, through proselytizing for converts.

Between 30 BCE to 10 CE there is much evidence in the Mishna of the split between Hillel and Shamai, but schools of philosophy are developed which keep up the schism. After the death of Hillel in 10 CE, we find mention of the Bet Hillel and Bet Shamai, obviously followers of the two, whose opinions are kept in the Mishna. More important than that one group was more liberal, the other less so, were their respective positions on Rome.

We return to Herod, that paranoiac king, who tried to build a Rome in Judea. If one cursorily reads Josephus, one would find Herod feeling the pressure of attack from all sides at the very same time that he is building a number of great institutions and places there. Some of his accomplishments have already been mentioned, such as Masada and the amphitheater at Caesarea, Tiberias, (named after the Tiber river in Rome). But at this time it is necessary to state that the famous Western Wall of the Temple where Jews now pray was also built by Herod, who is most remembered by traditional Jews as Herod, Y'mach Shmo, or *"may his name be wiped out."* This Wall is revered by Jews all over the world, even though it was created by Herod, the most hated Jew in history.

Herod operated in such a way that he killed every possible contender to his throne. He died in the year 4 BCE. His reign was followed by a number of attempts to succeed him. His death is followed by that of Hillel in 10 CE. Thus it should be noted that Hillel served as head of the Sanhedrin for most of that time in which Herod was the king, a fact seldom mentioned by most historians.

What now appears in Josephus is another explanation of the three sects of Judaism, in Book XVIII, Chapter I, section 2-6.

> *The Jews had for a great while had three sects of philosophy peculiar to themselves; the sect of the Essenes, the sect of the Saducees, and the third sort of opinions was that of those called Pharisees; of which sects, although I have already spoken in the second book of the Jewish War, yet will I a little touch upon them now.*
>
> *Now, for the Pharisees, they live meanly, and despise delicacies in diet and they follow the conduct of reason; and what that prescribes to them as good for them they do; and they think they ought earnestly to strive to observe reason's dictates for practice. They also pay respect to such as are in years; nor are they so bold as to contradict them in any*

thing which they have introduced; and when they determine that all things are done by fate, they do not take away the freedom from men acting as they think fit; since their notion is, that it hath pleased God to make a temperament, whereby what he wills is done, but so that the will of man can act virtuously or viciously. They also believe that souls have an immortal vigour in them, and that under the earth there will be rewards or punishments, according as they have lived virtuously or viciously in this life; and the latter are to be detained in an everlasting prison, but that the former shall have power to revive and live again; on account of which doctrines they are able greatly to persuade the body of the people; and whatsoever they do about Divine worship, prayers, and sacrifices, they perform them according to their directing; insomuch that the cities give them great attestation to them on account of their entire virtuous conduct, both in their lives and their discourses also.

But the doctrine of the Saducees is this; the souls die with the bodies; nor do they regard the observation of anything besides what the law enjoins them. For they think it is an instance of virtue to dispute with those teachers of philosophy whom they frequent; but the doctrine is received but by a few, yet by those of the greatest dignity. But they are able to do nothing of themselves; for when they become magistrates, as they are unwillingly and by force sometimes obliged to be, they addict themselves to the notions of the Pharisees, because the multitude would not otherwise bear them.

The doctrine of the Essens is this: That all things are best ascribed to God. They teach the immortality of souls, and esteem that the rewards of righteousness are to be earnestly striven for; and when they send what they have dedicated to God into the temple, they do not offer sacrifices, because they have more pure lustrations of their own; on which account they are excluded from the common court of the temple, but offer their sacrifices themselves; yet is their course of life better than that of other men; and they entirely addict themselves to husbandry. It also deserves our admiration, how much they exceed all other men that addict themselves to virtue, and this in righteousness; and indeed to such a degree, that it hath never appeared among any other men, neither Greeks nor barbarians, no, not for a little time, so hath it endured a long while among them, This is demonstrated by that institution of theirs, which will not suffer anything to hinder them from having all things in common; so that a rich man enjoys no more of his own wealth than he who hath nothing at all.

There are about four thousand men that live in this way, and never marry wives, nor are desirous to keep servants; as thinking the latter tempts men to be unjust, and the former gives the handle to domestic quarrels; but as they live by themselves, they minister one to another. They also appoint certain stewards to receive the incomes of their revenues and of the fruits of the ground; such are good men and priests, who are to get their corn and their food ready for them. They none of them differ from others of the Essens in their way of living, but do the most resemble those Dacae who are called Polistae(dwellers in cities).

But of the fourth sect of Jewish philosophy, Judas the Galilean was the author. These men agree in all other things with the Pharisaic notions; but they have an inviolable attachment to liberty, and say that God is their only Ruler and Lord. They also do not value dying any kinds of death, nor indeed do they heed the deaths of their relations and friends, nor can any such fear make them call any man lord. And since this immovable resolution of theirs is well known to a great many, I shall speak no further about that matter; nor am I afraid that any thing I have said of them should be disbelieved, but rather fear, that what I have said is beneath the resolution they

*show when they undergo pain. And it was in Gessius
Florus's time that the nation began to grow mad
with this temper, who was our procurator, and who
occasioned the Jews to go wild with it by the abuse of
his authority and to make them revolt from the Romans. And these are the sects of Jewish philosophy.*

Thus once again Josephus explains a basic difference between the Pharisees and the Saducees, especially
that the Pharisees taught that there was an eternal soul,
which is never mentioned in the Torah, that there is eternal reward and punishment after death, and also the importance of the Oral Law, along with the written Torah. In
addition they took over total responsibility for ritual matters, including what the High Priest could do in the temple
service. Also, they created the Maamadot to decentral-
ize the religion from the Temple, as well as teaching about
the father-God. Moreover, they made the Sanhedrin the
law of the land, so that even Saducees, who became magistrates, had to interpret the law their way.

These concepts now frame the Pharisaic ideas,
for all else is built on these rocks. If one understands
these as the foundation stone, then one should be able to
comprehend the almost immediate development
of Christianity with Jesus' death about the year 35
CE and with the almost simultaneous war against
the Romans which comes to fruition in 68 CE and
ends with Masada in 73 CE. *(Henceforth, unless
BCE is specifically noted, all dates are this era.)*

These two events are connected not only by the
fact that they took place in Judea, but also by what was
happening in the Roman Empire at that time. Because
the Romans believed that their Imperialism required that
they subjugate their populations harshly, they determined
that it was in their best interests to destroy any possibility of revolt. They practiced the policy of massive movements of populations, breaking up of family ties and visible violent punishments of their enemies. One of their
most successful techniques for the latter was crucifixion.

Jesus, re-introduced here, has to be placed in the

context of Jewish History. First of all, it should be noted that there are no primary sources about Jesus, that is there are no eye-witness accounts; what we do know was written later, after his death. The fact that there are three parallel synoptic Gospels, Matthew, Mark and Luke, who attempt to reconstruct the life of Jesus, proves that there was more than one tradition. These gospels have internal contradictions, and even the same story comes out differently. Therefore, without spending too much space or energy, an explanation of Jesus will be attempted.

The earliest source for Jesus is Matthew, who opens his tale with 17 verses of the genealogy of Jesus. He takes him from Abraham through 14 generations to David, 14 from David to the Babylonian Exile and 14 from the Exile to Jesus. Why this insistence on 14 generations? First, it is a multiple of the number 7, always an occult number to Jews. Second, the 14 generations represent 500 years, and Jewish History for Matthew is a matter of magic. There must be exactly 1000 years from David to Jesus to fulfill some apocalyptic idea that the millennium would bring the prophetic Messiah, the son of David. Thus, for those who believed that God was preparing the Jews for the return of their kingdom, there was the Jesus story. All through the gospels there are quotes from the prophets, rarely from the Five Books of Moses. For Matthew, Jesus was the fulfillment of the Pharisaic ideal.

We suggest that the first gospel is meant as a Pharisaic document, so the first genealogy is to prove that by patrilinear steps that Jesus was a son of David. But after doing this, Matthew immediately adds another story – not a Jewish idea, but rather Assyrian, that the Messiah was the son of the Father-God. To further complicate this vision, he adds another concept, foreign to Judaism, that three Magi, Zoroastrian astrologers, are also seeking the king of the Jews. From the beginning, it becomes obvious that Matthew tries too hard to prove Jesus' right to the throne.

The other synoptic gospels take other positions about Jesus, but they are written even later than Matthew. Without going into the whole Jesus story, it is possible to draw a number of conclusions. One, Jesus was certainly a Pharisee, since he accepts the idea of the Oral Law, believes in the Father-God, quotes easily from the Prophets, accepts the idea of the Messiah and certainly believes in resurrection. His positions are very close to those of the Essenes, a Pharisaic group or groups, who rejected wealth, sexual intercourse and saw themselves as agents for the End of the World.

The fact that Jesus indulges in discourses with the leaders, not yet called rabbis, would indicate that he followed the Greek approach for dialogue. He always begins his expositions of law with a question. So does the Mishna study law in the same way. But why in the gospels does Jesus have to perform miracles? Miracles are not required of the Messiah-Jewish style. One must turn to the Platonic system, in which the one and only means of proving that God exists is through the performance of miracles. Add to this the Immaculate Conception of Mary and the miracle of Jesus' birth. Every one is familiar with the phrase, *"God so loved the world that he gave his only begotten son, so that no one who believes in him should be lost, but that they should all have eternal life."*

One must again picture the two worlds which Plato postulated. God is in Heaven, and in order to save the world, which the nether God is plotting, He impregnates Mary, already a major miracle, to have a son, who would sacrifice himself to save the world. God is proved by miracles. If God can do anything, why can't he impregnate a Jewish woman? If you believe, then all is possible.

This is the mind-set that allowed Jews who were prepared by both the Platonic Mode and the Apocalyptic Way to conjure up that Jesus fit both ideals. By reading the New Testament, one must realize that much of the gospels are written in order to prove that not only is Jesus master of the miracle, but he is also the beginning and the end, or as it appears in Greek, the Alpha and Omega. Thus the Jesus figure fulfills the need of these people for a rationale for living and dying, both from the Pharisaic point of view. *For what is the meaning of Jesus' death without the resurrection?*

To summarize, Jesus is for some Jews the fulfillment of the prophecies, and the reason for life and death. As one Christian minister told me, *"If I did not believe in the Resurrection, then I would not be a Christian."* But for most Jews of that period, the requirements of a Messiah, according to the prophets, was that a Jewish state had to be created with the Messiah as king. At that time the whole world would turn to Jerusalem for its law and control and every person in the world would serve Jahveh. Since that did not happen, Jesus was not the Messiah.

Jesus really convinced only a small number of very devoted, who could not believe that he had totally died. Rather a new idea was suggested in the gospels, that God had taken his son up to Heaven, and that at a future date, Jesus would return. It became the role of these Hebrew Christians to convert others to believe in him. Since the early disciples were all Jews, the places they naturally turned to were the synagogues where they would be accepted. It was only with the arrival of Saul of Tarsus, known by his Greek name, Paul, that Christianity changed its whole outlook to a more universal position, that Jesus came not for the Jews, but to the whole world, and that the Pharisaic laws promulgated by the Sanhedrin would not apply to Christians. Christianity then became a major competitor to Judaism for converts.

In Judea, other events would take place which would change the role and content of Judaism. Josephus describes the period as one full of intrigues and oppression of the Jews. This is the period following the deaths of Herod and Hillel. It appears that there was an increasing amount of sabotage and murders perpetrated by those who were in opposition to the Romans and the Herod-ians. The premise here is that there were among the Shamai-ites those who were willing to do what had to be done, to rid the country not only of Romans, but also those Jews who were in league with the imperial forces.

Josephus also takes notice of a group called "Sicarii," so named because they carried a *sica,* a knife, which they used to kill their enemies. The context indicates that they were revolutionaries; Josephus calls them *robbers.* Once again the term, *robbers,* is a generic term meaning revolutionaries. We should recall that Jesus is placed on a cross between rob-

bers, and the crowd asked for Barrabas, one of the *robbers.*
The probability is that Barrabas was a leader of one of the
rebel groups, so recognized by the people.

It is about this time that Josephus concludes his history. Fortunately, he also wrote the *War of the Jews,* in which
he traces the history from coming to Jerusalem and the eventual defeat by the Maccabeans, up to the fall of Masada. In
fact, it is only because of Josephus that we even know about
the expedition against the Zealots by the Romans, for he was
an eyewitness.

Later Josephus will be used to explain a Pharisaic
position on resurrection and life after death as a Jewish
concept.

To return to the war against the Romans, it is necessary to detail the political-ethnic makeup of the residents of Judea in the year 66. Living in Judea at that time
were the following groups: Saducees, Beth Hillel Pharisees, Beth Shamai Pharisees; all sort of revolutionaries,
such as the Sicarii, the Fourth Philosophy, the Zealots,
Essenes and others who joined into apocalyptic groups,
mostly in the desert, Hebrew Christians, Roman citizens
and slaves, plus, if the Romans used their standard theory
of imperialism, diverse groups of peoples who were
brought to Judea in exchange for Jews who were dispersed
by the conquering Roman troops.

When the Romans defeated the rebels, including
the Beth Shamai group, they made league with the Beth
Hillel pro-Roman group, led at that time by a very skilled
rabbi, Yochanan ben Zakkai, of whom it is told that he did
exactly what Josephus did with the general, Vespasian.
Yochanan was an officer in the besieged Jerusalem, and
realized that there was no possibility of winning that battle.
He had himself carried out in a casket to the same general, and predicts that Vespasian would become Emperor, and
is honored by being granted asylum. The two stories seem to
indicate that this is one of the ways of being accepted as a
ward of the general and thereby accepting utter defeat.

More important is what happened as a result of this
act by Yochanan. With the total defeat of the Beth Shamai-ites

and their allies, the anti-Roman section was decimated. The Hebrew Christians moved out during the war, declaring themselves pacifists and migrated to the city of Philadelphia, which was the name at that time of Amman, Jordan.

From that point on, Christians played little role in Judea. They turned their attention to the Jewish Diaspora, and later to non-Jews.

The Apocalyptic groups basically practiced abstinence in sexual matters, allowing themselves to die out after several generations. What was left in Judea were the remnants of the Saducee party and the Beth Hillel Pharisees, led by Yochanan. According to myth, all that he asked from the Romans was a place to establish a school at which he hoped to preserve Judaism according to Hillel.

That myth must be destroyed for it is absolutely not true. What he received was far more than a school, rather a college, along the lines of the College of Cardinals of the Roman Catholic Church. Whereas prior to the defeat, the Sanhedrin was essentially the law-making body of Judea, after Yochanan, it became, with the power of the Roman Empire behind it, the major force for the direction of Jewish life in the Roman Empire. From the year 70, it is possible to say that all Judaism is Hillelite and no opinions afterwards were according to the Shamai position.

Yochanan, because he was not a direct descendant of Hillel, could not be a Nasi, nevertheless acted temporarily but firmly to establish the new Sanhedrin outside the area of Judea. He moved it to Yavna, or Yamnia, which is near the Mediterranean coast, rather than inland, such as Jerusalem. It was in Yavna that major decisions were made which have created the Judaism we now practice, regardless of philosophy. The initial act of the new Sanhedrin was to add additional material to the Canon, namely, the third section of the Hebrew Scriptures, called either Holy Writings, or K'Tuvim. The rabbis, having added this group of books, made a most interesting comment, *"With the completion of these books, nothing more may ever be added, because the voice of prophecy has left Israel. "*

This leads to the definition proposed in the section on the Judah Literary Society, and the ideology of those writers, for then that statement makes a great deal of sense. By these words the rabbis were notifying the Jews and the Romans that nationalism was dead. Henceforth, Judaism would be only a religion of laws and practices, not a form of national spirit. This position was the Hillelite one and perfectly acceptable to the Romans.

For the first time the term, *Rabbi*, was used. A moment should be spent to indicate some of the misconceptions about this word. Rabbi is unanimously translated as *teacher.* The Hebrew word for *teacher* is *moreh* for a male and *morah* for a female. Rabbi, to be more precise, means, *"My lord,"* or as it is used in medieval England, *m'lord.* The term does not appear in literature until about the year 40. Hillel was never called *rabbi,* and he died in the year 10. Any attempt to call Jesus a rabbi is simply designating him with a term that was not current in his life time; nor was he a member of the Sanhedrin. which would have allowed him to be called a "rabbi."

It appears that the term "rabbi" was a title of respect allowed by the Romans for the 70 ordinary members of the Sanhedrin. The Nasi was given a different title, *Rabban,* which in Aramaic would mean *Our Lord.* In Hebrew, he might be addressed as *Rabbenu,* but, for example, the first Rabban is always addressed as *Rabban Gamaliel.* The fact that the plural is used seems to be the famous "pluralis maistoris," that is, *majesty always speak of themselves in the plural.* Popes, kings and editors also use this device, when the singular would be preferable.

To return to history. The Temple had been destroyed, taking the cultic role from the Saducees, who based their claim for authority on the fact that they were the followers of the Aaronide tradition. In order to include the Saducees into the scheme of things, Yochanan and his group made a pact with them, that within the services and practices of the new Judaism, they were to have a special role. Thus, in every service, some note is made that Jews should look forward to the day when the Temple would be rebuilt and the priests would again be the functionaries there. Notice that no mention is ever made of the government, but only of the Temple.

As these Pharisees developed the prayer book as we know it, they added a Musaf service on Shabbat and Holy Days, in which the main function is to spell out the actual sacrifices that the priests had performed in the temple. Other accessions were the inclusion of the priestly benediction in almost every service, the Pidyon Haben, the redemption of the first born son, and the special place for the priests in the Yom Kippur Service. Also, the priest is always given first place in being called to the Torah. Finally, in the third section of the Canon, the Books of Chronicles were allowed to be included. These books are a history of the people from a priestly point of view, probably a Saduceean history.

Turn now to these books which were included in the Canon. The Megillot scrolls are the backbone of various holidays. Why were they included and others of equal merit kept out? Take the Book of Ruth, for example. It is essentially a love story between Ruth, a Moabite, and Boaz, a Judahite. Out of their love affair, forbidden by Jewish Law, David is a direct descendant, and thus David is a product of an intermarriage. Why would the rabbis place this into the Bible?

Or take the story of Esther, the Purim queen. She is encouraged to marry the King of Persia, certainly not a Jew, and yet she saves her people.

Thus, at the time of Yochanan, it obviously was important to let Jews and Romans know that intermarriage could provide both a male and a female savior. But the story of Ruth is only one way that David is changed. He is made the author of the Psalms, and thus the "sweet singer of Israel," and not the military leader that he was. And if the Messiah was to issue from David, quite possibly he might be a product of an intermarriage. The Messiah could then be a universal figure, rather than a national deliverer.

There was a major dispute about whether the Book of Esther should be included in the Canon. Many of the rabbis felt that the book was not a religious tome, since the name of God does not appear even once. Nevertheless, it remained, possibly for the Babylonian Jews who had created this myth for their life. It also once again fulfilled the wishes of the Roman conquerors that nationalism for the Jews was dead and that Judaism was unconcerned with intermarriages and conversions.

After all, if Esther could marry Ahashveros, why shouldn't other Jewish women be willing to intermarry with the sanction of the religious leaders?

In the Book of Lamentations, *Echa*, its first word, poses still another problem for the traditionalists. After all, the country and the Jewish government was destroyed by the Romans in 70, as well as the Temple. Yet no mention is ever made in Jewish religion of the government and national demise. Rather, Lamentations concerns itself with grief for the fallen Temple. Here again, a revisionist approach must be taken. Lamentations is within the spirit of the Hillelites who were opposed to nationalism, as were the Saducees. It was declared that both Temples were destroyed on the same day, the ninth of Av, Tisha B'av, when it was incumbent to mourn for the desecrated Temple, not the government. Solomon is also given the authorship of Proverbs (Mishle), no mean accomplishment for a man with so many wives and concubines, and also Koheleth and Ecclesiates.

Just as David is given the authorship of the Psalms, when it is perfectly obvious that several of them were written in Babylonia, so Solomon, another military figure, was made into a poet of love, for the Song of Songs was assigned to him, as well as the pithy sayings of Ecclesiastes.

A rationale for this transmogrification of military heroes must be given. The rabbis later even indicated that the Songs of Songs were not sexual, but rather an expression of God's love for Israel. The Catholic Church went even further, by declaring these erotic poems as expressing the love between God and the Church.

The rabbis added to all of the above the Apocalyptic book of Daniel, possibly to hold within the group some of the Essenes. Then they added the Books of Ezra and Nehemiah, which were probably of Saduceean origin, which speaks of the Theocracy of 450 BCE.

By no accident the story of the Maccabees was excluded. Up to the revolt, Judas was the hero and Chanukah a national holiday. But Judas was a warrior, and that would upset the Romans on the one hand, and the universalistic rabbis on the other. So the rabbis downgraded Chanukah to child's play, as they did with Purim. In the service of the synagogue and the prayer after a meal, during Chanukah, Judas is never mentioned, but rather Mattathias, the father, who was a priest. Again no military figure is permitted honor.

The most remarkable transformation takes place around the Passover Seder. The holiday, which should play up the military victory of Moses, not only against the Egyptians, but all of the other battles in the Exodus, certainly belongs to Moses, No figure dominates the period between Egyptian bondage and the arrival into the Holy Land more than Moses. The rabbis had to do something with him. First of all, they excluded Moses from the Haggadah, the order of the Seder for Pessach. He is not mentioned once. Yet over and over again, it is God and the miracles that are played and sung. Moses from that time on is called, Moshe Rabbenu; Moses, our philosopher-lawyer.

So, the four major military figures of Judaism – Moses, David, Solomon and Judah Maccabee – are, essentially, wiped out.

Were it not for the early Christian Churches, Jews would not have saved some of the remarkable writings. Some of the books were considered by the early bishops to be sufficiently inspired to be included in the Christian canon, and these are called the Apochrypha; others were saved but did not fit that criteria; they are included in the Pseudopigrapha, that is, books that supposedly were written by major figures but probably were not. Some Christian Bibles contain the Apochrypha. None have the Pseudopigrapha.

Thus, Yochanan, with the help of the Roman government was able to take over the reins of the Jewish establishment by calling it a religion, and by making the Sanhedrin the law-making body and judicial arm as well. The important difference between the period before and after 70 was that the Sanhedrin was now an official arm of the Roman Empire and not a sub-part of the Judean state responsible for Pharisaic activities. Henceforth, the Sanhedrin became that force of the total Pax Romana that related to Jews wherever they lived, and its power extended even to those Jews who lived in the eastern Parthian Empire.

It could be concluded that the defeat to the Romans was turned into a magnificent victory by those who either had no interest in the war promulgated by the Beth Shamai, or who had actively supported the Romans in the war. The year 70 became a watershed, and Yochanan was so successful in his venture that all Judaism is now framed in the Beth Hillel tradition, that is, anti-nationalistic, integrative in the outside society and liberal within the Jewish context. This should become more evident as the history unfolds.

To recapitulate, from Herod's reign, basically 30 BCE, the Sanhedrin was a two party arrangement with the leadership in the hands of Hillel and his followers. Shamai led the nationalistic opposition. For almost 100 years that arrangement was maintained until by force, the Shamai group took over, ordered the war, and lost. Those who made peace were able to denationalize Judaism in its practices, its Holy Books and, in particular, its structure.

The services were reorganized without the Temple, but always with references to the Temple which someday would be rebuilt and sacrifices restored. The concept of the Messiah was radically altered from that of a descendant of David, who would restore the state according to the prophets into a teleological ideology. He would signal the end of the world, when time would stop.

Jews were not prevented from intermarrying and proselyting the pagans to become Jews. During the next several centuries, Judaism was winning more converts than Christianity. It is said that the wife of one of the Roman emperors became a Jew and favored Jews in the royal court. It will not be until the beginning of the fourth century that there was a radical change in the attitude of the Roman Empire to Christianity.

It is certainly true that the Romans treated their Rabbinical appointees quite well, so that at least the leadership of the Sanhedrin were well paid, so that they could maintain their position in the Roman court. At the same time, Rome continued its program of "Divide and Conquer." That involved the heavy taxing of the people, the taking of large number of slaves, the breaking-up of families and the mass moving of indigenous people and replacing them with persons of other national areas. The whole purpose was to create a new people, which would constitute a "Pax Romana."

So for most Jews, the period of the Roman occupation was one of terror, deprivation, slavery and exile. In fact, it was in this period that the philosophical base for the term, *Galut* (exile), came into existence. It then became a part of the rituals and beliefs of the Jews.

6 ✡ THE EXPANSION
OF THE ORAL LAW: MISHNA, TALMUD
AND THE MIDRASH

For the Pharisees there were two laws: the Written Law, now in three parts, and the Oral Law, which was the bailiwick of the Sanhedrin. None of the Oral laws was written, but there was a statement that the written law should not to be memorized nor the Oral Law written down. It became, as it developed, a fluid legal system, to which the rabbis turned their attention.

It should be understood that since most of the oral laws was created during the Roman occupation, they were at least in consonance with Roman common law, and must have drawn some of their substance from that foreign law base. To pursue it quite another way, nothing came into the Oral Law that would be in opposition to Roman common law or would create problems with the authorities. No one should ever consider that the Sanhedrin was an independent body in a society that practiced *Separation of Church and State.*

How did the rabbis respond to possible conflict between Roman common law and Jewish law? They preached a philosophy of *Dina D'malchuta Dina.* This translates precisely that the law of the country, despite what Jewish written or oral law might say, takes precedence. For example, if a Jewish soldier in the Roman army had to work or fight on the Sabbath, the rabbis confirmed that he had to work or fight, even if it meant violating his conscience.

One of the concomitant results of the Roman policies, which began with Pompcy in 63 BCE through the time of Yochanan after 70CE, was the development of a major Diaspora of Jews in the Roman Empire. There had been earlier communities in Babylonia and Persia, and into near-by North Africa, but now we see evidence of small Jewish settlements in the farthest reaches of North Africa, England, France and Germany. Wherever the Roman legions went, there were Jews along as either slaves, military or merchants. It should be obvious that Jews many miles from Yavne would have difficulty maintaining their traditions and keeping up with communal activities. We might suppose that the variation in religious practices by these far-flung communities must have been wide. Literacy was not as prevalent as one is led to believe from Jewish sources. This is confirmed by the many discussions of the rabbis about which is the correct tradition or which is the more correct.

It is during this period that the legal term, *Halachah*, came into existence. Halachah, which means in simple Hebrew, the *Way* or the *Path,* should appropriately be translated, when one is talking about Jewish Law, as *Proper Way*, as distinct from those which had developed differently. So much of what we know today as Jewish Law is based on decisions made during this period, although much of it was not written down until many decades later. Sometimes there was no real basis in law for decisions, and then they would try to find a justification within the written law. In many cases, the argument strained credulity. Nevertheless, from Yochanan Ben Zakkai's time, a principal role of the rabbi was to clarify the positions of Jewish Law for Jews in the Roman Empire.

One method of clarification has become a classic means of determining case law in many western states. The methodology is as follows: a question is sent to the authority in charge. The respondent then repeats the question and then gives his opinion. This happens today when someone asks the attorney general of a state for a legal opinion on a matter. He will then restate the question, and then frame his opinion based on the law as he views it. Unless someone challenges that opinion, it has the weight of law. During the rabbinical period a similar process developed.

For example, assume that a leader of the Jewish community in Rome has a problem posed to him for which there is no ready answer available. He would, on behalf of the community, send a letter, an epistle, to the Sanhedrin for clarification. That is called in Hebrew a *Sh'elah*, a question. One of the rabbis, after some discussion at the Sanhedrin, would be designated to answer, and he would direct an epistle back to the community, first copying the question and then providing all type of variations of possible decisions. If there was general agreement in the Sanhedrin, he would give the majority position as *Halachah*. This would constitute an answer, a *T'shuvah* in Hebrew. This program began a method of fostering universality of law through the She'elot and T'shuvot (plural). These were not only sent back to the original writer, but copies would be distributed to the major cities of the Diaspora. This was not, however, the corpus of the Oral Law, but rather a pragmatic device for particular cases. Not every part of the Halachah was amenable to *Responsa,* another term for this process. There probably were many variations throughout the different communities. Beyond this, even in Palestine, it was not possible for every Jew to know what was expected of him if he had to depend on oral transmission. The need to write out the Oral Law would become even more pressing for the world Jewish community, but the time was not yet ripe.

As the Roman Empire became more and more oppressive, the revolutionary spirit appeared to have been revived. For how long could the Jews follow the peaceful path of Yochanan, which was essentially one of accommodation to the Romans? In several areas in the empire Jewish revolts took place, especially in North Africa. Finally, that spirit of Shamai began to appeal to more of the Palestinian Jews, and under the leadership of Simon Bar Kochba (the son of the Star) or Koziba, in 135, a revolt was promulgated. His name is a strange one, for the star had always been identified with David and Solomon, and reflected that national Jewish spirit. The revolution was actively furthered by some members of the Sanhedrin, mainly the leading intellectual, Rabbi Akiba. It may be assumed that other rabbis also played a role in this revolt. The revolt failed and Akiba and a number of the rabbis were publicly killed in a mortifying way, which was the Roman method of handling traitors.

This revolt signaled a major decline of the Sanhedrin. The Romans forced the group to leave Yavna, move to the Galilee – first to a town called Usha, and then to Sipphoris, both away from Yavne. There was a seeming decline in the quality of the rabbis, but it also appears that the power which the Roman government had granted in 70 had dissipated. The Jewish population of Palestine, as the Romans preferred to call it, decreased, because increasing numbers either lived in the Roman Diaspora, or moved to the Parthian Empire to the East. In the East they found less oppression, less taxation, and the local communities seemed to have been more accepted by the reigning powers.

By the end of the second century, there was more evidence that the Roman empire itself was beginning to lose power. Revolts were taking place in all corners, and the commerce and taxation, which fed the appetite of Rome, were insufficient to maintain their economy. Judea was also showing the effects of having its land stripped of all of its trees in order to build the Roman fleet, and the crushing taxation, as well as the splitting of families, eroded the leadership of the Rabbis.

Recall Axiom II: "Whenever a society is in decline, its leaders attempt to capture the past, either by writing history, or by canonizing the legal system."

About the turn of the third century, the Sanhedrin was led by the Nasi, Judah. Interestingly enough, although he was the Nasi, he is always referred to as Rabbi, not Rabban, the term previously used for the head of the Sanhedrin. Judah felt that the time had come to save the past, which was a violation of the Pharisaic law, that the Oral Law should never be written down. He postulated that when the law is being violated, it is perfectly permissible to break that law in order to save the Law. He ordered the writing down of the Oral Law, with some of the variations of time and place. The writers added stories about the law and about the previous rabbis, to punctuate the Law.

This codification, done about the year 200, became the book called the *Mishna*. Mishna can mean either repetition or teaching. This book, written in fairly classical Hebrew, is divided in six parts or volumes. They are Zeraim (seeds), Moed (holy days), Nashim (women), Nezikim (damages), Kedoshim (holy things) and Taharot (ritual cleanliness). Thus the Law after Judah was essentially contained in these six volumes. It should be indicated that there are side issues within each of these volumes and within the first, essentially dealing with agriculture, its initial chapters are entirely devoted to prayers, not agriculture.

One of the enigmas in this first section was that it began with prayers. Obviously this is the most important aspect of Jewish life, and as a result, its first issue.

I,1. From what time in the evening may the Shema be recited? From the time the priests enter the Temple to eat their heave-offering until the end of the first watch. So, Rabbi Eliezer; But the Sages say: until midnight. Rabban Gamaliel says: until the rise of dawn. His sons once returned (after midnight) from a wedding feast. They said to him, 'We have not yet recited the Shema.' He said to them, 'If the dawn has not yet risen, you are still bound to recite it.' Moreover, whenever the Sages prescribes 'until midnight' the duty to fulfill the commandment lasts until the rise of dawn'. The duty of burning the fat pieces and the members of the animal offerings (in the temple by the priests) lasts until the rise of dawn; and for all the offerings that must be consumed on the same day, the duty lasts until the rise of dawn. Why then have the Sages said: until midnight? To keep a man far from transgression.

This is the very first law of the Mishna, which in a sense is the first written law since the Torah. What can one draw that make some historical sense of these laws? Obviously, the most important prayer for the rabbis was the Shema. Recall that this story is written down some 130 years after the destruction of the temple. Yet the rabbis are still impelled to relate the prayers to the temple service. But this time, the rabbis had already developed the order of the prayers and a multiplicity of prayers both in the shortened version and the longer ones. The former led off with Baruch Atah Adonay, the other with Baruch Atah Adonay Elohenu Melech Haolam. They developed prayers for eating, drinking, washing the hands, seeing a rainbow, seeing twins or a miracle. There are prayers when one sets off on a journey, and one when one returns. Hundreds of rabbinical prayers are recorded and there are probably many more that were never recorded.

Special prayers were written to conclude a session of learning (Kaddish), and there were special prayers for the New Moon, rain, dew; and that goes on and on. Although no theory for the multiplicity of prayers is given, it appears that the rabbis felt that the more one invokes the name of God in prayer and the more expressed qualities credited to God, the more possible it would be for a Jew to reach the Kingdom of God in Heaven. It became incumbent for a Jew to set times for certain prayers daily and other prayers at other appropriate times.

There were of course differences of opinion among the rabbis. In the Mishna, we find hundreds of references to disputes between Beth Hillel and Beth Shamai, the two succeeding schools of legal philosophy. In all cases the Halachah,the Way, was according to Beth Hillel, except for eighteen ordinances promulgated during the war with the Romans in the year 70 when the Beth Shamai took control of the Sanhedrin. Judah was a follower of Beth Hillel, and since the Mishna took on the character of the new constitution for the Jews in 200, all subsequent law was in accordance with their thinking. The Mishna,therefore, must be considered a Hillelite book, and all Judaism since then has been either following that position, or reacting to it.

When one speaks of Judaism as a religion, it must be in the framework of the Roman impression on all religions of the western world, a sect bounded by theology, rules and beliefs. That is why whenever traditional Judaism has enunciated a kind of Zionism, it has overwhelmingly been in the area of restoration of the Temple, not the state of the Jews. Whenever Jews are considered in the body politic as a religious grouping, they must respond in Hillelite answers rather than in nationalistic terms. Non-religious Jews and even anti-religious Jews, when confronted by the Christian community for identification, must respond in religious terms. In America, where the majority of Jews are not personally identified in any organized way, it is expected that the response would be in a religious manner. On the other hand, in societies, such as Russia and Poland, both pre- and post- revolution, where the Jews were given national recognition, Jews were able to respond in different terms, in various shades of nationalism.

To continue. Judah, through the written Mishna, created the means for universalizing the Oral Tradition. The Halachah, both in the Roman Empire and in the Parthian Empire to the east, was constructed on this written text. Building on other texts which contained some explanations of law which did not enter the Mishna, the Sanhedrin in Palestine for the Roman Empire Jews and the academies (yeshivot) of the Parthian Empire began to evolve wider interpretations and expansions of the Mishna for eastern Jews. The former were in conformity with Roman common law, and the latter in Babylonian and Persian within the spirit of the indigenous Babylonian and Persian laws and customs. Thus, those laws and explanations in the Mishna contain some Latin words in explanations, whereas in the discussions in Babylonia, there are Persian and Aramaic words from the East.

During this period, after 200, a new form of rabbinic literature developed, known as the *Midrash,* meaning interpretation. The rabbis attempted to teach ethics and morals through sermonic materials, based as far as is known, on the two parts of the Bible that are non-nationalistic, the Torah and the scrolls or Megillot, which occur in the third and latest section of the Bible. These sermons are generally verse-by-verse and some times word-for-word elucidation in moral and ethical terms. The person who extrapolates the text and expounds the text is called a *Darshan,* with both words, Midrash and Darshan, deriving from the same root, D-R-SH, meaning *to explain.* It can be surmised that the Midrash was a step in distancing Jewish communities from the nationalistic philosophy of Beth Shamai, and, to an extent, to foster the dominant positions of Beth Hillel.

For it was the Midrash more than the Talmud, the compilation of the Oral Law and its later expansions, that shaped the illusions and dreams of the Jewish people. The Midrash became the base for much of the material which mothers taught their children, and the details of Jewish life that were expounded by fathers and teachers to the children. In the expansion of the simple texts of the Bible and scrolls, Jews began to create fables which, more than laws, embodied Jewish life. Rabbis seldom taught from the Talmud, the basic body of Jewish law, but rather preferred to teach the values from Midrashic sources and stories.

Beginning with the third century, the basic texts were the Mishna of Judah and the various Midrashim. Based on the theory of the Midrash, it should be obvious why the rabbis did not comment on the prophets. There were also other legal and sermonic books, but they never had the impact of these two. In addition, as it occurred in every Eastern religion, there was an underbody of mysticism and theoretical philosophizing. Much of that Jewish mysticism had to do with certain mysteries as enunciated in the Torah and the Midrashim. There was much speculation about Elijah and how he disappeared in a chariot up to heaven, and the story of Adam and Eve, as well as the end of the world. Two key items of Jewish mysticism were Paradise and Elijah, the beginning and the end of the world.

The Meaning of Death

Much thought was also given to death, and what happens after death, following the Greek philosophers who dealt in great length on what happens to the soul after death. Does it go into another living being, such as another human, or into an animal, or does it stay in limbo between this world and the next, waiting for God or gods to decide its faith? The rabbis devoted a great deal of thought about this subject, and created prayers which are still in use today, embodying their theories of life after death.

Two of the most well known prayers, *El Moley Rachamim* (Lord, full of mercy), which is said before mourners and at *Yizkor* (Remembrance services) and the other, said every morning, *Hanashamah sheh'natati bi* (the soul which Thou hast implanted in me), express the idea of the soul coming pure from God and returning to God pure. Also, the idea that the Messiah would come down the Mount of Olives to Jerusalem, began the desire of many Jews to be buried on the east side of the wall, so that when resurrection takes place at that time, those who are buried there will revive to greet the Messiah, who would arrive on a white donkey, entering the Holy City from the East.

Parenthetically, an essay written by Josephus on Hades, which he wrote to Greeks (philosophers), explains what Jews believe about death and life after death. It is reproduced totally, because of the importance that Josephus gives to the Jewish idea of Resurrection at the end of the first century CE.

1. Now as to Hades, wherein the souls of the righteous and unrighteous are detained, it is necessary to speak of it. Hades is a place in the world not regularly finished; a subterraneous region, wherein the light of this world does not shine; from which circumstance, that in this region the light does not shine, it cannot be but there must be in perpetual darkness. This region is allotted as a place of custody for souls, in which angels are appointed to them, who distribute temporary punishments, agreeable to every one's behavior and manners.

2. In this region there is a certain place set apart, a lake of unquenchable fire, whereinto we suppose no one hath hitherto been cast; but it is prepared for a day afore-determined by God, in which one righteous sentence shall deservedly be passed upon all men; when the unjust, and those that have been disobedient to God, and have given honour to such idols as have been the vain operations of the hands of men as to God himself, shall be adjudged to this everlasting punishment, as having been the causes of defilement; while the just shall obtain an incorruptible and never -fading kingdom. These are now confined in Hades, but not in the same place wherein the unjust are confined.

3. For there is one descent into this region, at which gate stands an archangel with an host; which gate when those pass through are conducted down by the angels appointed over souls, they do not go the same way; but the just are guided to the right hand and led with hymns, sung by the angels appointed over the place, unto a region of light, in which the just have dwelt from the beginning of the world; not constrained by necessity, but ever enjoying the prospect of the good things they see, and rejoice in the expectation of those new enjoyments which will be peculiar to every one of them, and esteeming those beyond what we have here; with whom there is no place of toil, no burning heat, no piercing cold, nor are any briers there; but the countenance of the fathers and of the just, which they see, always smiles upon them, while they wait for that rest and eternal new life in heaven, which is to succeed this region. This place is called The Bosom of Abraham.

4. But as to the unjust, they are dragged by force to the left hand by the angels allotted for punishment, no longer with a good-will, but as prisoners driven by violence; to whom are sent the angels ap-

pointed over them to reproach them and threaten them with their terrible looks, and to thrust them still downwards. Now those angels that are set over these would drag them into the neighborhood of hell itself; who when they are hard by it, continually hear the noise of it, and do not stand clear of the hot vapour itself; but when they have a near view of this spectacle, as of a terrible and exceeding prospect of fire, they are struck with a fearful expectation of a future judgment, and in effect punished thereby: and not only so, but where they see the place (or choir) of the fathers and of the just even hereby are they punished; for a chaos deep and large is fixed between them; insomuch that a just man that hath compassion upon them cannot be admitted, nor can one that is unjust, if he were bold enough to attempt it, pass over it.

5. This is the discourse concerning Hades, wherein the souls of all men are confined until a proper season, which God hath determined, when he will make a resurrection of all men from the dead, not procuring a transmigration of souls from one body to another, but raising those very bodies, which you Greeks, seeing to be dissolved, do not believe (their resurrection). But learn not to disbelieve it; for while you believe that the soul is created, and yet is made immortal by God, according to the doctrine of Plato, and this is time, not be incredulous; but believe that God is able, when he hath raised to life that body which was made as a compound of the same elements, to make it immortal; for it must never be said of God, that he is able to do some things and unable to do others. We have therefore believed that the body will be raised again; for the earth receives the remains, and preserves them; and while they are the seed, and are mixed among the more fruitful soil, they flourish, and what is sown is indeed sown bare grain, but at the mighty sound of God the Creator, it will sprout up, and be raised in a clothed and glorious condition, though not before it has been dissolved, and mixed (with the earth).

So that we have not rashly believed the resurrection of the body; for although it be dissolved for a time on account of the original transgression, it exists still, and is cast into the earth as into a potter's furnace, in order to be formed again, not in order to rise again such as it was before, but in a state of purity, and so as never to be destroyed again. And to every body shall its own soul be restored. And when it hath clothed itself with that body, it will not be subject to misery, but being itself pure, it will continue with its pure body, and rejoice with it, with which it having walked righteously now in this world, and never had it as a snare, it will receive it gain with gladness. But as for the unjust, they will receive their bodies not changed, not freed from disease and distempers, nor made glorious, but with the same diseases wherein they died; and such as they were in their unbelief, the same shall they be when they shall be faithfully judged.

6. For all men, the just as well as the unjust shall be brought before God the Word; for to him hath the Father committed all judgment, and he in order to fulfil the will of his Father, shall come as Judge, whom we call Christ. (The sentence from the semi colon is probably a later insert by a Christian editor as are other Christological references in succeeding sentences). For Minos and Rhadamantheus are not the judges, but he whom God and the Father hath glorified; concerning whom we have given a more particular account, for the sake of those who seek after Truth. This person, exercising the righteous judgment of the Father towards all men, hath prepared a just sentence for every one, according to his works; at whose judgment-seat when all men and angels, and demons shall stand, they will send one voice, and say, Just is the judgment; and the rejoinder to which will bring a just sentence upon both parties by giving justly to those who have done well an everlasting fruition; but allotting to the lovers of wicked works eternal punishment. To these belong the un-

*quenchable fire, and that without end, and a cer-
tain fiery worm, never dying and not destroying
the body, but continuing its eruption out of the body
with never-ceasing grief: neither will sleep give ease
to these men, nor will the night afford them com-
fort; death will not free them from their punishment,
nor will the interceding prayers of their kindred
profit them; for the just are no longer seen by them,
nor are they thought worthy of remembrance. But
the just shall remember only their righteous actions,
whereby they have attained the heavenly kingdom,
in which there is no sleep, no corruption, no care,
no night, no day measured by time, no sun driven
in his course along the circle of heaven by necessity, and measuring out the bounds and conversions of the seasons, for the better illumination of
the life of men; no moon decreasing and increasing, or introducing a variety of seasons, nor will
she then moisten the earth; no burning sun, no Bear
turning around (the pole), no Orion to rise, no wandering of innumerable stars. The earth will not then
be difficult to be passed over, nor will it be hard to
find out the court of paradise, nor will be any fearful roaring of the sea, forbidding the passengers
to walk on it; even that will be made passable to
the just, though it will not be void of moisture.
Heaven will not then be uninhabitable by men, and
it will not be impossible to discover the way of as-
cending thither. The earth will not be uncultivated,
nor require too much labor of men,, but will bring
forth its fruits of its own accord, and will be well
adorned with them. There will no more generations
of wild beasts, nor will the substance of the rest of
the animals shoot out any more; for it will not produce men, but the numbers of the righteous will
continue, and never fail, together with righteous
angels, and spirits (of God) and with his word, as a
choir of righteous men and women that never grow
old, and continue in an incorruptible state, singing
hymns to God, who had advanced them to that hap-*

piness, by the means of a regular institution of life;
with whom the whole creation also will lift up a
perpetual hymn from corruption to incorruption,
as glorified by a splendid and pure spirit. It will
not then be restrained by a bond of necessity, but
with a lively freedom shall offer up a voluntary hymn,
and shall praise him that made them, together with
the angels and spirits, and men now freed from all
bondage.

7. And now, if you Gentiles will be persuaded by
these motives, and leave your vain imaginations
about your pedigrees and gaining riches, and philosophy, and will not spend your time about subtilties
of words, and thereby lead your minds into error,
and if you will apply your ears to the hearing of the
inspired prophets, the interpreters both of God and
of his word, and will believe in God, you shall both
be partakers of these good things, and obtain the
good things that are to come; you shall see the ascent
unto the immense heaven plainly, and that kingdom
which is there. For what God hath concealed in si-
lence (will be made manifest), what neither eye hath
seen, nor ear hath heard, nor hath it entered into
the heart of man, the things that God hath prepared
for them that love him.

8. In whatsoever ways I shall find you entirely;
so cries the End of all things. And he who hath at
first lived a virtuous life, but towards the latter end
falls into vice, these labours by him before endured
shall be altogether vain and unprofitable, even as a
play, brought to an ill catastrophe. Whosoever shall
have lived wickedly and luxuriously may repent; however there will be need of much time to conquer an
evil habit, and even after repentance his whole life
must be guarded with great care and diligence, after the manner of a body, which after it hath been a
long time afflicted with a distemper, requires a stricter
diet and method of living; for though it may be possible, perhaps, to break off the chain of our regular
affections at once, yet our amendment cannot be se-

*cured without the grace of God, the prayers of good
men, the help of brethren, and our own sincere repentance and constant care. It is a good thing not
to sin at all; it is also good, having sinned, to repent; as it is best to have health always, but it is a
good thing to recover from a distemper. To God be
glory and dominion forever. Amen.*

Josephus confirms many of the points previously
made about the beliefs of Hillelite Judaism - the resurrection, the conversion techniques, the belief in repentance,
study and the Platonic system of two worlds separated
by Chaos, where mortal man can never cross that void,
but God can reach down and perform a miracle, since God
can do anything. What is almost Danteish is the description of Heaven and Hell, as well as the area that is the
precursor of the end of the world. What is more interesting is that there are still people who believe in this today.

With the completion of the Mishna, the Jews enter another era, which can be labeled the Talmudic Age.
Those who are mentioned in the Mishna are called
Tannaim, an Aramaic word, which in Hebrew would be
Shannaim, or teachers, but particularly those who are
the actors of the Mishna, which is derived from the same
Hebrew word. In this post-Mishnaic time, the discussants
are no longer called Tannaim, but rather, *Amaraim,* meaning speakers, coming from the root, A-M-R, meaning to
say or speak. The literature of this period is sometimes
called Tannaitic, even though it includes the Amaraim. In
later periods, reference would be made to a *Tanna,* and
that would mean that statement would be made by a
Tanna, an expounder in the Mishna, whereas an *Amora*
appears after 200.

As previously mentioned, the Mishna became the
backbone of Jewish Law in both the Roman Empire as
well as in the Parthian. In the academies around Baghdad,
in Sura, Nehardea and Pumpeditha in the East, continuing discussions went on, allowing for expansion of the
Law that could easily fit into the mold of Zoroastrian (Persian religion) law. In the West, the discussions starting at

Yavna, for political reasons as well as economic, and moving to other parts of Palestine, took place within the context of permissible Roman Law. Now there began to be a bifurcation of Jewish Law, eastern and western. It is important to understand that there were substantial differences between these two milieus.

In Palestine, Judaism was faced with the growth of the Christian Church as an offshoot and competitor for converts. Both organized religions paid court to the same Roman emperors. Each had to justify its existence as the New Israel to the powers. As a result neither saw much good in the other. It is no accident that some of the early bishops of the church were zealous anti-Semites. The Jewish leaders also employed the same sort of attacks, many of which were later censored by the Roman authorities from Jewish texts and prayers.

The conflict between Judaism and Christianity would have continued on a fairly equal basis had not the life and opinions of Constantine early in the 4th century played a different role. Constantine, the Roman Emperor, who had converted earlier to Christianity, became increasingly anti-Jewish. About 325, he promulgated some imperial decrees which proclaimed that conversion to Judaism was grounds for death, and those who abetted the conversion would also be put to death. It was Constantine who forced the rabbis of the West to declare that anyone who comes for conversion should be told in no uncertain terms, that the answer was "no!"

Thenceforth, Judaism almost ceased to be a proselytizing religion, whereas Christianity, with the power of Constantine, and then his sons, became more effective in adding to their numbers in the West. It is possible that had Constantine not played his role, the Roman Empire, because of the number of converted Jews and their natural growth might have become the Holy Roman Jewish Empire.

One can, when studying the decline of Rome, recognize certain facts that led to the idea that Rome was beginning to fall, and it was losing its vitality and spirit when the Roman Empire became the Holy Roman Empire. Under the pressure from Christian bishops in the Empire, many anti-Jewish acts were part of the new establishment. Jews were slaughtered, forced to wear outfits which would easily identify them, and life was made increasingly difficult. More and more Jews moved into the friendlier area of the Parthian Empire, where they were a fairly large identifiable group, particularly along the Euphrates River. Hegemony began to shift to these academies as the Sanhedrin became weaker.

In the Roman Empire, where the Palestinian Sanhedrin held sway and expansion of the Oral tradition embodied in the Mishna was taking place, the rabbis must have felt the impending doom of their institutions. Actually, it took almost a century after Constantine, about the year 400, and not too distant from the date of the fall of Rome to the Visigoths of the North in 410 CE. The rabbis there decided to write out the discussions and conclusions of the Sanhedrin, in order to save the past, for no one knew what might happen if the Roman Empire were to fall to the pagan Goths.

Out of this calamitous period came a remarkable set of books, usually called *Jerusalem Talmud,* or in Aramaic, *Talmud Yerusalmi.* The interesting fact is that not one word of it was written in Jerusalem, and the final redaction took place in Tiberias on the Sea of Galilee. One edition of this Talmud has a more appropriate name, *Talmud Ma'aravi,* or the Talmud of the West. Unfortunately, there is no complete collection of the Western Talmud, and some sections have seemingly been lost forever. Nevertheless, enough has been saved to indicate the style and ideology of this Talmud. It is very succinct and what is available is about half of the size of the Babylonian Talmud.

The Talmud, to repeat, is essentially case law, with many stories which are built up one by one. Each section of a law is divided into two – the first is the Mishna, which is part of the discussion by the rabbis of the Sanhedrin. This is always followed by either an extended discussion by the leaders of the Sanhedrin in Palestine, in the Western Talmud, or by the discussions in the Yeshivot in Babylonia. The second part is called *Gamara,* or "Finishing."

For an example: the first item in the Mishna discusses when the Shema should be said; this is followed by the discussions. In the Talmud one part of this Mishna is written, which takes about two or three lines in some editions; then the Gamara would be based on those discussions about each sentence. In the Talmud, that could go on for some twenty or thirty pages. Included in that lengthy discussion would be some of the debate, mostly in Aramaic, although sometimes in Hebrew, where the advocates for different positions would expound them. They would tell stories to defend their positions, or quote some earlier figure to justify that expression.

The Talmud has *Halachah,* the Law, as it finally was determined, and *Agada,* the stories, which usually also have a moral tone to them. (Incidentally, Sanhedrin members who were called Rabbi or Rabban had no similar designation in Babylonia.) What can be said with certainty is that the Western Talmud was developed in the Roman Empire, whereas the Talmud Bavli (Babylonian) was created in the Persian Empire. Thus one Talmud reflected the milieu of the West, the other Talmud, the East.

By the end of the fifth century, it must have been clear to the rabbis that the empire of the West was in a state of collapse, which was enough to cause the rabbinate in Palestine to save their statutes and discussions. Following the aforementioned Axiom, the Jerusalem Talmud was completed approximately in the year 400. One author estimated that about this period two-thirds of the Jews in the world lived in the Persian Empire, the balance one- third in the Roman Empire. This fact alone might explain why the Jerusalem Talmud never was a major force in the creation of Jewish Law.

Soon after 400, Rome itself was captured by the Visigoths, and Jewish History turns itself to the East. The eastern empire was also beginning to have problems with the far-flung peoples there and revolutions were taking place in many sectors. It took an additional hundred years for the decline to be recognized by the leaders of the Jewish community. But about the year 500, they, too, decided to codify their legal creations and discussions, and from

500 until the present day, we are able to talk about a Code of Law for the Eastern Jews. It totally reflects the Persian influence, and many words of Persian origin are in this Talmud, just as there are many Latin words in the Western tome.

Many of these words have been incorporated into the Hebrew language, as if they were Biblical, even though they are found only in the Babylonian Talmud. For example, *Sandak,* the man who holds the male at circumcision, *Pundak,* an inn, *Bustan,* a garden, are Persian in origin.

Today, and for almost 1500 years, Jews who speak of *The Talmud* always refer to the Babylonian, and never to the Western version. Why should a people who have centered its history in Palestine, choose the Babylonian Talmud over the Palestinian one? Scholars have tried to address this question and proposed various theories, most often it is because the Eastern Talmud is better written, more comprehensive, and more relevant.

The theory here is quite different – the Babylonian Talmud became the authority inasmuch as the vast majority of Jews extant after 500 were Oriental Jews, or at least lived in the Orient, and were ready to accept the authority of those in power in the Babylonian Jewish community there. Simply by the weight of numbers, political and economic powers, the Academies of the East were able to exercise hegemony over these Jews.

In Baghdad its Jews play the center of the world for Jews. It was there that a direct descendant of Hillel led the community and there were three major academies to whom Jewish communities turned to for religious advice and counsel. In Baghdad, the Jewish community had a very surprising organization. The heads of the academies of Sura and Pumpeditha were given a title of *Gaon,* not a Hebrew word, but probably Persian.

During the Persian period, a new position developed as head of the organized Jewish community, responsible to the Persian government. His title in Aramaic was *Resh Galuta,* or if it had been in Hebrew, *Rosh Hagalut,* which means "Head of the Exile." The title name is clouded in obscurity, but eventually the position was assigned to a direct descendant of Hillel, who, it can be recalled, was called the

Babylonian five centuries before.   A new myth was created that Hillel was directly in the line of King David who, therefore, if not the Messiah or a precursor of that Messiah, was eligible to be the king of the Jews. In a sense, what happened was another of those great transmogrifications of history, where a religious leader, like Hillel, is changed into a national hero, and then becomes a symbol for national renaissance. Hillel, who had started a school of rabbinical thought that preached and fostered political internationalism, became in Babylonia, the symbol of a national king. The Resh Galuta became the official representative to the court of Baghdad, and, we can surmise, was also rewarded both by the Parthian government and by Jews who might seek favor at the court.

Later it should be noted that a major conflict developed in Baghdad as to which seat of Jewish power was to be pre-eminent; the secular Resh Galuta, or the head of the Academy. The same clash occurred between the Pope in Rome and the Emperor of the Holy Roman Empire.

The Talmudic Era ended, with most of the Jews of the world not only living in the Parthian Empire, but under the leadership of the Jewish community of Baghdad, with the Resh Galuta and its Academies.

To recapitulate, the approximate relevant dates since Alexander are the following:

Alexander the Great	333 BCE
The Maccabean Revolution and the Rise of the Pharisees	165 BCE
Fall of the Hasmonean Dynasty and the Rise of Rome in Judea	65 BCE
Herod becomes King and Hillel becomes Nasi of the Sanhedrin	30 BCE
Hillel dies, Rise of Bet Hillel and Beth Shamai	10 CE
Probable death of Jesus	35 CE
Destruction of Temple and the National State of Judea. Beginning of Hillelite Sanhedrin under Jochanan Ben Zakkai at Yavne. Closing of the Jewish Bible	70 CE
Rabbi Akiba and Bar Kochba Revolt	135 CE
Mishna codified by Judah	200 CE
Jerusalem (Western) Talmud	400 CE
Babylonian Talmud	500 CE

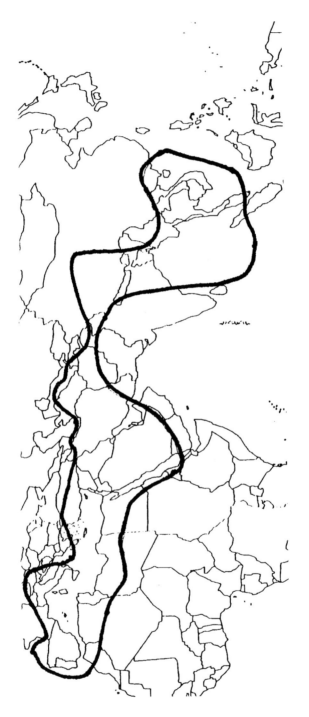

ISLAM EXPANSION

7 ✡ JEWS IN THE ISLAMIC WORLD

Half a millennium has passed since the time of Jesus, Hillel and Herod. The Roman Empire had been destroyed by the northern invaders and the area had lost its vitality. In the East, the Parthian Empire had also begun to fall apart internally and externally. For the first time in centuries, there was no major force to pick up the pieces of the great empires.

Psychologists have a term to describe the period between the preceding time and the next explosion. They call it the "Latency Period." By that they mean that between the stages of childhood and adolescence, there is a term of life, where there does not seem to be an expression of any growth. The child simply stands still. It is almost as if the child holds itself in, developing the resources to expand towards adolescence. The hormones are just beginning to move. In much the same way, one can almost say that the previous world entered a latency period in which nothing seemed to be happening, as though the world was charging its energies for something new.

It took another 122 years for a rather unprofound event to occur. The flight of Mohammed from Mecca served to trigger a spiritual revolution, which was followed by a military success, as vaunted as Alexander's some thousand years before. Mohammed himself was successful in capturing the Arabian peninsula, and by and large, to convert almost all of that area to Islam.

But it was those who were the next three generations of followers of Islam who created the Islamic Empire, the vast crescent which extended from Southern France and all of the Iberian peninsula in Europe, across great parts of North Africa, and into various parts of Asia Minor, up into the Balkans, far into Asia, including much of India, Burma, Indonesia and even some parts of the Philippine Islands.

No empire in history had ever extended over such a geographical spread. It was not only the physical space, but the fact that all of this became a united force in the short space of 100 years. And, of course, the fact that some 75-80 per cent of Jewry lived in this area placed an enormous burden on the leadership of the Jewish community.

It is most important to take a broad look at this Arabic-Islamic Revolution. With the writing down of the Koran, "that which is to be read," of the words and thoughts of Mohammed, that form of Arabic, the language and script of Southern Arabia which he used, became the official language of Islam. It was used at every service, from every Muezzin and Mosque, in every legal document and every journal. It can easily be said that Arabic became the "Lingua Franca" of the Islamic World.

This was not the only development. For the first few generations after Mohammed, there were a great number of internecine battles, for political power and for religious purity of thought. The major struggle was about who was to succeed the Prophet after his death. The battles continued until about 750, when the Caliph of Baghdad, that same Baghdad of the Parthian Empire, took control of the vast areas of the whole expanse. This was the famous Haroun al Raschid of Sheherazade fame and the 1001 Nights.

Haroun created in Baghdad a new Athens, which became a center for Islamic dynamism, unknown since Alexander. He saw himself as the reincarnation of that young Greek, and resolved to more than duplicate what Alexander had achieved by building on the Hellenistic ideas. He ordered all of the libraries to be reopened, and insisted that everything in the libraries be translated into Arabic. A new term came to be applied at this time, the Golden Age of Islam.

Since Plato was obviously the most important philosopher of Hellas, he would have to become the most important thinker for the Arab Empire, but since Plato was now in translation, those who now fell into Platonism were called Neo-Platonists. Academies were the method of education for the Greeks, so Haroun had to create similar institutions. He ordered the creation of the institution now called the University of Baghdad.

With the consolidation of the Empire in Baghdad, an enormous expansion of the economy on a world scale took place, with caravan routes extending from Japan and Northern China through all of Asia, North Africa and into Europe, particularly Spain and Portugal. Because the relationship between Jews and Muslims was extremely close in Asia Minor, it extended into most phases of this empire. This was the beginning of the Europeanization of the Oriental part of Jewry. Of course, there had been Jews in Europe since the Roman conquest, but with the coming into the Middle Ages, the history of the Jews shifts, not only in space, but also in kind.

To try to put this into a historical perspective, this story is taking place about 750. If one were to look at Europe at this time, the area was a disaster, due to the breakup of the Roman Empire. The spiritual stagnation of the Roman Church fell prey to many individual leaders who chopped out parts of the empire for their feudal courts. During the period 750 CE to 950 CE, Baghdad became the center of the universe.

The plight of the Jews was not always good, for they were considered *Dhimmi,*non-believers, and at times their life was degrading. The fact that education and literacy were common in the Jewish community helped to make the Abbasid dynasty more than a little dependent on Jews. At times, a majority of the court were Jews.

Baghdad began a process of using its excess capital for cultural purposes – in line with Axiom I. It was during this period, with over a century of use of the Koranic Arabic, that Arabic became the folk language of peoples of the Empire, both Muslim and others. Jews became masters of the language, as well as Aramaic, and they also had a reading knowledge of Hebrew. From Baghdad sprang a flood of new literature, such as *Omar*

Khayam, Thousand and One Nights of Sheherazade, and music in an Arabic mode. Inasmuch as the universities were built along the Greek lines, we find the beginning of a new science, *algebra,* an Arabic word, and *alchemy,* also an Arabic word; and they devised a better way to write mathematics, which we call Arabic numerals, using Arabic letters to represent decimal numbers.

Philosophy became the hallmark of the schools, and in general, philosophic debates were held primarily over Platonic philosophy. Schools of Arabic Neo-Platonism began to arise. Arabic architecture, which in California is called Spanish-style, developed wherever the Arab culture flourished. This was the beginning of what historians often call the Arabic Golden Age. Historians also labeled Europe at the very same time as being in the brutal Dark Ages.

The Jews who lived in the Arabic world profited well from their association with the caliphs, emirs and cadis, the leaders of the Arab sphere. Jews also attended the universities, studied Plato, submerged themselves in science, literature, even to the extent of writing poems, songs and secular literature in Arabic. Some even tried writing in Hebrew, but most of that was reserved for purely religious matters. The Exilarchs lived in great luxury in Baghdad as the national representatives of the Jews in the caliph's court. They received tribute from the Jewish communities around the world, just as the Caliph did from his people. This luxury readily indicated that the leaders of the Jewish community fared well during most of this Abbasid period.

The Jewish academies around Baghdad still received questions from all over the world on religious matters and their responses were scattered back to the fold. Their reference was the Oral Law as encompassed by the Talmud, the Midrash, and whatever commentaries were available at the particular time. Within the Muslim world, debates and conflicts took place between those who said that the Koran was the final word and those who maintained that besides the Koran, Mohammed also delivered an Oral Tradition to his followers.

Thus, almost in parallel to the Pharisees and the Saducees, Islam had to deal with the problem of the Koran, the written word and oral traditions. Sects of Islam were created not only as to whom was the proper prophet-designate, but which direction Islam should go. The fight continues today on the front pages of the world's newspapers. For the purposes of this book, it should be noted that a similar argument should have and did take place in the Islamic Jewish community. You should recall that all books at that time were prepared by copyists and that errors and omissions were bound to happen whenever one document was copied for another.

These developments began to shape the Jewish community. Under the impact of the Islamic community arguing about the real Koran, disputes took place over what was the real Torah, there being differences between scrolls. Secondly, a movement to undercut the religious and economic power of the heads of the academies, and like the Muslims, go back to the original book. The third development related to the impact of philosophy on Jewish scholars.

It was during this period that a group of scholars determined to set the authoritative Bible for Jews. They attempted to finalize the conflicts over spellings and misspellings, added and omitted letters and words, and to create a uniform text. These scholars, Massoretes (bearers of the tradition), refined as well as they could the text of the Bible. They also created the musical designations for every word of the text. What eventually resulted from their work is the standard Hebrew text, which we use today; it is obviously called the Massoretic text with all the vowel signs in place.

Related to the first issue was the development of major attacks on the rabbis and Talmud by a group of Puritan Jews, who demanded a return to the original Bible and without any of the Oral accretions that had developed over the centuries. They proposed that Jews should return to the primitive ways of the Bible, a sort of new Saducee approach. They called themselves *K'raim*, or those who follow the K'rah, "that which is to be read," as opposed to the inclusion of Oral Tradition of the Rabbis. Today we call them *Karaites*. This was the first group since the beginning of the millennium to challenge the leadership of the Jewish community. The Karaites lived in the Oriental areas, and accepted Muslim laws and institutions as their public law, but religiously interpreted the Bible in a strict constructionist way.

In the Oriental community of Jews, the Karaites provided, a different brand of Judaism, even up until World War II. At times they were part of the Jewish community, and frequently, not. Hitler, who found the greatest numbers of Karaites in Russia and in the Balkans, made no distinction and left very few Karaites to this world. There are still some in Israel, but they are becoming lost in Jewish assimilation.

The third facet of Islamic life has had the most powerful and lasting effect on Judaism and Jews. When Plato became the philosopher of Islam, it was only natural that the rabbis had to prove that Plato was really the philosopher of Judaism. It was the head of the Babylonian academy, Saadia of Fostat, Egypt, who not only led the rabbinical attack on the Karaites, but also wrote the first Jewish Platonic philosophy since the writings of Philo of Alexandria some eight centuries earlier. In fact, there does not seem to appear a single Jewish writer until Saadia to involve himself in Platonic ideas. Only under the spell of the Islamic universities, which had by now spread to Cairo, Kairuan in Tunisia, Fez in Morocco and even to Cordova in Spain, did interest in Platonic philosophy become important to Jewish leaders.

Saadia lived in the latter part of the 9th and the first half of the 10th century. The power of the Baghdad Empire was beginning to decline, along with the power of the Exilarchs, who although claiming descent directly from Hillel, really represented the national ideas of the people. The academies represented the rabbinical concepts. Saadia was brought in to head the academy of Baghdad, by now the most important, because he was an Egyptian, and therefore was not seen as a threat to the Exilarchs.

He became the most important opponent of the Exilarchs for power. Eventually, he won, and shortly afterwards the office of the Exilarch ceased to exist.

Saadia set the tone for the whole series of Platonic philosophers to expound their ideas in Jewish life. This neo-philosophy could never have developed without a similar movement in Islam. As was pointed out previously, the Caliphs sponsored culture, and one part of their program was to translate all books and scrolls. Plato was translated, which caused a great stir in the universities. As this uncovering of the Greek past was brought to life in Arabic, and building on Pythagorus and other Greek scientific ideas, the Arabs began to invigorate Science and Mathematics. Plato had few answers in these areas, so he became the thinker for poets, mystics and inductive thinking. It was only when the Arabs discovered anew the writings of Aristotle, Plato's student, that a real ideological clash began in Academia.

It was the first time that there had been major clashes of philosophies since the Athenian period. We begin to see about the end of the millennium, a major attack on the premises of Platonism, or rather, Neo-Platonism. This came from those who saw more truth in Aristotelian style of thinking, that is, essentially, deductive, or scientific. Whereas the Platonists saw all things in the universe as bifurcated, the others began to see that Nature was more integrated. Rather than two worlds, the later thinkers viewed the world as one with gods and God as part and parcel of the world.

It is possible to label these two ideas as binary and unitary. Since the 10th century, this has been one of the major problems before the philosophical community. Is God in the world, or is God in heaven, as the tradition has always stated, or is God part of our world and of necessity bound by the same rules of Nature as everything else in Nature? Those who have studied American History will recall the debates between the Transcendentalists and the Immanentists, that is those who believed that God was above and beyond this world, and those who thought that God was in the world. This is essentially the same conflict.

The controversies in philosophy began in Baghdad and soon spread to all of the universities around the empire. It continues in our day, albeit in different forms. For the purposes here, an important figure rises in this period, as the stage is set for the Golden Age in Spain.

8 ✡ RISE AND FALL
OF THE SEPHARDIC JEWS –
MAIMONIDES' MAJOR CONTRIBUTIONS

To set the stage for the next development in the Jew
ish saga, it is necessary to return to the Baghdad of
850. The caliph at that time had begun to differentiate
between the Muslims and the other Dhimmis, the non-
believers. He had just passed an ordinance that required
Jews to wear a "yellow badge of shame" on their outer
garments to distinguish them from the believers. In the
previous century, life for the Jews in the Islamic Empire,
was, in general, good for them, although internecine fights
made the caliphs incapable of holding sway over all the
various parts of the Empire. They began to lose control,
and, therefore, one should expect to see a swing of power
away from Baghdad. What actually happened is that the
real power of the Empire shifted to the west, to the Cadi
of Cordova, and for the purposes of explanation here, the
change of leadership of the Jewish community also moved
to Spain. The beginning of this is reflected in that conflict
between the Exilarch and the head of the Academy, the
Gaon.

The community went to Egypt for a person to head
the academy in Baghdad in much the same way and purpose that Herod had gone to Babylonia for Hillel to head
the Sanhedrin in Jerusalem, some 950 years earlier. Probably by going outside the community, it was felt that Saadia
would be no threat to the Exilarch, but, as we now know,
this turned out not to be true.

Saadia was the first substantial Jewish philosopher
since Philo of Alexandria in the first century, and he al-

ready showed the influence of Aristotle. Under the influence of the Karaites, he wrote a dictionary of Hebrew. Moreover, he wrote a prayer book, a Siddur, probably because there was such variation of prayer books in the Jewish communities around the world. As Gaon, he masterfully took on the Karaites who had made much progress in the Empire. The major importance of Saadia was that he signaled the beginning of the end of the Exilarch by preempting the power of the national group and shortly thereafter, the Gaonate. As Babylonia and Baghdad began to lose its control of the Islamic world, so did the Babylonian Jewish world begin to yield its power to the Western part of the Arabic Empire. This begins the end of Babylonia as the center of the Jewish world, and the rise of the Emirate of Cordova.

Very little intellectual or cultural creativity came out of Baghdad after its power waned, either in Arabic or Jewish. Cordova and its Emirate rose and the indication for Jewish History is signaled by the appointment of Hasdai ibn Shaprut as both the treasurer of the Emirate and as the Nasi of the Spanish Jews.

Hasdai was born in 915, when the Islamic Empire was already showing major signs of disintegration, at least as far as control in the West. The Spanish communities had already begun weakening their ties with the Babylonian academies. About this time, the ruler of Cordova, Abdarrachman III, began the process of unifying the areas of Muslim Spain. He did so externally by warring and defeating the Christians in the North, but also by developing friendship and solidarity with the various indigenous peoples of Spain, including the Jews. Industries were created in the peaceful area, and commerce increased with many of the Mediterranean countries.

Hasdai was from a wealthy and intellectual family, which moved to Cordova from the town of Jaen, because the Caliph assigned a number of favorable commercial assignments to Hasdai's father. Hasdai became, subsequently, a favorite of the Caliph and due to his great intellectuality, he was useful in military and economic interests of Cordova. As he became more popular, he used his skills to foster Jewish learning and culture. Just like among the Muslims where there had been a flowering of poetry, fables, music and science, so followed the Jewish experience. Jews, who had initiated international trade out of Andalusia and Granada, began to develop their own jargon, a proto-Spanish, written in Hebrew, which became first a commercial language and then the folk language of Jews in the Iberian Peninsula. This language is called Ladino and is still spoken by Sephardic Jews today.

Hasdai promoted Jewish academies in Spain, as the Babylonian ones were sinking into obscurity. In these academies Jewish law and tradition were not only permitted to find a home, but further explorations of the law were encouraged. He also promoted Jewish literature, especially poetry, both religious and secular. Most importantly, the creation of the academies helped to shift the sphere of influence from the East to the West.

Beginning with Hasdai, we have what has been called the *Golden Age of Spanish Jewry.* Jews, both Sephardic and Ashkenazic, would look to Spain as the high point of the Diaspora, and certainly the most creative area. All of this development took place in a period of some 250 years, and effectively ends with the departure of Maimonides from Spain to Northern Africa and then eventually to Egypt. Out of this period we have magnificent poetry for the synagogue, called *piyutim,* which are still used in the prayer book; and writers whose works affected the western world, such as the three Ibn Ezra's, Moses, Judah and Abraham; and the philosopher-poets, Judah Halevi and Samuel Ha-Nagid.

Spain became the focus of the Jewish commercial ventures, not only in the Muslim world, but also within the Christian part of Europe. In addition, we have evidence through the letters of Isaac of Tudela, Spain, of his visits with Jewish communities all over the Far East, as he traveled what came to be known as the Silk Route. It was not only in commerce that most of the Jewish world looked to Iberia. It was in the areas of philosophy and Jewish Law that all eyes turned. Whether it was to the famous Isaac Alfazi (from Fez, Morocco), or the Ibn Ezra's, or Judah Halevi, or the Kimchis of Southern France (my direct ancestors) or eventually to Maimonides, it was to the Spanish area, including Morocco and Southern France, that Jews turned for their religious and cultural ideas.

It was the scientific approach of this time, the beauty of Ladino folksongs and stories and the religious feelings generated by the melodies created in Spain, that permeated much of Jewry of the South.

Ashkenazim and Sephardim

Now, it is time to take up the meaning of the terms Sephardim and Ashkenazim. Since Jews were multi-lingual and literate, they were able, under Islam, to play a unique role in commerce. Jews were encouraged to become involved in shipping and trade, and many of the early cartographers were, perforce, Jewish. The fact that there were no copyright laws then, one of the ways Jewish mapmakers could protect their product was to assign Hebrew names to places on the map. The most western place mentioned in the Bible is *Sepharad,* so the Hebrew word was placed on the early maps of the Iberian Peninsula. In the same fashion, the Rhine River Valley, which was the entrance to the Northern Continental Europe was given the Hebrew name, *Ashkenaz,* which had a northern connotation in the Bible.

As these maps came into common use among traders, those who lived in Spain and Portugal were called Sephardim, and those in Christian Western Europe were designated as Ashkenazim. Furthermore as the Spanish Jews crystallized their order of service and their academies began to exercise more leadership among the Jews of Islam, and the order of the service and the traditions of Spanish Jewry became more the norm, we can recognize the hegemony of Spain over all parts of the Empire. So it is probable that Yemeni Jews would accept the authority of the Spanish rabbis and therefore become Sephardic Jews in practice. Not all Jews in Islam accepted this arrangement, and a number of Islamic Jews did not accept the rule of Spain, and they are not Sephardic. This is the reason that in Israel, there are now three classifications of Jews: Ashkenazic, Sephardic and Oriental, meaning eastern Jews who do not operate under the aegis of the Sephardic Chief Rabbi.

Into this unique scene of the time entered Maimonides, his Greek name; or Moses Ben Maimon, his Hebrew name; or Rambam, which is the acronym for him, based on the first of his letters of his name plus Rabbi. Born in 1135, he embodied to a great extent the scholar-teacher. Early in his life, he became a physician, which tied him to the more deductive sciences, rather than the reflective and inductive thinkers of the Platonic school. He found himself more at ease with the neo-Aristotelian ideas. He determined that there was a need for a compilation of a code of law for the Sephardic Jews. Codes of laws are usually written when the people under the law are not following those laws.

To repeat what we have expressed earlier, whenever a code of law is prepared, it means that the era of that law is near or at the end, and represents a signal for the future, or a compilation of the past. It was obvious that Maimonides felt that the Sephardic Jews of that and the next generation were losing their way.

His first major tome, *Mishneh Torah*, a Repetition of the Law, is written in fourteen chapters. The Hebrew way of writing fourteen is Yad, that is Yod, for ten and Daled for 4. A nickname for the Mishneh Torah was Yad Chazakah, which is translated as *A Strong Hand.* In the Yad, Maimonides attempted to bring some order to the Talmudic discussions over the Law which had occurred since the origin of the Oral Law, through the Mishna, Talmud, as well as later commentaries, as of the twelfth century.

In his introduction, he stated what he thought were the most important beliefs of Judaism. Included in this were the description of the major ideas about God and the Messiah. It is here that Maimonides affirms the belief in the coming of the Messiah, which became the song of the Hitlerian concentration camp martyrs, called *Ani Maamin.* The ideas of Maimonides were incorporated into the prayer book and are called the thirteen I*karim,* or

Articles of Faith. This codification was not accepted universally by all the rabbis of that time, but it signaled the need for some clearing of the haze as to what was Jewish Law and belief.

For the purposes of his book, Maimonides was severely castigated for his ideas by extremely conservative scholars. The work was essentially for the Jewish community and was to enable ordinary Jews to not only understand the laws, but also appreciate the reasoning behind so many of them.

Later in his life Maimonides wrote for a more scholarly audience, his philosophy which he entitled *Moreh Nevuchim,* normally translated as "Guide for the Perplexed," but a more accurate translation would be "A Guide for the Confused." Maimonides probably would not have written such a title unless there was a large number of Jews who were confused about their understanding of what Judaism entailed. It is a major tome, which has over the centuries inspired new thought, not only in the Jewish community, but among Christian and Islamic scholars. It aimed at developing a modern interpretation of Jewish faith and the philosophic and scientific ideas of that period. Maimonides introduced Aristotle to the Jewish world, and was the integrating force for Jews, who from then on saw their Judaism in terms other than the traditional.

Plato and Aristotle

It becomes necessary at this point to contrast Aristotle to Plato. Plato has been previously described as dualistic, mystical, poetic and pessimistic. Aristotle is much more scientific, precise and in a strange way, Unitarian. Implicit in Aristotle's ideas is the idea that Nature is not to be seen as dualistic, but rather that all of Nature must be ruled by one law, and that God must be bound by that same law. Implicitly, this philosopher denies the idea of miracles, for miracles require the Supernatural, and for Aristotle there is no supernatural entity.

We find also a basic difference between a Platonic thinker and one who follows Aristotelian lines of thought. If one believes in miracles, then one must believe in the intervention of the Supernatural. If one does not believe that there is a supernatural being, but rather that God or Gods are in this world, then no miracles can occur for everyone and everything is bound by the same rules of Nature – *miracles are distortions of nature.*

This distinction is important to understand! Miracles are part of the world in which the deities play with those in the natural world. If something happens that does not follow rational logic, then there are basically two explanations. The first, the Platonic, explains that the deity has decided to manipulate the rules of Nature. We call that a miracle. The other way of thinking tries to explain the occurrence in some rational way, as scientifically as possible, and if that is not possible, the answer is that we do not know enough to explain the situation. This methodology is Aristotelian.

Maimonides introduced to the Jewish community what is called the *allegorical interpretation of miracles.* He wrote that the Bible was written for ordinary people, not philosophers. Ordinary folk would not be able to understand certain events without the explanations of miracles. Academics, however, had no need for an explanation where God enters intrusively into events. God could no more perform miracles than could anything else in Nature. In other words, there had to be a scientific reason for every event in the Bible which is called a miracle. It is the difference between inductive thinking and deductive reasoning.

For example, the flood at the time of the Exodus is brought about by God with his uplifted arm. That is the way the Bible and the Haggadah tells it. Maimonides had great difficulty with this way of handling the story. What he tried to do was say that there must have been a wind storm, a tidal wave or some other reasonable way to explain the parting of the waters. Other Biblical miracles are explained in the same way. What Maimonides seemed to say directly was, "I accept the Bible, but I do not accept the reasoning of the Bible."

From that time forward, with the rise of Arabic science, all religious ideas have had to deal with the choice between the style of Plato or Aristotle, even if never paying tribute to either. The question is simply this: How does one react to the past doctrine? Is it immutable, not only in what is handed down, and in what manner? If one questions the past interpretations, is it legitimate to create new ideas, or does one use the Yiddish expression, "Es shteyt geshribben," meaning it was so written and it may neither be changed nor reinterpreted?

This conflict continues today between those who accept the literalness of the Bible and belief in the Bible as it is, requiring either a Leap of Faith or a rejection of rationalism, and those who demand and insist upon a rational and scientific approach. Maimonides, by his creative genius, took the latter position, and by doing so, can lay claim to being the first Reform Jew of the modern era. Since his time, the conflict has had to be confronted by Jews, Christians and Muslims as well. Many have accepted the challenge and have moved from orthodoxy in various ways. Others have simply accepted the tradition as impervious to change and common understanding. The latter believe that the Bible is precisely what God wanted it to be, and if there are things in it which bother the mind, so be it.

Maimonides is also the symbol of the beginning of the end of Islam in Western Europe. From about 1250, those Sephardim who were still in Spain and those who were forced out, first by reactionary Muslims and then by the invading Christians, became more and more mystical, and in a sense, more Platonic. For with the rise of the Rationalism among the scientific philosophers, a counter movement arose in both the Jewish and Muslim communities.

This anti-rationalistic movement created a new Mysticism known as *Kabbala,* a Jewish mystical expression countering the scientific method.

To return to the Axiom – whenever a society suffers a traumatic experience, it tries to save the past and turns to mystical approaches to explain the trauma. Picture the Sephardim of the Iberian Peninsula who have lived through the Golden Age. They have lived under generally favorable conditions for some centuries, productive, culturally above average and protected by a benevolent monarch. They see their whole world collapsing and they can not understand it. The impending trauma turns them to the occult, the irrational, for they can find nowhere a rational explanation for what has happened.

About this time in Spain and southern France, a Sephardic mystical movement arose, sparked by the Bible of the Kabbalah, *Zohar,* the Book of Splendor, which became the focus of those who turned their attention to esoterica and the occult. The fact that the Kabbalah arose at the same time as the downfall of the Golden Age occurred served to reinforce the theory of the previous axiom.

From this time on, the Sephardic World became less a forward looking, progressive force, but rather it turned more to the past and end-of-the-world speculation. This is duplicated by what happens in Islam, as Muslims are forced out of Spain, and are replaced by the most reactionary Christians, egged on by the forces of the Inquisition. By 1498, all remnants of Judaism had been wiped out of Spain and Portugal, and those who remained in that area either had become Christians, pseudo-Christians or were exiled to other countries.

Most Jews who were able to escape the torture or auto-da-fes of the Inquisition followed their Muslim brothers to North Africa, or to the Ottoman Empire, which had arisen by now, with its capital in Turkey. Others went to Italy, joining an older Sephardic group from Spain and Portugal, to areas not beholden to the Pope, or to Holland or England. Except for those few who were able to move to other parts of Europe, most of the Sephardim remained living among Muslims. Both the Jewish and Muslim religions went into decline simultaneously, and the creativity that had developed in Spain ended. Little has been left of this legacy except for constant reminders back to that glory and hope for the end of the world. So the saga of the Sephardim in Spain is concluded.

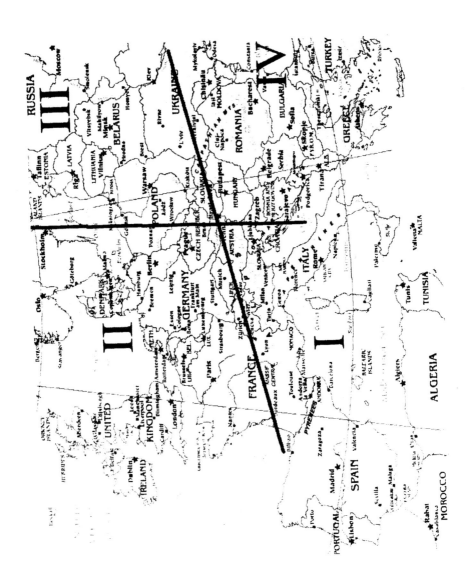

9 ✡ MELLMAN'S QUADRATIC THEORY OF EUROPEAN JEWISH HISTORY

It is at this point that it is necessary to introduce a didactic tool in order to create a theory of European Jewish History. This is an important device since most American Jews are products of that continent. This theory is almost humorously titled the *Mellman Quadratic Theory of European Jewish History.* It was developed in order to pictorialize the various threads of Jewish life which one finds on the American Jewish scene today.

To explain the theory, we have divided the map of Europe, before World War I, into four quadrants, because most Jews, particularly the Jewish population in the United States, are descendents from European immigrants. The vertical and horizontal lines cross at Vienna, which for centuries has been known as the "Crossroads of Europe." There are major lines of travel in at least six directions radiating from Vienna. *One caveat though: there is obviously no absolute accuracy in the precise direction or placement of either line.*

Quadrant I – The Sephardic Area:
The lower left quadrant includes Spain, Portugal, Southern France and Italy. This area, designated as Quadrant I, is called the Sephardic Quadrant, and for these purposes after the Inquisition and expulsion from Spain and Portugal, only Southern France and Italy are involved. Southern France plays a most interesting role with Napoleon, and Italy with the rise of the Renaissance.
Quadrant II – The Napoleonic Area:
Quadrant II in the northwest includes the British Isles, Northern France, Western Germany, Holland, Bel-

141

gium, Switzerland, and with some deviation of the lines, all of Scandinavia, as well as what was Czechoslovakia and Western Austria.

Quadrant III:
Quadrant III is the area of Northeast Europe, which includes the present Baltic States of Estonia, Latvia, Lithuania, Northern Poland, Great Russia and White Russia.

Quadrant IV:
Quadrant IV includes all of the Balkan countries of Rumania, Hungary, Bulgaria, Greece, Yugoslavia, and Southern Russia, including, Ukraine, Moldavia and Podolia.

Quadrant I
It is necessary to go back in time to explore Quadrant II. Jews have been living in this sector, all of it, since the rise of the Roman Empire and at least since the capture of Judea by Pompey in the year 63 BCE. There are records of Jewish tombstones that date from that period, as well as some correspondence back to Palestine. It is said that Jewish communities were in touch with the Palestine Sanhedrin and were in tune with the traditions of that body. What is surely certain is that from the time of Constantine and the Christianization of the Roman Empire, the life of the Jew in Western Europe was hardly pleasant. One papal decree and council after another earned their keep by passing severe restrictions against the Jews.

There are few documents about Jewish life in the area, but what we can learn from Church documents, and from the results, Jews were forbidden to live with Christians, to trade with them, to employ Christians, and finally, the Fourth Lateran Council of 1215 forced Jews in all parts of the Holy Roman Empire to live inside a walled community within a city, called a *Ghetto.* These were usually the worst habitable areas. Moreover, Jews were required to wear special garments and a badge denoting that they were Jews, and treated like animals. The Christian guilds of various smiths excluded Jews from their membership and restricted Jews from all businesses. As a result the only businesses left to Jews were rag dealers, second hand clothes, pawn broking and to some extent, fine metal smithing.

Jewish communities, beginning about the year 1000, with the First Crusade, suffered the most violent acts by these soldiers of the Christian God. Communities were pillaged, women raped and synagogues burned and stripped as the Crusaders traveled along the Rhine River, and then down the Danube on their way to conquer the Holy Land from the Muslim infidels. The Roman Church had by this time consolidated its position in the Empire, so that almost any king, marquis, baron or other feudal lord was forced to do the Pope's bidding, in attempting to extend the Church's influence wherever the Muslim lived.

For the next 500 years, the Church Triumphant used whatever device it could to force out any heretics, including Jews. Whether it was by Lateran Council, or by Bishops haranguing the masses into hysteria against the Jews, it resulted in the creation of ghettos, false tales of Passover plots, selling Jewish communities to royalty, or the holding of public disputations between Christian clergy and forced appearances by the leaders of the Jewish community. They burned the Talmud and finally demanded death or conversion by fire during the Inquisition. The Church and its allies succeeded in creating a Jewish history primarily of tragedy and destruction.

Paralleling this destruction, about 1000, we begin to see a rise of Jewish scholarship. Some five hundred years after the close of the Babylonian Talmud was completed, the first major personage emerged in Central Europe, a Rabbenu Gershom of the German city of Mayence. He issued a number of *Takkanot*, or decrees, having to do with social legislation among the Jews. He is most prominently known as the one who abolished polygamy for Jews. But he created as well a social contract for the Jews in his orbit for rules in business and interpersonal relations. His most prodigious feat was to introduce the program for Torah and Talmud learning, which spread rapidly along the Rhine on the German as well as the French side. Soon Jews began to have commentators on both the Torah and the Talmud.

Generically, those people who wrote comments to these books are called *Tosaphists,* or adders. Before discussing these individuals, it is important to take up the most famous commentator of the Bible and Talmud, *Rashi,* again an acronym, for Rabbi Sh'lomo Yitzhaki. His acronym comes from the R-SH-I, the first letters of his name, and in Hebrew, wherever possible, the "ah" sound is placed between consonants.

Rashi, born in 1040 died in 1105. He studied with the pupils of Rabbenu Gershom and then returned to his hometown of Troyes, France. There he took on the task of commenting on the Torah and most of the Babylonian Talmud. His style was so succinct and direct, quite in contrast with the sermonic material used, that reading Rashi soon became the universally accepted way one studied these documents. In fact, until recently, it was considered improper to study the Torah without the Rashi commentaries attached. The expression often used, in Yiddish, "Chumash (the Five Books of Moses) und Rashi." Rashi tried, based on his own understanding of Hebrew, to give the ordinary meaning of the text. This was in sharp contrast to the Spanish Jewish scholars, whose general intent was to find philosophical and scientific meanings behind the writings of the past.

Rashi so influenced the future schools where these subjects were taught, that for centuries the style of Rashi was emulated by his successors, the Tosaphists. It is said that the style of Rashi had a great effect on those scholars who began studying the Bible critically, and opened the door for the Reformation.

It was about this time that the Crusades began wreaking havoc on the Jewish communities in Quadrant II. So the period of the Tosaphists is parallel to that of the Crusades, which were exciting to the Crusaders, but not to Jews who happened to be in the way on their paths to glory.

The Jews of this area, which was called the Ashkenazic region, added two facets to Judaism, which were different from the Sephardim: The first is a very interesting twist to Hebrew. They who were furthest away from Palestinian Hebrew, softened some of the letters and vowels. For example, take the word, *Shabbat.* The *t* at the end may originally have been more like the *th* sound in the ears of the Ashkenazim. In time, the word was transformed to a soft *s,* so that the Ashkenazim pronounce the same word *Shabbos.* The *ah* sound became an *aw* sound, and so for Northern Jews, the word was *Shabbaws.* In addition, where words had their accents in the last syllable, like German, the accent shifted to the next-to-last. So Sephardim would say *Shabbát* and Ashkenazim, *Sha'baws.* Parenthetically, even today, Germans, attempting to pronounce the "th" sound, will still say, " Ze dinner is on ze table."

The other contribution of major force was the creation of a Jewish language, developed primarily from early German, but written in Hebrew letters. Originally called Jüdisch, this language became Yiddish. The jargon, like Ladino, probably started as a commercial lingo, so that only Jews could read the bills, orders and instructions. Eventually it became the folk language for the Ashkenazim, as Ladino did for the Sephardim. The Germanic and French Jews, living as they did among Christians, created a number of rites, which paralleled their neighbors. For example, the *Jahrzeit,* the remembrance of the anniversary of a dear one's death, was created by German Jews, and has subsequently been adopted by some Sephardim, This memorial is almost a perfect parallel of the Catholic Requiem.

They also introduced the Bar Mitzvah to parallel the confirmation of the Christian boys, and the breaking of the glass at the end of the wedding. Originally, that ceremony was introduced to drive away evil spirits, but somehow as time progressed, it became a symbol of the destruction of the second temple. Since Aristotle had not yet had his effect on Christian Europe, it is safe to say that the overwhelming ideas were in line with the Platonic thinking of the traditional church. It is well known that mysticism and outright superstition were rampant in Europe. It is no accident that parallel to the Golden Age of Islam, the European society was labeled by historians as "The Dark Ages." There is no doubt that the average Jew surrounded by Christian ignorance and superstition would also adopt some of these same general practices.

But to better understand the Ashkenazim, it is necessary to turn back to Italy, which was destined to play a strange and important role in the change of Quadrant II. Many Jews who were forced to flee from Spain and Portugal were accepted into some of the ducal kingdoms of Northern Italy. Interestingly enough, the Inquisition had little effect on these kingdoms which were not directly under the control of the Popes. These Jews, many of whom were called Marranos, or Jews by birth, forced by the church to become Christians publicly, once out of Spain, mostly returned to Judaism. They were, in general, the cream of the Spanish Jewish intellectuals and brought to Italy the philosophy, the languages, the business skills and the love of life that had been part of the good Jewish experience in Spain. They all spoke a number of languages, including Latin, Greek, Hebrew and probably many others.

Coming as they did around 1250, to such places as Florence, Venice, Milan and Genoa, they must have had some effect on the courts of the Doges. It is tremendously exciting to hypothesize that the influence was so great that the Jews may have initiated the idea of the Academy, for about this very time we find the first Academy in Florence, about 1440, which had as its purpose the study of Plato and other Greek philosophy. It is out of Florence that come the remarkable achievements and great contributions of the Italian masters. They include Da Vinci, Boticelli, Dante, Fra Lippo Lippi and so many others who benefited from the remarkable development of the Italian Renaissance. It started in Florence, almost everyone agrees, but the unusual part of the whole matter is that the first evidence of the intellectual and artistic growth came from the Platonic Academy which arose about the middle of the 13th century. Is it too much to assume the growth of the academy coincided with the arrival of the first Spanish Jews to Florence and other non-papal states?

There is at least a coincidence of time, but even more so, the idea of academies and colleges was part and parcel of the Jewish baggage, and it would be only natural that the doges, who were dependent upon the Jews for their commercial successes in the Mediterranean and in northern Europe, would respond to them intellectually as well. This is the same Italy which was in the Dark Ages just prior to this period. Something must have triggered this unbelievable transformation of the Western

World.

Coupled with the intellectualism of the Spanish Jews were their apparent skills in international commerce. By the middle of the 15th century there was a significant rise in the number and power of Jewish bankers in Northern Italy, particularly in Florence, Venice, Mantua and Ferrara.

Returning to Axiom I of this book, that whenever there is excess capital, one should expect a rise in the cultural life. This is precisely what happened in the northern part of Italy. Not only was there a tremendous rise in the economy, as evidenced by the stories of the enormous estates and homes which became prominent then, but literary and creative arts begin rising like a Phoenix out of the ashes of the Dark Ages.

At this very time one can also notice the rise of Italian universities, modeled very carefully after the Platonic academies which were the epitome of Arabic culture. Who better than the Jews to play this cross-cultural role? The Roman Catholic Church played a very negative role in this, excluding as well as it could, the Jews from the body politic, but the Northern states to a varying degree did not follow the Church's teaching on the Jews.

One other piece of evidence of the literary renaissance was the increasing study of Hebrew by Christian and Humanistic scholars. It almost became a trademark of the scholar that he studied and publicly professed his interest in Hebrew. Of course, this led not only to a reading of the Bible in the original, but also to a study of other Jewish classics in Hebrew. Beyond that, the scholars who wished to learn from Arabic had to depend on the Jewish savants from Spain and the Middle East to translate the works into Latin or the vulgate, the people's jargon.

It may be coincidence, but it should be obvious that the Jews played some role in the development of the Italian Renaissance. What also happened was the development of a Jewish Renaissance with great advancements in Talmudic studies, in Bible commentaries and on the artistic side, secular writings by Jews as well as artistic and musical contributions. Jews were intimates of Dante and Michelangelo. A Jew was the first "Pope's Musician." Soon after the invention of the movable type printing press, a most famous Jewish printing company was established in the town of Soncino, near Milan, in 1483. Called the Soncino Press, it has been involved in major Jewish publications since then, including the Bible, the Babylonian Talmud in translation, and many other texts in use in synagogues and temples all over the world.

What then develops in Italy is a class of Jews that parallel the patron in the Christian community. They were not only the bankers in the community, but as in Spain, they represented the Jewish Community before the government, and beyond that, they supported the Jewish and general culture far beyond what might be expected. They became the embodiment of the "Renaissance Man." It is no accident that many of the most illustrious writers in Italian literature are Jews, such as Carlo Levi, Alberto Moravia and Carlo Primo.

Religiously, however, Italian Jewry became a stilted and conservative force, hoping mostly to retain the past. Liberal forces in the Jewish community looked to other places to express their values. Nevertheless, Jews were, in general, looked up to in Italy, even in Rome, except by the church and by the fascists after their merger with Nazi Germany.

Many of the Jews who had been forced to convert to Christianity by the Inquisition, and become Marannos, but after emigrating to northern Italy, returned to their mother religion. They were able to play a major role in trade with the Ottoman Empire traders, many of whom were Sephardic Jews who had escaped from Spain and Portugal, to land in Egypt, Turkey, Greece and Palestine, all then under the Ottomans. It was also these former Marranos, who developed trade between Italy, particularly Venice, and the Rhineland ports, for Holland had welcomed these exiles, as did the city of Hamburg.

To return to Quadrant I. After 1492, we see almost no more visible Jews in Spain or Portugal, although there remained some Marranos who kept up their trade with relatives who had left for other parts. The trauma for the Spanish Jews was overwhelming. Those who followed the Muslims and settled either in North Africa or in the Ottoman Empire turned inward and mystical, and, by and large, turned away from the philosophical and intellectual to the Kabbalah, Jewish mysticism. Those who moved to the Balkans and Palestine became involved with pseudo-messianic movements. As far as the Quadratic Theory, they had moved into Quadrant IV.

A part of that neo-messianic movement had its greatest effect in the city of Safed in the Galilee. Under the leadership of a number of rabbis, mostly from Spain, but also some who had lived in Germany, a new movement was created, which should be called "the Sephardic Chassidic Movement." This is to distinguish it from the well known Chasidic movement of today which is Ashkenazic, although, as will be shown later, there is a real connection.

The Safed group was developed around the personality of Rabbi Isaac Luria, the Ashkenazi, who is known by his acronym, ARI. This stands for the words, Ashkenazic Rabbi Isaac. But it also is the Hebrew word for a lion, the eternal symbol of David and his tribe, Judah. In addition, Luria played on the prevalent mysticism, built on the Kabbalah, and especially the book, Zohar, the Bible of Jewish mysticism. This Sephardic Chassidic movement, although based in the north of Palestine, was the first Zionist movement in modern times, and made much of the fact in the new rituals which they developed. These Chassidim, flavored by the pessimistic mysticism brought on by the fall of the Golden Age in Spain, began to see themselves as the precursors of the Messiah.

The theory of the mystics about the Messiah was that the Savior would come when the world was at the lowest possible position. Of course, the refugees from Iberia would certainly have seen that the world was growing more evil, and for Jews even more so.

It should be noted that not only had the Sephardic Jews been dispersed, but the Ashkenazic Jews in Northern Europe had also suffered terribly from the Crusades and the increasing pressure of the Roman Catholic Church's insistence on the ghettoes, and general demeaning of Jews. It was in this environment, that the new Chassidic messianic movement developed. Luria, the Ari, created a group which, except for Shabbat, lived a very austere life with ritual baths and midnight watches. But on Shabbat, joy was encouraged through singing, and dancing, and old customs were invigorated during the Shabbat.

The Chassidics would walk east from Safed before Shabbat to greet the sunset earlier, recognizing that the further east one went, sundown came earlier. In addition, they created poetry to welcome the Sabbath, including the famous, *L'cha Dodi.* Incidentally, this poem has ten verses, two of which are about the Sabbath, and the other eight are about preparing for the Messiah, the son of David.

The Shabbat was to be celebrated in joy, so other religious songs were created, such as *Z'mirot,* which were sung after meals, all for the purpose of praising God. Then in order to extend the Shabbat, the Havdalah service was made the crown of the day and was delayed as long as possible. The theory behind this was that when the Messiah comes the world would be *Yom Sh'kulo Shabbat,* a day completely sabbath. This phrase is included in the grace after meals. The mystics had developed a theory that the heavens, where all the souls of Man would be contained, would be a place and time where no work would be necessary, and that all of the time would be spent in study, contemplation and song. In a sense the Chassidim were practicing a type of sympathetic magic, celebrating Shabbat as a symbol of the place of "Life after Death."

Luria and his followers had a tremendous effect on the Eastern Sephardim, and even incorporated an order of service, which is called *Nusach Ha'ari,* which includes many references to mystical ideas and angelology. Building on the immense pessimistic mysticism of the Kabbalah, a whole new development of Eastern Sephardim was created, which had a profound effect on that group, and on present day Judaism. Clearly these chassidim were not only involved with Kabbalah, for they were also Talmudic scholars, having established new Yeshivot in Palestine, but had the sense of impending doom and resurrection for Jews.

One of the rabbis, Joseph Caro, seeing that there was total confusion about the law, spent his days preparing a Code of Laws, printed in 1565, which soon became the new Bible for these Sephardic Jews. This codification, *Shulchan Aruch,* or the Prepared Table, once more follows the Axiom, that when a society feels a trauma, it tries to save the past. The Shulchan Aruch with its immense details of how to keep all the requirements of Jewish Law, deals with much that is nowhere in the Bible or the Talmud, including such small details of how to wash one's face, which direction to face in the synagogue and the necessary prayers to be said before sex, as well as minutia dealing with proper dress and food. Certainly the Shulchan Aruch contains the legal and communal requirements for all Jews, yet it was primarily related to customs of Eastern Sephardic Jews.

The Shulchan Aruch, several centuries after the codes of Maimonides, captured the minds of the Sephardic rabbis, and began to have an influence in the European communities. This book was amended by a Rabbi Isserles in Europe and that version became the *Bible of the North.* With the death of Luria, and in the vacuum created by the events in Spain and throughout Europe, it appeared to many Jews that the world was going to hell. It could not get worse, and therefore a succession of pseudo-messiahs saw themselves and were seen as the "Chosen One of God." Among those who should be mentioned are David Reuveni and Shabbatai Zvi. The latter was by far the most successful in creating a Messianic movement around himself. It should be noted that both men were Sephardic.

Zvi, a devoted Lurianist, was able to attract Sephardic Jews from Palestine to Amsterdam and Hamburg. In fact, he was so impressive, that synagogues all over the world celebrated his birthday, and on that day the young men wore the royal colors, green and white. About 1665, Zvi officially proclaimed himself the Messiah. Throngs followed him wherever he went, and special pilgrimages were organized to see the Messiah in the Holy Land . A number of these accompanied Shabbatai to Constantinople, where he went to convince the Sultan that he should be given the Holy Land for a kingdom. The Turkish authorities, fearful of violence, put Shabbatai in prison. He was then given his choice – become a Muslim or die. He chose to become a Muslim and the followers of Zvi were crushed.

Most of these followers retreated further into mysticism and read the conversion as still one more evidence that the end of the world was near. Others, wanting to further the movement, embraced Islam and created a group which was somewhat like the Spanish Marranos. They were outwardly Muslim, but at home they practiced a form of Judaism. These people were called *Donme* and remained a visible group in Turkey and Greece until Hitler.

This period of mysticism and Messianism was punctuated by great debates in the rabbinical community between those who were Kabbalah-oriented and those who were more inclined to the rational exposition of Law and Torah. The calumny and bitterness between these rabbinical opponents were so sharp that many leaders were actually forced out of their positions into exile. One more item needs to be added. Since the time for the Messiah had arrived, one group was founded by Frank, a Polish Jew, who dabbled in mysticism. After a trip to Turkey, where he learned more of the Messianic movements, he declared himself a king and developed a court of followers. Since the Law was there to be kept, in order to bring on the Messiah, he therefore ordered for his followers that sexual promiscuity was perfectly permitted and more so, sex was a completely religious act to be actively pursued. This group of Polish Jews, or possibly from Podolia, on the Romanian border eventually accepted either the Catholic Church in Poland, or the Greek Orthodox in its areas. There is some evidence that a small group of Frankists were still around in the twentieth century.

Quadrant II

From 1498, except for Southern France and Italy, the European position of the Sephardim was erased from the Quandrant 1 area. Sephardic Jews either lived within their Islamic homelands or left for Italy, Holland, England or parts of the Rhineland, where they established a new Sephardic presence. The difference must be understood. Those who went into the Muslim area became, by and large, mystical and sentimental about Spain in the past. There was little creativity from this group other than the mystical Luria movement.

Those who went into Christian Europe entered the area at a time it was beginning a whole new period. The time was the era of discovery, exploration and colonization, but also when Northern Europe had begun to learn and add to the Italian Renaissance. England, France, Germany, Holland, Switzerland and Austria became interested in the love of knowledge and art in a way unmatched since the Arabic Golden Age. Sephardic Jews who entered these countries were able to play an emphatic complementary role.

It is necessary at this time to place in perspective how the Italian Renaissance migrated north. As far as we can determine, the Italian academies for the study of Plato and the classics were fostered by Catholic orders that were not directly under the influence of the Pope. These orders, such as the Franciscans, Dominicans and others, began to use the technique of the academy to teach philosophy and the Bible. They created *scholas* in the Holy Roman Empire, before going north to establish similar academia in other countries. These scholas were the precursors of the famous universities of Europe, such as Grenoble, Sorbonne, Heidelberg, Jena, Utrecht, Oxford and Cambridge.

At these scholas philosophy was taught in dialogue form in Latin and Greek, and the Bible in Hebrew and Greek. For those students who passed the first examinations, they were entitled to call themselves Baccalaureates, or Bachelors. When that student was able to proceed to a level where he was able to tutor other students in the fundamentals of philosophy, then he was granted another title, Maestro, or Master. Finally, if he was able to advance to the level of becoming a maestro of maestros, he would, of course, become a Doctor of Philosophy, the highest title of the academic program. These academies were started in Italy, but soon were taken up by the itinerant monks into the other parts of the Empire. *(Readers should note that there is a remarkable relationship between the Schola and the Jewish Schul.)*

The fifteenth century becomes a watershed for Europe. A simple listing of the giants of humanism in Europe. In Italy, we have Leonardo Da Vinci, born in 1452, Botticelli, 1447, Machiavelli, 1469, Lorenzo Medici, 1449, Pico della Mirandola,

1462. In the North, Gutenberg, 1397, Martin Luther, 1483, Erasmus, 1466, Tyndale, 1490, Copernicus, 1493, Zwingli, 1484, Rabelais, 1490 and John Knox, 1505. These astonishing figures all emerged out of the same soil of intellectualism and ferment. All were early figures of the Early Renaissance which accompanied the rise of capitalism, rationalism, and Protestantism, that takes place in the next century.

Feudalism is beginning to crumble in the Holy Roman Empire, and the individual lordly and churchly provinces are starting to dissemble at this very time, when a more universal approach to the world seemed necessary. Since the Jews were still part of the feudal world, they must react to what is going on around them and they did! In Quadrant II, which is Northwest Europe, Jews were essentially the subjects of the feudal lord, and outside the pecking order in the typical estate. The Jews usually lived at the mercy or sufferance of the Lord, Earl, Count or Graf. They generally had no rights, and unless the Jews paid excessive taxes and travel levies, were always in great jeopardy. Those who were permitted to live in cities, were by order of the Lateran Councils forced to live in the ghettos of the cities, most of which were along the Rhine River Valley.

The Jews of this area developed a jargon, similar to Ladino in Spain and Portugal, which was a proto-German with Hebrew, and Aramaic words written in Hebrew. This language was originally entitled Judisch, with an umlaut over the **u**. This patois eventually became the Yiddish in Eastern Europe, where the umlaut was somewhat transfigured. This language, which was initially a commercial language in code for Jews, soon became the folk language for Jews living in the Rhine Valley.

It is in this area that the Court Jew arose. Like the famous Suss, made popular by Leon Feuchtwanger in his novel *The Jew Suss,* a group of Jewish bankers developed in the Rhine Valley, who were able to finance the courts in their gaudiness and infamous wars. These Court Jews were involved with other Jews who could help raise funds on an international level. They created connections between Hamburg and Venice, Amsterdam and London, Frankfurt and Vienna.

But even these Court Jews were confined to ghettos to which they had to retreat at night unless they were able to obtain expensive special passes. These ghettos were fenced and gated, of limited space, and if the Jewish population increased beyond what the area could hold, then there were only two alternatives, either arrange to move to another less crowded ghetto or another country, or, build up! Construct taller buildings! It appears that the first town houses in Europe, that is building more floor space above the allocated ground level, started in the ghettos of western Europe. Later, there will be discussion about the move to Poland in the fourteenth century,

This book, in attempting to make learning history easier and more understandable, creates at this point an innovation. Many people who study Western European History are faced with one of the dullest and most arduous tasks of learning the names, causes and effects and results of the series of wars which take place in this quadrant between 1492 and 1798. These conflicts include the Thirty Years War, War of the Roses, War of the Oranges, Hundred Years War and so many other smaller ones that this period becomes even more difficult to understand.

Many adults have expressed this feeling of frustration about this era. I attempt to solve the problem by calling this period the *Three Hundred Years War,* from 1492 to 1798. This is almost precisely what happened in Western Europe. There was a series of wars one after another with brief periods of detente in between. The sum total of the three hundred years of war ended with the map of Europe being approximately what it is today.

By the fifteenth century, the beginning of the Renaissance, you can begin to see the origins of the ethnic and national differentiation in Europe. A person could now distinguish an English literature, different in style and tone, and of course, language, from French or German literature. Folk music and dance also are recognizable. What is beginning to happen with the breakup of the Holy Roman Empire is a division of parts, according to the native language and culture. Certainly this can be labeled the *Rise of Nationalism.*

The prime result of the Three Hundred Years War is the shaping of present Western Europe.

In the seventeenth century a magnificent figure, Baruch Spinoza, enters the scene in the Dutch community of Amsterdam, where his family had arrived from Spain as a consequence of the Inquisition. His Hebrew name was Baruch Spinoza, but was given the Latin name, Benedict. Spinoza built on the Aristotelian works of Maimonides and created a new identification for God. For his God was Nature, and his philosophy is called Pantheism. It is not necessary to fully detail his philosophy, but sufficient to recognize the Maimonidean connection.

The new Jewish community of Amsterdam, feeling threatened by the possibility of being found to have heretical thoughts within it through Spinoza, excommunicated him. What this meant was that Jews were forbidden to have social contact with him, and that he obviously could not be married or buried under Jewish law. Had he been living today, he would have undoubtedly been called the premier Jewish philosopher, but unfortunately he lived in the seventeenth century.

Earlier, in the fifteenth century, Gutenberg's discovery of the movable type press changed forever the intellectual life of the known world. Whereas, previously, only the priests and a few layman of the Christian world were literate, now it became possible for every person to have his own printed books instead of handwritten manuscripts. The impact on the Church was most evident. Now a Bible could be read by all, and it was not too much later that the heresies of Jan Hus in Bohemia, Luther in Germany, Calvin in France, Henry VIII in England, John Knox in Scotland and others sought self-determination.

These Protestant reformers soon founded their own churches: in Germany, the Lutheran; in England, the Anglican; in Holland, the Dutch Reformed; in Bohemia, the Moravian Church; in France the Huguenots; in Scotland, the Presbyterian, and in Switzerland. the Calvinist churches. The remarkable fact is that in every case the church was based on national origin, and soon became the established church in that country. Where the Catholic Church was able to be the victor and the majority, it became the established church. Many areas of the three hundred years conflict were developed on religious lines, but the national spirit was probably more dominant. So, in Protestant countries, the Catholics became the second class religion, whereas in the Catholic countries, the Protestants were the underlings. But in every case in the second quadrant, the Jews were third in line, which placed them in a precarious position, for if the Jews took a position on either side, they were considered the traitors of the other.

It has been indicated in this quadrant that there was a rise of intellectualism, Nationalism and Protestantism. Additional "ism's" will be added to more adequately explain the period in this sector. With the defeat of the Spanish Armada in 1588 by the British, the major colonial powers were all in this quadrant. Colonialism was the major force in expanding markets and allowed land-based countries to expand their abilities to have more raw materials, far more than heretofore possible. For example, England, with the power of the fleet, was able to see itself, not as a small island off the continent, but as a world-wide power. So it was with Holland, Germany and France. No longer were physical boundaries drawn on a map the determinant of a country, but rather where one could place one's flag.

Add to this, the changing nature of economies and it is possible to see the rise of international capitalism, another ism, and then must be added an adjunct of all of the above, industrialism.

All of the above was affecting Quadrant II. For the average person in this area, it must have been an awe-inspiring period, with culture exploding, science playing its hand, political devices falling right and left, religious certainties being tossed about, and for the first time, instead of divine rights of monarchs, one could begin talking about the "Rights of Man." For the Jew, it was a particularly strange milieu, for although there were many Jews who were able to spread their wings in this breathtaking air, most Jews in this area were still caught in the post-feudal society. They were still the scapegoats for petty tyrants, still had to pay enormous taxes, still lived in ghettos, and still were, at best, third class citizens even in the more enlightened areas. All of this would begin to change at the end of the Three Hundred Years' War.

How were the Jews organized at this time? Many history books on Jewish history write in abundance about the Kehillah of eastern Europe, but so far not one has dealt with the western European community, especially the northwest. The Kehillah, which was the mode in Eastern Europe, was quite different from the others. The difference was Establishmentarianism – that is, the designation of one church as the authorized one in a state, either Protestant or Catholic; in every case, the Jewish group was always in a third position. Moreover, it was generally accepted that the Jews were nothing more than a religion.

In a sense this was a product of the old Roman Empire declaring Judaism as a *religio licta,* a permitted religion, but also by extension, the fact that the Holy Roman Empire retained this tradition. It was, therefore, natural that Jews would be seen as another religion, albeit a despised one. By contrast, Eastern Europe Jews were considered one of the many nationalities, so that they were viewed in a different category. It is necessary to recognize this distinction to understand Jewish history there. The Jews were a religious group, paralleled by Catholic and Protestant groups.

It should never be assumed that Jews during these 300 years were anti-Zionistic. Internally, Judaism still kept its prayers about the return to Zion, the rebuilding of the Temple, and still operated on a semi-national level, so that Jews took responsibility for other Jews out of a sense of national destiny. However, as far as legal authorities were concerned, and outward appearances, the Jews were simply another of the multiplying religious groups.

To go back to the organization, at least as far as Germany was concerned, the structure was called *Gemeinde.* This German word means community, and was the parallel to the parish of the Catholics and the synod of the Lutherans. In Germany, where most of the Jews of this quadrant lived, they organized along religious lines. The leaders of the community were usually the richest of the area and were called Parnasim. Every Jew was automatically a member of the Gemeinde and was taxed according to his income.

For example: if a Jew was taxed by the government 100 marks, and the Gemeinde had determined that the needs of the community were 10% of the total imposed tax, the total tax would be 110 marks; government retaining 100 marks, the Gemeinde the other 10. For this the Gemeinde had responsibility for keeping the records of births, deaths, divorces, etc. In addition the regional government held the Gemeinde responsible for the acts of its members. Beyond this, the Gemeinde hired all employees for purely Jewish concerns, such as rabbis, ritual slaughterers, shamasim or synagogue functionaries, doctors and nurses of Jewish hospitals, teachers of the Jewish schools and other persons in the employ of the Gemeinde. Also, if a person wished to move to another community, he had to have permission from both gemeindes, the one he was leaving as well as the one he intended to join. The old gemeinde had to be sure that he had no outstanding gemeinde debts; the second one had to receive references for acceptance.

Thus the government in exchange for collecting the Jewish Tax was able to exercise some control over the Jews. Certainly the Parnasim were completely beholden to the state, not only for the Gemeinde, but also for their own personal wealth in the economy. It is important to understand that although the Gemeinde had the records of the community, the records really belonged to the State. All Gemeinde employees were considered as state-employed, and kept their jobs as long as they did not create problems for the Count, Graf, City or whatever or whoever was in charge. Obviously, no employee of the state wishing to retain his or her position would oppose an action of the State or the Gemeinde for fear of loss of position.

Rabbis of these communities were particularly in jeopardy since it was they who delivered sermons and who many times wrote articles for journals which might include inflammatory or defamatory material. It was not unknown for the head of a particular state, prior to unification of Germany, to refuse to allow a certain rabbi to become the gemeinde rabbi.

The system itself forbade the sort of social activism that Americans take for granted from our leaders. In addition, it must not be forgotten that the records of the gemeinde belonged to the state and may help to explain how simple it was for Hitler to determine who in Germany had had Jewish great-grandparents and was thus labeled Jewish.

The whole question of the third class Jewry remained hidden until the end of the 300 Year's War when those who took power after the French Revolution, preaching equality, had to try to come to terms with this matter. Since the Revolution seemingly abolished the old regime, the rights of the average man was highlighted. Frenchmen became citizens of France with a phrase following it. If one was a Protestant, then he was a French national of Protestant religious persuasion. A Catholic had a similar designation. But for many Frenchmen, granting the same to the Jews was very difficult, inasmuch as Jews had traditionally been the pariah in both of these camps. In addition, Jews, in their prayers, still spoke of the return to Zion. Nevertheless, there was a great sentiment to grant Jews citizenship, a new concept in nationalism.

Recall that in France that there were two type of Jews, Sephardim of the Mediterranean, and those from Alsace-Lorraine, Ashkenazim. The Sephardim saw themselves as the elect over those speaking Yiddish-Rhinelanders.

The discussion lasted until Napoleon took over the French Empire, just before the end of the 18th century, when as General Bonaparte, he issued a proclamation in which he promised the Jews of the Near East that he would restore to them the Holy City of Jerusalem. When he declared himself emperor, he did pass some discriminatory legislation against the Alsatian Jews. But it was in the year 1806, when Napoleon exercised his greatest contribution to the status of the Jew, for after consulting with some of his Jewish friends of southern France, he convened an Assembly of Jewish Notables which he created as a new Sanhedrin of 70 persons. At this assembly, the Jews pressured by Napoleon, agreed to a resolution that the Law of France superseded Jewish Law, and where there was a conflict, French Law was pre-eminent. Also they announced that intermarriage was not against Jewish Law. The following year, Napoleon posed twelve questions to the now 80 leaders, who overwhelmingly voted to acclaim the superiority of the State to Jewish Law, encouraged Jews to go into all professions, especially the Army, but at this time they were hesitant on the intermarriage question.

What is even more important from the Sanhedric declaration was the impact on the Jews, not only in France, but as Napoleon expanded the empire, Jews in other countries accepted the idea of citizenship in their own country. Napoleon established the Consistoire, the ruling body of the Jewish community, which, with the approval of the government, chose the Chief Rabbi and insisted that the Jews begin the process of seeing themselves as nationals of their own state with the religious adjective. In Germany, Belgium, Holland and Austria, the Jews developed a program similar to the Consistoire, which was a religious self-governing body responsible to the government. So the Rabbis and the leaders of the Consistoire and the Gemeindes of German speaking states became pawns of the state, including their responsibility to provide Jews of conscription age for the military. In addition, these arms of the Jewish community became the force for the state imposing its values on the Jews.

When Napoleon decided to conquer all of Europe, and was successful all the way into parts of Russia, he instituted the French constitution, wherever the French army won. For Jews, living in ghettos, Napoleon was the savior, for it meant that, for a time, they were equals of their neighbors. In Germany, many Westphalian Jews named their children, Napoleon, and when Jews were expected to assume surnames, there was at least one Jew, who changed his name to Schonheit, German similar to

Bonaparte. All of this was happening in the first decade of the 19th century. In Italy, many Jews threw off their chains of the ghetto and walked to Paris with their freedom.

So Quadrant II is where the first evidence of the granting of equality and freedom to the Jews occurred in modern times, if only for a short time. The exchange for this freedom was for Jews in this area to give up any idea that they would be a nation within a nation, That Jews were now to be considered as a cohesive religious group in Quadrant II, was to be a determining factor in what happened religiously there. Immediately after Napoleon's Sanhedrin and his victory in the lowlands of Belgium, Holland, in German towns of the Rhine, it was almost a natural event that some Jews began to try to move out of the medieval vise that had been placed upon them.

When one adds to this the new philosophies, the Biblical studies, the openings to the universities for Jews with possible professions available, we find Israel Jacobsohn, in Prussia, eastern Germany, building a synagogue, in which he wanted to strip away the Orientalisms in Judaism. An organ, the backbone of the Lutheran services, was introduced, and then sermons in German, again in parallel with the Protestant move. The change was so great the Prussian government, probably at the urging of the more conservative Jews in the Gemeinde, forced the closing of his synagogue. Jacobsohn then moved to Hamburg, to the west, where he formed another one closer to his taste.

Much that was going on in intellectual thought at the turn of the century was predicated on the thinking of one professor at Heidelberg University. This teacher, Georg Hegel, had as much effect on intellectual and political life as anyone in modern life. It is necessary to now bring basic philosophy to bear, for much of what happened in Europe in the century developed upon different understandings and applications of Hegel.

First of all, let it be noted that philosophy prior to Georg Hegel in the last decade of the 18th century was static philosophy. Plato and Aristotle were still the powers to be reckoned with. Their philosophies were adequate in a society in which there was seemingly little visible change. But with the printing press, many inventions, discoveries and new science, the world was moving much too fast for these two. About 1790, Hegel promulgated a philosophy of progress, explaining why, at this particular time, there seemed to be so much new and exciting developing.

That is what he basically wrote in unbelievably prolix German. Building on Kant, who postulated that an idea has energy and direction by itself, and Newton, who proved that a weight in motion has energy, and if it meets another weight, both will change and there will be a release of energy, Hegel developed the idea of philosophy of progress.

Using Greek, as all philosophers did then, he called an idea, *Thesis.* When a thesis comes into conflict with an opposite idea, the *Antithesis,* they intersect. And when two ideas meet, a new Thesis is developed, containing the best of both ideas, forming a *Synthesis.* This Synthesis has a new direction and power, and there is released ideational power as well. This new Thesis then intersects with still another Thesis, creating another process, and so on. Each new direction and release of energy produces progress.

This philosophy captured the intellectual world in Western Europe. In economic terms this led to Marx producing *Das Kapital,* which led to the rise of socialist movements, all based on the dialectical idea of economic forces. In the field of sociology there developed champions of class struggle.

In Psychology, Freud, later used the concept of the struggle between the *Id* and the *Superego*, determining the *Ego* of an individual.

Hegel was challenged to hypothesize what would be the final Thesis of this world. He proposed that the two most eminent ideas in the world were Religion and Nationalism. Being the German Protestant he was, he then indicated that the final word would occur when the Purest Christianity and the Purest Germanism would meet in dialogue. Since he was also essentially a Platonist, he meant that when Christianity had cleansed itself of the Oriental and cultic parts, and Germany could rid itself of its non-Teutonic influences, then the end of the world could take place. The implications for events in Germany in the twentieth century should be obvious. But since Germany was the most intellectual, the most cultural in the world and the German universities were the acme of the academic heap, and it was in Germany that the real Protestant Revolution had begun and reached its highest point, all else was obvious.

Over 50 years ago, I heard the famous author, Ludwig Lewisohn say, "There is no greater music than German and German Literature is far superior to any other."

Hegel captured the intellectual life of Europe, and of course, the German people loved his conclusions, especially if they were Protestant. If, however, they were Catholic, they simply indicated the purity of the line of the popes from Peter. The Jews, who wished to embrace Hegel, had another problem. But this was soon solved by Jewish philosophers. For them, it was obvious that Hegel was correct, since there was no greater philosopher in the whole world. But he had a mote in his eye. He chose the wrong religion, that is, the child religion not the mother, which was much closer to the truth, obviously.

The new German rabbis in the first half of the 19th Century and their followers were so certain that they were on the right track, that they proceeded to try to eliminate anything in Judaism that smacked of Orientalism. Keeping kosher was therefore not important, since the only reason for kashrut was hygienic, and obviously, no country was more diligent about its hygiene than Germany. Shabbat, or Shabbos as they called it, could just as well be on Sunday, for who knew which day was the first, and in Germany all businesses and schools were open on Saturday. It would be unwise if Jews were required to compete and not be open on Saturday. Second day holidays were eliminated as rabbinically ordained to remind Jews that they were in exile. After all, no Jews in Germany were in exile, since they were "full" citizens, and none of them wanted to go to Palestine, for they were at home in Germany.

If that were true, then any relationship with the Holy Land as the looked-for homeland of the Jews had to be denied. Also it would certainly not be necessary to believe in a personal Messiah who would lead all Jews back to Jerusalem at the end of time. So the Messiah idea began to shift to the concept of a Messianic age, very much in tune with the Hegelian idea of the final synthesis. Jews in Germany felt that they could do without any of the trappings of the previous values of Judaism. Berlin and Hamburg were their Jerusalems – no Zionism for them. To top it off, they introduced the organ and family pews to the temple, much in the manner of the Lutherans who tried to redefine their religion after Luther.

Thus we had the origin of the German Reform movement. Completely convinced by their new freedom, their sophistication and their worldliness, it posited that Judaism was the next Thesis in this world. One should only try to recollect that Germany was the home of Mozart, Beethoven and Bach, Heine, Goethe and the finest universities in the world. In addition it was becoming obvious that Germany was taking the lead in bringing forth culture and commerce, in which the Jews played an active role.

Although it is not necessary to detail the contributions of German Jews to Reform Judaism, it is more important to review the previously mentioned Gemeinde. Through this state-controlled Jewish community, religious social action was out of the question. Rabbis were free, in general, to speak on ritualistic matters, but not on the application of Judaism to social problems. When the first rabbis from Germany came to the United States in the 1830's and 1840's, they thought they had come to a place where the lack of governmental intervention in Jewish life so extraordinary that one rabbi stated that in one hundred years all Americans would become Jews – again a Hegelian synthesis.

It was possible for the Gemeinde to exercise major control over every Jew in his personal, professional and even social life, if the leaders so wished. Many German Jews saw the double disadvantage to themselves of being a controlled Jew, as well as part of a dis-established religion. For them being a Jew was an *Umglueck*, a tragedy. Thus it became easy for upward striving Jews in the Enlightenment which developed in the late 18th century in Germany to want to have freer access to positions in the majority religion. Recall, that all universities were in the hands of the established religion. So Moses Mendlessohn, the most erudite Jew in Berlin, who translated the Bible into German so that Jews could learn cultured German, found his son, who wished to be a banker, accepting Lutheranism, Berlin's religion, and his grandson to be the champion of Bach, the Lutheran Organist and Superior Musician, and Felix felt it necessary to write a Reformation Symphony in honor of Luther.

Heinrich Heine, wanting desperately to become a professor in a German university, also converted. In Austria, where the established religion was Roman Catholicism, Gustav Mahler, converted to Catholicism, so that he could become the conductor of the Vienna Philharmonic. He, also felt that he had to prove his conversion, so he wrote a Resurrection Symphony. Mahler did however, insert into his writings little Jewish melodies, as if to say that he did not relinquish his identity. Still, all of his life, he was known as the Jew Mahler.

Such a conversion even took place in the United States, when Serge Kousevitsky was required to become an Episcopalian to become the conductor of the Boston Philharmonic. He, too, proved to remember his traditions and people by placing in his will that his papers were to be donated to Israel.

Many, too many, Jews trapped in other positions inside a restricted society, opted out to the majority religion. It was much later that gemeinde countries created another option – *Konfessionlos* – that is, without a religion. In that case, quite a number of Jews opted out, choosing to be such, insisting on being atheists or agnostics. Nonetheless, the great bulk of Jews remained faithful to their people and faith.

In Germany Jews tended to be either Radical or Conservative Reform on one side or Ultra or Modern Orthodox, on the other. Remember, Jews in Germany were only Jews by religion. In either case, the leaders of all synagogues were expected to wear top hats and morning coats to services, as a symbol that they were still Germans.

In Germany with the rise of the intellectual life, Jews, particularly those who were university trained, began to research their past. The reformers, in order to prove that Judaism was always abreast of the times; and the orthodox, in order to demonstrate that they, too, could show that they were not obscurantists. Out of this milieu developed a most interesting institution, *Der Verein des Kultur und Wissenschaft des Judentums,* the Society for Culture and Science of Judaism. This organization set up by Leopold Zunz and Samuel David Luzatto was aimed at exploring in a critical and scientific way the past of Judaism. The purpose was to demonstrate the efficacy of the Jewish past, and that it was not dying, but rather, in line with Hegel, part of the final synthesis.

This institute became the groundwork for the development of German Reform and the soon-to be created Conservative Judaism, which was promulgated first at the Breslau Academy by Dr. Zachariah Frankel. The Verein fostered more than simply the writing of classical and technical papers and journals, but more importantly, it laid the groundwork for integrating modern knowledge and skills into a search for truth in Judaism. Of course, many of the early papers were apologias, meant to show to Jews and others that Judaism was the Hegelian ideal. Nevertheless, the style, dedication and the critical processes have energized Jewish scholarship since the early 1800s.

To summarize the material on Germany, in particular, northwestern Europe in general, the following determinants have helped to mold the community, the religious reactions and the impact on American Jewry since that time: the structure of the Gemeinde, the impact of Napoleon, the philosophy of Hegel, the drive of Marx and his followers, and the essential establishmentarianism of the German body politic, making religious groups a part and parcel of the government.

Later, as the waves of immigration to the United States takes place, each one of these facets will be demonstrated to have shaped the American Jewish community. It is certainly true that the German Jewish community has had much more than its share of input to the development of the American Jewish community.

Finally, it is certain that the Quadrant II is the area out of which American Reform Judaism developed, although its phenomenal growth has taken place here in the Americas.

Quadrant III – The Litvak Area.

This sector is assuredly the most difficult to describe. It includes the areas of Estonia, Latvia, Lithuania, Northern Poland up to Galicia, Great Russia and White Russia. In 1993, if one looks at a map of Eastern Europe, including almost all of the territory east of Germany, and south, almost to the Carpathian Mountains, the backbone of Europe, one sees a major diverse society with many different nationalities, languages and histories.

In another context, it should be seen as the northern part of the Russo-Polish territory. The area should not be seen as a fixed sector, but rather a generalized northeastern quadrant. The fact that it has been labeled *the Litvak sector,* does not indicate that all within it were Litvaks, that is Lithuanians, but rather that there was a pervasive ethos that is different from that of west-Germany, and that of the the fourth quadrant. The overwhelming force has been called *Litvak,* or Jewish Lithuanian.

Although there were probably some Jews in this area earlier, the beginning of major immigration took place as a direct result of the First Crusade, which began in 1096. According to some sources, the first of this group came from what is the Bohemian part, or the German-speaking part of what was to become Czechoslovakia. Because many Jews were forcibly converted to Christianity, those who were able decided to head eastward, since the areas in the west were the sources of the Crusades.

From that time on, there was a continuous flow of Jews both from Northern Germany and from Bohemia in the South. Among the towns where Jews could be found were those near Austria, such as Krakow, Posen, Kalish and Silesia. *(Recently there was an exhibition of Jewish artifacts from the Great Synagogue of Krakow which may be the earliest Jewish religious building still left in Poland.)*

It was natural that these communities developed commercial ties with their co-religionists in the West, and so there was a growing connection between the Polish Jews and the ghettos on the Rhine, which were dominated by the Jewish bankers. These bankers were able to create markets for whatever could be produced in the Polish area. This was certainly facilitated that both ends of this commercial venture would be conducted in Yiddish. Although Yiddish was mostly based upon 11th century German, it contained at that time many French and Spanish words, which is evidence of Sephardic influences. The very fact that it was written in Hebrew letters, as Ladino had been for the Sephardim, is further evidence that Yiddish was used as a kind of inside code for commercial purposes. The varying dialects of Yiddish developed out of the areas of Germany and Austria from which the people came.

Thus, for those who came to the most northern part of this quadrant, probably took the shortest route from the west, and so brought with them the German dialect of the area nearer the North Sea, where the German was called Platt-Deutsch. This area uses far fewer umlauts than those from the South. That is why those in the North ate *Kugel,* while those from the area further south ate a different variety, called *Kigel.* Even gastronomically there was a difference, since the North was more industrial, and less agricultural. They therefore had more flavorings and garnishes, than those who lived off the land. Kugel generally has sugar, and raisins, while Kigel is simply noodles or potatoes, eggs, oil and possibly salt.

In addition, those in the north learned later about processes to keep food from spoiling by smoking, which the Germans had already developed. Thus the delicatessen foods which in America have come to be called Jewish, were either created in the North or were developed in Germany and transplanted. For example, smoked salmon, lox, was only known in the Baltic areas of the north. The fish delicacies of the South were river fish and usually scavenger such as carp, out of which gefilte fish was made. Had it have been in the north, it would have been called "Gefulte Fish."

Back to the origins. It is necessary to describe Poland, which in the 11th century was much more important than Russia. It should be remembered that Poland is a Roman Catholic country, while Russia has been dominated by the Greek (Russian) Orthodox clergy. The clergy in Poland, as their counterparts in neighboring Germany, held vast land holdings and thus were antagonistic to the lords who had welcomed the Jews.

The Catholic clergy used their enormous powers not only to fight the lords, but also to encourage the peasants to take their out aggressions on the Jews. Finally, Bolislav of Kalish issued in 1264 a charter in defense of the Jews. That charter of privileges helped the Jews create a self-government that continued in various ways up to the Hitlerian period. In a strange way, the Jews were protected by the secular powers, but the church like its western sister, placed difficult burdens on the Jews. Whenever the lords were in power, the Jews usually were in good shape, however, whenever the church was in power, the Jews suffered badly.

The 14th century became a bellwether of change for Poland. King Vladislav abolished the former feudal divisions of Poland. And his son, Casimir, called both the "Great" and the "Peasant King," developed an economic program which included foreign contacts for commerce and industry, and even more importantly, he developed many large cities in Poland.

As a result, there was a large expansion of the need for workers and managers. Many of these positions were filled by Jews who came or were sent from the ghettos of the Rhineland. The Crusades were still going on. Under the principles of the Privilege Agreement, the Jews began to increase and develop their own self-government. Their numbers in Poland also grew because of the pogroms in Germany in 1348, when the Jews were accused of causing the Black Plague. Thousands of Jews fled certain destruction and the only viable exit was in the direction of Russia and Poland. By this time the ghetto residents had developed skills which earlier could be pursued inside the ghetto walls.

So, on the one hand, Casimir wanted an expansion of trade and communication with the outside world, and on the other hand, the Jews were the natural bearers of what he wanted and needed – skills, capital and communication ability. Most male Jews at this time were literate, and almost all Jewish females were also fairly literate. This allowed almost every Jew to be employed for more than simple hand labor. They could become bookkeepers, tax-collectors and other professions requiring reading and writing. At worst (or at best), everyone could communicate together in Yiddish.

Within the Polish-Russian system, with its various Slavic languages, Yiddish evolved with its own variations. It could be expected that those Jews who lived closer to Prussia in the west would add more German words and idioms. Those who lived closer to the Hungarian border added more Slavic and Magyar words in their language. So whereas there is a basic vocabulary and grammar to Yiddish, there are not only regional differences in the grammar but also dialectical variations.

Contrasting the third and fourth quadrant, there is the simple difference between the *shul* in the third quadrant and a *shil* in the fourth. In the third quadrant, Jews spoke Yiddish with the intonations of the Germans of the north with few umlauts, but the Jews of Quadrant IV used the German of the south part of Germany and Austria where they opened their vowels with umlauts. The language became one of the pieces of antagonisms that developed between the Litvaks of the north and the Galitzianers of the south.

Poland is a land which is full of natural resources. There are hundreds of rivers flowing to provide water and power. The land is very fertile and there are great supplies of mineral ores, coal and other mining possibilities. It was these very resources that allowed for the development of a working class even within the nascent capitalism that could grow in that area. What began in homes at first as artisan work, later became institutionalized with factories.

Over the years factories were capitalized by the banking houses of Jews in Germany, who were able to appoint the managers of these factories and so control the communities of these areas. By the 17th century there was the beginning of a type of colonialism in Poland, whereby the German Jewish banking houses, by and large, had tremendous investments in what was going on in these eastern Europe communities, where the raw products were processed by Jews, managed by Jews and all communications were in Yiddish.

A little state within a state had begun to emerge. A Jewish state in reality existed, even it had to pay to maintain the major state and endure war and pogroms. In fact, for many years there was actually a council which was the law-making body and court for the Jews. It began as a unifying force, some time in the middle of the 16th century and continued until 1764, when the Polish Diet, the law-making body of the Polish government, ordered the end of such a congress. The name of this group was *Vaad Arbah Aratzot,* meaning Council of the Four Lands. The four provinces were Great Poland, with Posen as its capital; Little Poland, Krakow as its leading city; Poland in Red Russia, which included Podolia, Galitzia, and its capital, Lemberg or Lvov, and Volhynia, with its capital, Ostrog, or Kremenetz.

These councils usually met twice a year, once at the time of the grand fairs in February, and the other in late summer. Although the major function of their work was legislative, many times the Vaad would issue proclamations on ethical and moral issues. It is interesting that legal matters were generally written in Rabbinical Hebrew and Aramaic, whereas the proclamations were usually written in Yiddish, which the ordinary folk could read in their own community or synagogue. Representatives of the communities sent delegations of parnasim (elders) and the great rabbis of the era. There was little attempt at democracy, for it should be remembered that the end of this self-government was in 1746, thirty years before the American Revolution.

One of the more interesting personages of this period was the famous Vilna Gaon, Elijah, who was probably the most prestigious of all the heads of yeshivot in the Quadrant. He seemed to have great power from the Lithuanian government and used his strength to build up the academy in Vilna. In the great struggles between the New Chassidim, he led much of the fight and helped to create a new movement, the *Mitnagdim,* which means opponents in Hebrew. The Mitnagdim were those who supported the original rabbinism, the power of the heads of the Yeshivot, and the more conservative politically in the Kehillah. Elijah of Vilna tried to stem the movement for modernism and Germanism in the Stedtlich, and was not very successful in his struggles against the Chassidic invaders of the South.

There is no question that Rabbinism grew enormously in Poland prior to 1792, with almost every community of any size having its own Yeshiva. Nevertheless, it will become obvious that the whole milieu of the rabbi had become sterile, involved in esoteric Talmud study, and picayunish discussions labeled pilpul or pepper, so far from the problems of the masses that it would open opportunities for other forces to undercut the authority of the rabbis. This is precisely what happened. In the Litvak and Warsaw areas, the German bankers and their cohorts attempted to Teutonize the Polish workers, and this was met by a parallel movement of the folk itself.

The *Erklärung* was an attempt by the German bankers to teach high culture to the masses. They tried to introduce German as a substitute language over the folk language. They also pushed German literature, music and philosophy (Hegel). In reaction, in the Jewish community three other movements developed: the Zionist, the Internationalists and the Nation Within a Nation. One finds in the literature of Poland and Russia an exploration of defining the Jew. Were they a religion or a people? If the Jews were a religion, were they like other eastern religions of Russia and Poland? If so, how could they modernize themselves? On the other hand, if Jews were seen as a people or as a nation, how were they to be organized?

A major dialogue in the Kehillah developed over these ideas. One should recall that nationalism rose first in the west. It took very little time for this new ideology to penetrate a sphere where there were hundreds of cultures and nationalities. Many of the working Jews began to see in the late 18th and 19th centuries an opening out of the oppression of the Jews. So in at least three other ways, a new element was added to the discussions in the shtetl – Nationalism.

Some, who adopted Polish or Russian as their cultural language, tried to express their longings for Jewish cultural nationalism. but this appealed to only a few Jewish intellectuals. For most other Jews who began to break with the rabbinical tradition, there were only two languages in which a Jew could express himself. For most, it became Yiddish, which was the folk language, and through Yiddish, a new culture would enable Jews to enter the New World. Those who chose this means were met with great opposition by the rabbis and a rift began to develop between this group and the rabbinical class and their followers. The battles encouraged the folk group to become increasingly anti-rabbinical.

The other group, seemingly more involved with the intelligentsia, came to a different conclusion. They felt that Yiddish was an imposition on Jewish Nationalism for it was a German dialect. They proclaimed Hebrew as the only true Jewish language. Further, the Diaspora had been the means of keeping the Jew from his Hebrew background, and from developing a modern form of Hebrew. So they began the process of creating Hebrew newsletters, journals and creative writing, which eventually led to the recreating of Hebrew as the modern language as spoken and written in Israel.

The term for this enlightenment in Yiddish is *Haska'lah,* with the accent on the second syllable; in Hebrew, the same word, has the accent on the last syllable. These two movements plus the other language movements began to have a remarkable effect on the communities of Poland and Russia. Major clashes in ideology took place, with one side always being the Rabbis, backed by their German brothers, who still believed that Jews were a religion only.

But it is the last two groups whose impact is still being felt in the world Jewish community. First, they both began to see a world beyond the shtetl. All sorts of developments in the West were finding their way into the East. As previously stated, western culture, deriving from the Renaissance, sprang forth in languages related to a people. So, those who wished to have a people develop, began bringing the great literature to Russia and Poland. Shakespeare, Goethe, Moiliere and others were brought, but not in the original language, but translated into Yiddish and Hebrew.

Out of this mass of culture, it did not take long for a Yiddish Grand Theater to be created which produced *Der Melech Lear* or *Faust,* in other languages. As opera, operettas and musical concerts were sweeping the western countries, Jewish musicians and composers emulated them. Concert halls and music theaters sprang up in the shtetl, and finally there arose the Hebrew and Yiddish theater. The purpose was not simply entertainment, but the liberation of the Jewish Folk.

Yiddish and Hebrew folk songs were composed, along with poetry in both languages. Many writers were creating new Jewish literature, and one can begin to see evidence of a Jewish Renaissance in this quadrant, for the 19th century was almost without parallel. The closest approximation would be the Golden Age of Spain. The present generations are still living in the shadow of that century's unfolding, with the cultural creation of Israel in Hebrew, the writings of the Yiddishists and neo-Yiddishists such as Isaac Bashevis Singer, Elie Wiesel and Chaim Potok. In addition, the many movies and theater offerings, such as *Fiddler on the Roof, The Fifth Season,* and *Yentl* are examples of that world.

Still, the major factor that played a role in defining the future of the Jew was the rise of nationalism in Europe, which ultimately added a new element to those Jews in the east. The acceptance of that issue by so many of these folk-Jews modified the cultural determination. It was possible to join two or three of these determinants into an ideology, and then create a group feeling about these ideas. A Jew might possibly support Yiddish, Zionism in very simple ways and socialism. That sort of Jew would then probably join the *Farband*, or on the other hand, should he choose internationalism as his political ideology, Yiddish and socialism, he would join the *Workman's Circle,* the Arbeiter Ring.

A more traditional Jew would hesitate to break away from his religious base and yet be attracted to Zionism, and thus would find his role in Mizrachi. Another could choose Hebrew, be anti-socialist, Zionist, and find his response in the Revisionist party, when it becomes a force.

Thus one could find within the shtetl, Kehillah representatives of the rabbis, Germanists, Polishists, Russophiles, Hebraists, Zionists of the far-left, not so far left, centrists, who were either Zionists or proponents of a nation within a nation, remaining where they were, and not looking to the Holy Land. All of this was going on in the many Kehillot of northeastern Europe. This magnificent dialogue en masse helped to create the Jewish Renaissance of Quadrant III. Each of these groupings created political parties, which could explain the multivariegated parties of Israel, since its founding in 1948.

For those in the United States, these various groups, when the enormous migration from this quadrant began in earnest in 1881, presented a panoply of organizations which were difficult to come together without a Kehillah. It took a rabbi from Lithuania, this very area, to develop an ideology, which somehow could incorporate all of these facets into a unified whole. That man was Dr. Mordecai M. Kaplan. His movement could only have developed in the marvelously creative area which is Quadrant III.

It is not meant as a disservice to the rabbis of that quadrant that little mention is made of their creative excitement and intellectualism. But they were doomed by their own pomposity and self-serving, as well as the final blows of Hitler, and were too tied to a past that could not be re-created. Nor can it be denied that there has been some resurgence of this Litvak milieu, especially by those who are religiously motivated. More of this when the United States is brought into the picture.

To recapitulate, what Quadrant III produced are the Conservative Movement, the largest and most dominant parts of the Zionist movement, the Jewish Labor Movement, the Yiddish Cultural Movement, including the emphasis on great musicians, the Yiddish Theater, not only the musicals which have been popular, but the fine offerings in Yiddish of Shakespeare, Moliere, and other great playwrights, as well as the Hebrew theaters, Hebrew and Yiddish newspapers and journals.

Quadrant IV --The Chassidic Area
This quadrant, in much the same way as the previous one, is fairly complex, and yet it must be understood as a macro-system. It includes all of the former Austria-Hungary Empire, east of Vienna, Rumania, Bulgaria, Yugoslavia, Greece, and for our purposes, Turkey and Palestine and Russia-Poland, including the following, Galicia, Podolia, Moldavia, Ukraine and Crimea. Anyone who has studied European History prior to World War I might have surmised that much of this area includes the countries of the Central Powers of World War I, excluding Germany, but includes a large part of what was southern Russia.

In a sense, southeast Europe and a part of Asia Minor has also been included. Referring to the First Quadrant, the

Sephardic sector, most of the refugees from Ferdinand and Isabella, and the Inquisition, either went to North Africa or further into the Ottoman Empire, centered in Constantinople. These Sephardim arrived in Turkey, Greece, Bulgaria, Yugoslavia, Rumania and even parts of Hungary. By and large their lives were in social and economic decline. As Axiom I indicates, that whenever a society goes into decline, that society will rely upon the occult, mysticism and into dispair. This is precisely what happened to the Iberian Sephardim who remained in a declining Ottoman Empire. They turned to Jewish Mysticism and one finds a tremendous increase in Kabalistic speculation and superstition. What had to follow out of this was the development of a messianic spirit, which initiated a whole series of false-Messiahs,

Earlier, we referred to Spanish Jews who had converted to Catholicism, but remained loyal to their Jewish background within the home The name given to these people is generally *Marranos,* translated by many as "pigs." (I have never been satisfied with this explanation. Jews would never call themselves pigs, and therefore propose the following: *The Hebrew word for "bitter" is "Mara." In Spanish, if one wishes to personalize an adjective, one adds "no" or in plural,"nos." For example, one may in Spanish describe poor ones as "pobrenos." Thus, the bitter ones became "Marranos.")*

Many of these Marranos emigrated to Holland and Italy, but most of them travelled to Turkey, where the Sultan welcomed them as essential contributors to his Empire. He created Jewish noblemen and women of some of the most illustrious of these Sephardim. Probably the most noted were the Duke of Naxos, who established the communities of refugees in Palestine, and Dona Gracia, who helped settle many other refugees. They developed large Spanish and Portuguese communities in the east, with major settlements in Salonika, Greece, Aleppo, Syria, Cairo, Fez, Sofia in Bulgaria, and more importantly in Tzfat, or Safed, Palestine. In Safed a unique group of rabbis, who were skilled in Spanish Jewish Mysticism, created a book called *Zohar,* meaning Glow.

These rabbis formed a group around a leading scholar of this variation of Kabbalah and called themselves *Chassidim.*

They will be called *Chassidim I,* to differentiate them from present-day Chassidim. Their leader was Isaac Luria. Since he had spent some time in the Rhineland, probably to study with mystics there of Ashkenazic Mysticism, he was given the title, *Ashkenazic Rabbi Isaac.* As previously mentioned, rabbis have always loved to use acronyms, such as Tanach for Torah, Neviim, Chetuvim-The Jewish Bible, or Rashi, Rambam, etc. In this case the acronym ARI, was his and in Hebrew it also means Lion. The lion has had significance for Jews, since that was the symbol of King David, and of course the Messiah.

Luria and his followers began to create a new variation of Judaism, with a great deal of mystic thought, messianism and angelology. To go back to early concepts, the Messiah was supposed to arrive when the world was at its lowest ebb. How low the spirits were after the Golden Age in Spain, with its wealth and breadth of knowledge destroyed, can only be imagined. That is what happened to the Jews of Spain who went into exile to Turkish hegemony. Out of this Chassidic I movement, came many of the poems and songs which are used on Shabbat and the Holy Days. For example, the Friday night, *L'cha Dodi,* was written by one of Luria's disciples.

These Chassidim reconstructed Shabbat, as a woman, a bride, who was to be worshipped. The Chaverim, those who were accepted into the fold of the inner group, would on Friday afternoon, walk east from Safed to greet the Shabbat, and would hold Havdalah service as late as possible on Saturday night, in order to keep the Sabbath longer. The theory behind this was that the End of "Time," that is the time of the coming of the Messiah, would be "Kulo Shabbat," that is completely Shabbat. Thus the mystical way to bring the Messiah closer was to totally devote one's self to the Shabbat, a time when one was constantly devoted to God and the Torah. One of the fables that developed was that the Messiah would come when all Jews totally observed the Shabbat.

To go back to the L'cha Dodi. Almost every Jew who has ever been to a Friday night service knows this poem. If asked to tell what it is all about, he or she would respond that it is meant to welcome the Sabbath. Reading the ten verses, one would find that only two of the ten verses are related to Sabbath, and the others are devoted to preparing for the Davidic Messiah, who is almost here.

These Chassidim developed their own order of services, which embodied the mystical qualities of the movement. This order is called *Nusach Ha Ari,* which means the order of services of ARI. This can be paralleled by the order of service in Germany and then in Northern Poland and northern Russia, called *Nusach Ashkenaz,* or the Roman order, *Nusach Roma.* This particular Nusach became very popular among the mystic Sephardim.

Obviously the Kabala played a great role in this group, which also led to many Sephardic superstitions. The most famous of these, adopted from the Muslims, was that of the evil eye, the *Ayin Harah.* The belief was that the Angel of Death, that is the "devil," could exact his reward through people whom he had endowed with the evil eye. These people could respond to anything said or done that did good or represented good, with a stare from his or her evil eye, which could bring death or terrible illness. Thus came into expression the *Lo Ayin Harah,* which became in Yiddish, *Kein Ayin Harah,* and then bastardized into *Kenahorah.*

Will the real Messiah please stand up?

These Chasidim and the false Messiahs had a tremendous impact on the Jews of the Balkans, who spread the word to those areas of the Austrian-Hungary territory, and eventually their effect was felt by their proximity to Ashkenazic Jews in the Carpathian Mountain areas, on the borders of Rumania, Bessararabia, and the Ukraine. Most important was the effect in the 1770's in a Carpathian area called Galicia.

It could almost be predicted that the end-of-the-world philosophy would create some personalities who saw themselves as the long-awaited Messiah. This is precisely what happened in Palestine. Several times, buoyed by the Lurian revolution, a number of men created movements around themselves, in which they were to be considered the Messiah. The most important one to arise was Shabatai Tzvi, who was able to mobilize support for his ideas from Hamburg, Germany to much of the Ottoman Empire's Jews.

The Shabbatean Movement was quite successful, so much so that eventually the Sultan stepped in, imprisoned Tzvi, and offered him the alternative of becoming a Muslim or death. To the consternation of his many followers, he chose to convert. A number of his people followed him into Islam, and were then called a Turkish word, *Donme*. This, too, created another type of Marrano, one who outwardly was a Muslim, but privately a Jew. The amazing fact about this group is that until Hitler's eradication of the Greek Jewish community, there were a number of Donme's living on the edge of a group of Jewish settlements in Greece.

The downfall of the major messianic movements forced the Sephardic community into itself, and it remained essentially unchanged, relying on its Ladino background, its Spanish milieu and the Kabalistic services and superstitions. It took the French imperial spirit, led by Premier Adolphe Cremieux, a Jew, who created the Alliance Universelle Francais, to begin an educational process, by starting schools for Sephardic children, in the French Empire, which included much of the old Ottoman Empire; and wherever there were Sephardic communities, the Alliance did its work of educating the young in language and modern technology.

The Alliance is still a strong force among many of this generation's older folk, who were taught not only French, but also a trade or profession, which many brought to the Western World. More will be told of the Sephardim, when the American scene is developed.

The major impact of the Sephardim of this quadrant was on the Ashkenazim, who were close to them in southeast Europe. In this area, the borders of countries were hardly visible and were easily crossed. In addition, the many national groups here gave more opportunities for both sects of Jews to find common cause. Since they shared at least one language, Hebrew, and possibly Aramaic, trade was not only possible, but very probable.

For those Jews, who in the 17th century and beyond, lived in the Carpathian area, life was tenuous at best. The many wars between the Austrians and the Poles, the Hungarians and the Russians were personal disasters for the Jews. Whether they were considered part of Catholic Poland, Magyar Hungary, Catholic Austria or Russian Orthodox Russia, the Jew was always at peril. Pogroms became regular events from the 17th century until early in the 20th century. In such distress, the poor and least educated of Eastern European Jews turned in great numbers to anything that might bring personal salvation and to follow their own kind of Messiah.

About 1770, such a Yiddish-speaking leader developed, following a series of miracle workers in the Carpathian mountains between Hungary and Poland. It is necessary to press on the Carpathian background, with the area of Transylvania as its core, which has become known as one of the centers of European mysticism, since about 1600. It should be remembered that this is the very locale of Frankenstein and Dracula. Many plays and operettas take place in this milieu, with its gypsy overtones, each one with seers, magic men and potions.

For the Jewish community of this area, which is roughly Galicia, in the 18th century, there were men, sometimes rabbis, who claimed to be able to heal, clear rashes, save marriages and help women to have children. These men were named *Ba'aley Shem.* One of them would be called *Ba'al Shem.* The definition of Ba'al Shem is simply "a man of God;" however in this context, it really has the meaning of "a man who has mystical ability to use the name of God for healing and other needs."

Since most Jews have heard of the Ba'al Shem Tov, the term has been mistranslated too often. Even such a brilliant expositor as Elie Weisel translates the three words as "Master of the Good Name." Since Shem is an indirect way to say God, the implication is that the Besht – the usual acronym for this miracle worker – was the Owner or Master of the Good Name. Familiarity with Hebrew construction would indicate that whenever there is an apposition such as Ba'al Shem, and another adjective is added, that the modifier applies to the first noun, even though it follows the last word. Therefore, the designation should read, the Good (or Best) Master of the Name (of God).

The above is not meant as academic drivel, but rather to place the Second Chassidic movement into some historical context. It is important that the reader understands the essential mystical and miraculous background. This became the battleground for the more than two hundred years of clash between those traditional rabbis and lay people, who tied themselves to the Vilna tradition of Quadrant III, and these Kabalistic wonder workers and their followers, who saw themselves outside the Pale of the structured community.

Built on the Sephardic style of life and yet in Yiddish, the Ba'al Shem and his various followers created Satrapies around Chassidic rebbes. (Sephardim until today call their Chacham affectionately *rebi.*) The rebbes sat in the style of oriental potentates courts to whom followers not only brought their problems but also their conflicts. Some of the classic Zadikim, as the rebbes were called, claimed extraordinary medical cures and direct communication with the Almighty. Literally within decades, the rebbes divided up Eastern Europe, capturing small and large communities, and in some cases demanded large scale support from their followers, most of whom were very poor.

Invariably, there were clashes between the followers of one rebbe as against another. Actually, there developed a kind of regional division of Chassidism, and the rebbe took on the name of the locality, where he held court. So we have the Satmar rebbe in Satmary, Hungary, the Gerer Rebbe, the Mohilever Rebbe, and the one who became the most famous, the Lubovitcher Rebbe, as well as a number of others. The most incredible part of this whole development was the fact that the eldest son of the rebbe succeeded him. Thus, whole dynasties of Chassidic groups became the norm.

Because the followers of the Chassidim were considered illiterate about Jewish Law and the Torah, and because the Besht taught that one need not be learned to be religious, the leaders of the Yeshivot of Quadrant III, at first, did not pay much attention if the rebbes took over the communities of the South in Quadrant IV, or areas outside of the Russo-Poland area. The Chassidim encouraged drinking and meditation away from the synagogue, and that was heresy.

But one of the disciples of the Besht decided to attempt a campaign to develop a movement in Lithuania. This man knew that if he were to be successful, he would have to appeal to the fairly intellectually religious Jew, especially those who were not terribly happy with the Kehillah leadership there. He therefore created a type of Chassidism which incorporated Talmudism and Mysticism. He did this by developing a three-pronged ideology. This philosophy is framed around three types of knowledge: *Chochma*-wisdom, *Bina*-understanding and *Daas*-knowledge.

By creating a new acronym, based on those three words, Ch, B, and D, and placing the *ah* sound, usual in acronyms, he created the Chabad movement, which is the Lubovitcher Rebbe's style.

His name was Zalman Schneour. Every rebbe for the past 200 years has been a descendant of Zalman, but not his son, for he had only daughters. Since that time, the rebbe has been named Schneerson. The last rebbe, who had been a permanent resident of Brooklyn, operated a vast network of institutions, with no visible responsibility to anyone. Without a doubt, he was the most powerful Jewish leader in the world today.

In 1989, he precipitated one of the most critical and potentially devisive arguments in recent Jewish history by forcing an Israeli Knesset debate, *Who is a Jew?* This argument had and has the possibility of enjoining a major schism between the Orthodox politicos in Israel and the rest of world Jewry. Fortunately the American Jewish Community, with some help of the centrist Orthodox in the United States, convinced the Prime Minister to cancel the debate. Nevertheless this issue will undoubtedly come again into the agenda of the Jewish community. The issue will center on the legitimacy of those who are not Orthodox, whether they are reform, conservative, secular or simply do not wish to state.

The Chassidic movements range from a liberal interpretation of the Jewish community to those who reject the whole concept of the establishment of Israel, even though their leadership and constituents live there and are protected by that government. One leader of such a group has gone to such an extreme to ask the Jordanian king for citizenship, rather than accept the present Zionist state. The Rabbinical and Kabalistic principle of this position is based on the concept of *Dochek et Haketz,* meaning " Pushing the End;" thus, by establishing the state forced the hand of God to end the world, and this can only come about through the Messiah, selected by God from David's descendants.

The Chassidim also adopted the style of clothing worn by the lords of the particular locality where they resided. These royal figures thus selected the long caftan, black hat and black shoes. The difference was that the Chassidim did not shave or clip their sideburns. The women were not given any rights except to take care of the house and bear children.

The rebbe held court, gave legal decisions, ordered marriages and divorces and created an aura of saintliness, through which health and disease problems could be healed. Soon, each rebbe created not only a feudal system, but each one also created a dynasty, with the saintliness being passed on to his oldest son, if there was one, or to a close member of the family. In order to insure the faith of those who were his Chassidim and his followers, acts of miracles and saintly words were credited to the rebbe.

The Chassidim, to further separate themselves from the Litvaks, selected the Sephardic prayer book, or *Minhag Sepharad,* since so much of the traditions which were carried to the poor were of Sephardic origin. This, too, must have been some of the reasoning behind those who were opposed to the Chassidim.

Consequently, it is perfectly proper to place both Yiddish speaking Ashkenazim and Ladino speaking Sephardim in one didactic area. Each fed off the other. More so did the Chassidim draw on the Kabala and superstitions, as well as the prayer book of the Sephardim. The Sephardim, on the other hand, escaping from the rigidity of the Muslim area, were able to penetrate the Austrian-Hungary area, which had been ceded to it from Poland at the end of the 18th century.

It is from this area that the great bulk of Orthodoxy came to the United States at the turn of the 20th century, which brought the large masses of Jews here.

The four quadrants of the Mellman Theory are now complete. Let us review the four areas again.

Quadrant I begins with the Golden Age in Spanish and Portuguese Jewry and flows through the exile and the inquisitions as they took place in the Iberian Peninsula. 1492 marks the division of Spanish Jews into three parts – those who remained within the Muslim orbit, those who escaped into Holland and England, and those who made their way to the New World as either Jews or Marranos. In all three cases, the creativity, which had taken place after the Arabic Golden Age, retired into the doldrums of maintaining the past or seeking mystical solutions for the trauma, which had been inflicted upon the most productive and cultured people that ever lived.

Others were admitted to the Free States of Northern Italy, who helped set the stage for the rise of the Renaissance. These saw themselves as Jews by religion, but this religion included secular songs, romances and other facets of a thriving culture. However, that civilization was bound by the past and has not yet in the almost five centuries added much that can be considered new, modern or creative. Yet, there are many signs that the Sephardim internationally are awakening and making the moves to preserve and move the Ladino culture into the 21st century.

Quadrant II is that area which includes England, France, Germany, Holland, Switzerland, Belgium, Austria and all of the Scandinavian countries. It is in this area that one basically finds the Gemeinde mentality and structure of the community, in which the government controls and owns the Jewish community, through the appointment of the leaders of the Gemeinde, or Board of Deputies, for the country or province. One must never forget that in the Gemeinde the taxes are collected by the state and distributed by the state, to the parallel of the Diocese and the Synod. In addition, since Napoleon, Jews in this area were considered only a religion. It is therefore natural that as modernism touched this Jewish community, the only changes would be in the Reform Movement which had its origin in this quadrant.

Quadrant III is that area Northeast of Vienna, that is, Poland, Northern Russia, Lithuania, Latvia and Estonia. This particular sector was populated by those who escaped from the ghettos of Western Europe, starting with the Crusades, but encouraged by the Polish kings and the Jews' rich relatives along the Rhine River. Together, they created "company" towns along the major and minor rivers of Poland and Russia. The largest of these became the *shtetlich* of Jewish life, with industry the determining factor. In this area, Jews were considered another nationality among all of those in eastern Europe. As modernism hit this region, and the fact that the community was fairly independent of the government, it developed both religiously and secularly. Too, with the rise in the 18th century of Marxian philosophy, there developed Jewish political parties, both native and Zionistic. All of this created a multi-faceted Jewish community, each part represented inside the Kehillah. Much of what we call Jewish culture was created in this quadrant, as well as what later became the Conservative movement.

Quadrant IV is the real meeting ground of the Sephardim in Muslim surroundings, and the poorest of the Ashkenazim, the ones most distant from the culture and intellectualism of the North. Superstition and Messianism played a tremendous role in the development in this sector. Out of this Quandrant comes the Eastern Sephardic tradition as well as Chassidism of the Ashkenazic-Yiddish speaking poor. It is from this area that we have the largest number of the Orthodox community in the United States today.

10 ✡ THE QUADRATIC THEORY COMES TO AMERICA

Having created the bricks on which to build the next step towards moving the Jewish community of Europe to America, the reader may be able to understand the unfolding of the history of American Jewry.

Quadrant I

The first Jews to enter the American continent were Sephardic Jews who had been forced out by the Spanish and Portuguese Inquisitions. It was fortunate that the Spanish Jews who went to Holland and England, having played a major role in the industrialization of those two countries, were able, despite the vicious anti-Semitism of Peter Stuyvesant, to settle in New Amsterdam in 1654. Since one of the provisos for their admission was that they had to provide for their own services, they immediately created institutions, such as they knew from Spain, the first being a cemetery.

The number of Sephardim was never considerable. But they would soon be found in a number of the coastal towns; all were involved in international trade, primarily with their cousins in England, Holland and Venice, as well as those living in other coastal cities here. Eventually, Sephardim became visible in Philadelphia, Charleston, Savannah and in Newport, Rhode Island. These men were intensely involved in the Yankee Clipper trade, which involved trade with Africa for slaves, picking up molasses and other raw materials in the Caribbean, depositing those in the colonies, exchanging them for raw materials of the South, mostly cotton and tobacco, and then proceeding north to exchange these for finished products manufactured in the Fall River towns of New England. Having completed these transactions, they would then take the woven yarn and cloth to England or Holland for final manufacturing. The cycle would continue in much the same directions, with the ports sometimes changing.

By the time of the American Revolution, the Sephardic Jews were secure and considered part and parcel of the American scene. For historical reasons and economic connections, many of them were Tories, with great allegiance to England. Nevertheless, an estimate of the total number of Jews before 1776 would approach 2,500 or about 750 families. After the Revolution, many of the Colonial Sephardim, now supporters of the King, fled to Canada, or back to England, their role being taken over by Jews who had supported the revolution.

Between 1776 and 1812, there was little increase of Jews in the United States. The main theater for the world had turned to France with its own revolution and the rise of the Napoleonic Empire. Napoleon lifted the spirits of many Jews around the world because he promised full citizenship and greater freedom in his empire. However, with the fall at Waterloo, the Congress of Vienna, led by Metternich, divided Europe and in those countries where there had been supporters of Napoleon, mass banishments took place. As was previously pointed out in the European Quadrant II, Jews were among the greatest advocates of the New Regime. After 1815, there was also a fairly large number of affluent Reform Jews in Germany who probably had no thoughts of emigration.

The Jewish Publication Society Year Book of 1902-03 lists the 1818 Jewish population in the United States at 3,000, as estimated by Mordecai M. Noah. Probably half were of Sephardic background, the other half, Ashkenazic. By 1824, Solomon Etting, in that same edition, gives the count as about 6,000. Probably most of those who came were Ashkenazim, so that by that time, there were three times more Ashkenazim than Sephardim, there being no particular reason for Sephardim to migrate to America.

Quadrant II

The immigration of German Jews coming to America between 1815-1848, is labeled "German II," for there had been some earlier immigration from that area, but it had been insignificant. and it is so titled to distinguish it from the initial waves of Germans. The importance of this group is that they were what may be called "Napoleonic Jews," who saw themselves as Jews by religion. Their relationship was still with the old country; they were still under the influence of Hegelian ideals, and felt that the orders of the Congress of Vienna were a distortion of the True Germany. At first, these German Jews joined the Sephardic synagogues and institutions in the major cities on the East Coast, but as soon as their numbers became sufficient in a particular location, Ashkenazic organizations were established. Instead of addresses in Ladino from the clergymen and leadership, now these Jews wanted and received their learning from German-speaking scholars, as well as in English. This occurred in New York, Philadelphia, Baltimore and Savannah.

It should be noted that, simultaneously, the German Reform Movement had begun in Hamburg and several other cities. Shortly after that, a call for an organ was requested by the congregation in Savannah, as more German Jews entered that community. All rabbis there were born and trained in Europe, bringing with them a specific orientation and predilection. Obviously, it would take years for such a person to become acclimated to the political and social climate of the country where he was now living.

By 1840, the American Almanac, as quoted by the Jewish Publication Yearbook, estimated the Jewish population at 15,000, still not much more than the total Jewish population of the state of Indiana or the city of Seattle, Washington today.

It is precisely during this period that we begin to hear of rabbis being brought in from Germany to lead Ashkenazic congregations. The most notable was Rabbi Isaac Mayer Wise, who found the political climate in the United States so breathtaking that he proclaimed in 1848 that in one hundred years everyone in America would be Jewish. Wise was an amazing organizer; first, he established the Union of American Hebrew Congregations, so called because he originally wanted to include all synagogues here in the group. In time the UAHC proved to be too radical for the more traditional rabbis and congregations.

These German II immigrants, mostly petty bourgeois, founded many of the synagogues which are the giants of reform temples today. They fostered the same ideas of the early German Reform Jews as only another religious group, and that Judaism was only a religion. Therefore, the synagogue became the center of their Jewish world. This did not prevent them from organizing social clubs and philanthropic associations. Probably the most important of these clubs was the Independent Order of B'nai Brith, founded in 1843, as a sort of Jewish Masonic order, with rituals, cloths and structures, modeled after the Masons.

Many other similar groups were also founded by these German II Jews. A fascinating fact is that until the United States entered the Allied side in World War I, fighting against Germany, B'nai Brith still conducted all their rituals in German. In fact, the ritual still used by that organization is almost a word-for-word translation from the original German. For example, during a regular meeting, the president on calling one of the officers for a response, says, "What say you?" which is an exact translation of "Was sagt Ihr?"

The members of this wave of immigration kept very close ties with *Mother Germany,* with the men going back to find wives, sending their children to German universities, and, of course, keeping their mercantile connections, all of which meant continuing to speak German at home. This tradition was passed on to the next wave after the Revolution of 1848. During the period of 1815 to 1848 there was in Europe, especially in Germany, the rise of the socialist parties highlighted by La Salle and Marx. Again Hegelian philosophy was the spur, that progress was taking place in Europe and that Germany was the flint stone of that change. Many middle class Jews found a refuge in these discussions and political parties, for all spoke of freedom and democracy in various degrees. One must recall that in Germany the Jews were still treated as third class citizens, not being able to become professors at the state universities, conduct their symphonies, become judges in the state courts; even the rabbis had to be approved by State authorities. Only the rich Jews really had privileges, and they, too, were restricted.

In 1848, in central Europe, Germany and Austria both had socialist revolutions in which Jews played prominent roles. The successes of these revolutions were short-lived by counter-revolutions, which defeated the socialists. As a result, many Jews and others were exiled from both countries. They sailed to many shores, many to the United States, where they were accepted by their cousins who had been the second wave of immigration.

This post-1848 wave, German III, which continued for a number of years, also saw themselves as Jews by religion only, however they added another facet to the Judaism of their motherland-social action. Whereas the German II group wanted merely to modernize the rituals and format of Judaism, these new immigrants fostered a vision of themselves as "repairing the world," *Tikkun Haolam* are the Hebrew words. They literally fell in love with the Prophets, whom they truly believed to be the original universalists, whose words spoke of Social Justice, Charity, Brotherhood and the Age of the Messiah. They created in America a new form of Judaism, far different from anything that might have been allowed in Germany, either by the State or by the leaders of the Jewish Community there.

The statistics which are now brought to bear are fascinating. In the Jewish Year Book's statistics, M. A. Berk is quoted in his estimate for 1848, that "the number of Jews in the United States was 50,000." This would indicate, if true, that the number of German III group that had arrived were more than twice the total number of Jews that had been here in 1840. Once again a wave of immigration to America out-numbered the number of Jews who welcomed them. This leads to still another theory to be projected here: the *Theory of Overwhelming Waves of Immigration.* By this we mean that, at least for a while, each wave of immigration outnumbered those who were here previously, and by their numbers overwhelmed the culture and practices of the older group, and forced some accommodation.

As America expanded west, it was the German III group who made effective use of opportunities in the West and the South. They were aided by their banker and jobber cousins in the Eastern cities, and became the shopkeepers and department store owners. These adventurous Jews also became the most philanthropic supporters of charities and the arts wherever they settled. They became "Our Crowd," which more than any other group created what has been called the "Organized Jewish Community." The names of these illustrious families include Guggenheim, Schiff, Rosenwald, Seligman, Schoenberg (later changed to Belmont), Sulzberger, Ochs, Gimbel, May, Straus and Warburg.

It was the group of these wealthy and conscionable leaders of the Jewish community, who created a number of major institutions for their own part of the community, but also in later years earned the honorable titles of philanthropists, not only for their work for Jews, but for the disinherited of the American scene. It is true that many of these men became wealthy in not always legal fashion, but later they helped to create funds which enabled millions of Jews and non-Jews to further themselves in this country.

As America itself was spreading westward, and the period of coast-to-coast exploitation of the land and its products went on, Jews of German III were to be found in almost every town of any size, not only as the merchant, but frequently as the lawyer or judge and even as a sheriff. Several of them became enormously wealthy and powerful for their ability to develop the great mining interests in the West. Some were the founders of department stores in the medium-sized towns of the Northwest Territory or in the Plantation South, or as the Goldwasser family (now Goldwater) did in Phoenix or the May family in St. Louis. They then were able to become part of the networks of their relatives in the East Coast cities of New York, Philadelphia, Baltimore and Boston.

It was after the Civil War that the German III leaders expressed the wish to recreate the Gemeinde mentality on the American soil, and to lay the groundwork for the increasing number of Jews who were continuing to come to America. The breadth of this immigration will be more evident by the next quote from the American Jewish Year Book.

William B. Hackenburg, in 1880, was able to give a precise number of Jews in the United States as 230,257.

Discounting any increase from the previous number which would come from births, the fact is that there had been a five-fold increase in the Jewish population since 1848. The numbers on the continent had now become more significant, and those arriving were literate, and in some cases scholarly Germans, who could build on the efforts of their fellow German Jews. It is certainly true that by 1880 the American Jew was overwhelmingly of German origin, with the greatest amount of freedom, and where, with talent, almost anyone could succeed.

At this point, it may be helpful to include a table of the figures quoted.

1818	3,000
1824	6,000
1840	15,000
1848	50,000
1880	230,257

So, in the short space of 62 years, the number of Jews had increased by a hundred fold, almost all of them of German extraction. It is certainly true that some of these were from Eastern Europe, but the numbers were probably inconsequential.

It is the period of the German III group that the first major Jewish organizations of what we now call the "Organized Jewish Community" were formed by the group which was categorized as "Our Crowd." What is unusual is that one can find the same group of leaders of this group in almost every organization. They include Jacob Schiff, Mayer Sulzberger, Dr. Cyrus Adler, Cyrus Sulzberger, Daniel Guggenheim, at least one of the Warburgs and one of the Lehmans. Those who have read the Birmingham book on "Our Crowd" will recognize their names. Among their contributions are the following: Hebrew Union College, Union of American Hebrew Congregations, Hebrew Free Loan Society, Young Men's and Young Women's Hebrew Association, and so many other of the precursors of the gamut of Jewish organizations which are taken for granted in most cities today.

A reader will notice the predominance of the word,

"Hebrew" in these designations. That was no accident for these German III Jews had come from a milieu where the word "Jude" even in the 19th Century was considered derogatory. The German Jews hated the word, so they considered themselves Hebrews, and Yahudim were those Jews from Eastern Europe who spoke Yiddish and were lower on the social scale than were the Hebrews. As the German Jews became wealthier, especially as leaders, they took control of these organizations.

One of the remarkable organizations that they created, within the aegis of the Union of Hebrew Congregations, was the "Board of Delegates on Civil Rights" in 1872. Its purposes were:

> *To provide the means for the relief of Jews from political oppression and unjust discrimination and for rendering them aid for their intellectual elevation.*

Imagine such a statement happening a century and a quarter ago. One should understand that Rabbi Isaac Mayer Wise, who created the UAHC as an organization of all American congregations regardless of their leanings towards liberalism or orthodoxy, had intended that this group represent all Jewry. This organization followed a previous one created in 1859 in New York by the German III group called the Board of Delegates of American Israelites, to protest the infamous Mortara case in Italy. The Mortara case concerned a Jewish child who was kidnapped for the purpose of forced baptism. This was probably the first time that there was a Jewish lobbying arm in the United States. Unfortunately, the Board of Delegates collapsed because of the start of the Civil War and also because of the cultural cleavages that had already manifested themselves internally. (Notice again that the German Jews avoided the word Jewish in the title, and that their concern was with other people whom they called Jews.)

The genius of these German III Jews was their ability to create organizations, fund them and provide top leadership whether on the national or local level. There was never any attempt to practice democracy in the groups, but rather there seemed to be a *noblesse oblige,* which the top leaders accepted – that they were the appropriate people to run these operations. It was the Americanization of the old Parnas system of Germany and the Gemeinde. In fact, it was accepted that when a father died, his son took his place. By 1870, the immigration from Germany and Austria began dropping off, which gave the Jewish leadership energy to turn itself into creating an American Jewish life. Thus in 1875, the UAHC commissioned Isaac Mayer Wise to create the first seminary for rabbis here, Hebrew Union College. Since he was the leading Reform rabbi in Cincinnati, it was established there. It is no accident that Cincinnati is probably the most German of all the American metropolises, and it was the same for the Jews there.

Then with sufficient graduates and other rabbis who considered themselves Reform, Wise convened the Central Conference of American Rabbis in 1889. This was the first organization of American rabbis and represented the most prestigious congregations from Boston to San Francisco, including many smaller ones in the midwest and south.

The more traditional American rabbis were not so well organized, yet they were beginning to have their weight felt as the numbers from Eastern Europe were increasing. Certainly, the Sephardim remained a small, yet an important part of the community, because of the standing of so many of their leaders in the general life, and because they were the "Grandees" of the community. The Sephardim concentrated their efforts behind the Spanish and Portuguese Synagogue in New York, another in Philadelphia and several smaller ones as well.

Quadrant III

At this point another major change occurred in World Jewry, which has had and is continuing to have a tremendous affect on America Jews. The year 1881 signaled a significant downgrade in the Russian approach to the Jewish question. Czar Nicholas III, with the active direction of the procurator of the Russian Orthodox Church, Pobedonetzov, began a program for eliminating the Jews from Mother Russia. His plan was geared to compel one-third of the Jews to emigrate, another third forcibly converted to the Russian Orthodox Church *(forced conversion has always put extraordinary pressure on Jews everywhere)*, and the balance to starve to death. From this program came the infamous May Laws, which began the emasculation of the Jews in their Shtetlich. Power was taken away from their own communities, quotas were enforced on the number of Jews who were able to enter schools and professions, and thousand of Jews were forced to move from established towns and cities, especially Moscow.

It became very obvious to many Jews in Russia and Germany that something had to be done for the entrapped Jews in Czarist Russia. The primary focus of concern were those Jews who lived in Quadrant III. Beginning earlier, but in 1881, the Litvak area saw the *enforced* departure of many Jews. These Jews went wherever they could find an open door. Many went to Mexico, other parts of Central America, to every liberated country in South America, England, France, Palestine, South Africa, Canada, Australia and New Zealand. However, the great bulk of them came to the United States. Again, it is necessary to turn to the American Jewish Yearbook, which adds another line to the Jewish statistics list. Isaac Markens estimates that in 1888 the number of Jews in the United States at 400,000, an additional 170,000 to the 230,257 of 1880.

More startling is a later estimate in 1897. David Sulzberger offers the statistic of 937,800 Jews, which would mean that almost 600,000 had arrived from Quadrant III in those seventeen years. One can only imagine the feelings of "Our Crowd," who were the acknowledged leaders of the American Jewish community, as they faced the prospect of so many of their co-religionists, but were a different sort of Jew. These were the Yahudim, who spoke Yiddish and were not cultured or as fastidious as the German-speaking Jews. The institutions which the German III group had developed were primarily aimed at their own people. New methods and institutions had to be created for the new immigrants. And so they created more organizations and supplied the funds and their time. HIAS, the Hebrew Immigration and Aid Society, was given responsibility for taking care of Jewish immigrants, guiding them to many Jewish-sponsored social welfare agencies in the community where they were headed, providing programs for the children, English and Americanization classes, housing where necessary, loan funds at no interest and camps for the children. And if that were not enough, they made sure that these new immigrants would not try to enter their religious establishments.

Jacob Schiff and his New York group, with the strong assistance of the German bankers in 1883, helped to create the Jewish Theological Seminary. In line with initial premises, which were indicated in the discussion of Quadrant III, the same sort of connection between the German bankers and the rabbis was maintained. It is possible, although difficult to prove, that German bankers in Germany helped to establish the connections. Nevertheless, since 1881 until the present day, a most unusual relationship has been maintained between the scions of the German III families and the Litvak religious establishment, represented by the Jewish Theological Seminary. For decades the Chairman of the Board of JTS was always a member of Temple Emanuel of New York, the focus of German III religious activity. When a number of years ago, Arthur Goldberg was asked to become the chairman, he immediately joined Temple Emanuel, although his own family background was deeply in Quadrant IV.

As far as Russia is concerned, a scenario is offered. Starting in that magical year of 1881, when a community or shtetl was threatened in Quadrant III, the German bankers who had investments in the industry of the town would arrange for the Hamburg Line or the Amsterdam Line to set up the departure of one whole segment of the community to leave together. A ship would come to Riga or Konigsburg, Memel or Danzig. The managers of the industry and the relatives of the bankers would be given first-class staterooms on the ship, as befitted their station. Also with them in first class would be the rabbis, who had been their partners in the Kehillah at home. Second class would be occupied by the subsidiaries of these two groups, which might include the teachers and the schochtim (ritual slaughterers) and other religious functionaries, as well as the foremen of the factories. In steerage would be the laborers, who had been the lower class in the community.

They would be taken by boat to one of the destinations parallel to the one in Germany. For example, should they have arrived in New York, the boat would arrive at Ellis Island, and the émigrés would be met at the boat by the representatives of IIIAS. Obviously the first class passengers were helped off the boat first, given some considerations, and easily sped through the process. Then those of the second class, given a little less help from the HIAS people. Finally, those in steerage would be handled. After clearing their physicals and interviews, they were taken to the Lower East Side, which was as far away as possible from where German Jews lived, which at that time was Harlem and the east side of Central Park. The geographical distance could be measured in miles.

The other organizations of the community would have provided, by this time, a Settlement House for all sort of social and educational programs to keep the adults and children involved. With the help of the European Baron De Hirsch Fund, a synagogue would be provided as well as a rabbi, who would conduct services and provide Jewish education for the children in Talmud Torah. In addition, and this is one of the most fascinating instruments that "Our Crowd" created, was the *Industrial Removal Society,* again funded by the De Hirsch Fund. This organization offered incentives to those immigrants, who would agree to move to a smaller and distant town, with the hopes that they would become farmers. Another part of this program was the *Jewish Agricultural and Industrial Aid Society,* funded by De Hirsch with the express purpose of teaching young Jews agriculture.

Its charter stated:

"The encouragement and direction of agriculture among Jews resident in the United States and their removal from crowded sections of cities to agriculture and industrial districts;

"The granting of loans to mechanics, artisans, and tradesmen and accumulate savings for the acquisition of homes in suburban, agriculture and industrial districts; and

"The removal of industries, now pursued in tenements or shops in crowded sections of cities, to agricultural and industrial districts."

Through this organization and its intertwining directorships and their relatives in other communities, a number of immigrants were encouraged to leave the big city on the Atlantic for other places. What seems to have been the process was that the New York leader would contact one of his relatives in Louisville or Indianapolis, or, as in the case of my grandfather, Little Rock, Arkansas, to accept a number of Jews who would be helped to settle away from New York. What is significant is that the descendants of some of these very people are still in farming in New York, New Jersey, Pennsylvania and even as far away as California.

To return to the Jewish Theological Seminary. When the leaders of the Wilna religious community made contact with the leaders of the German III group, it was obvious that there was a need for a Yeshiva that would parallel the famous one which the Wilna Gaon had headed. So Jacob Schiff and his friends helped to establish the JTS for the Litvak group. To be sure, JTS was established as an Orthodox style seminary, and it was only with the arrival of Dr. Solomon Schechter, from England that the term *Conservative Judaism* was applied to the movement.

The symbiotic relationship which developed between the Conservative Movement and the German III Jews has continued through a number of generations. This can best be recognized by the radio and then the television program, *Eternal Light,* which was sponsored by the JTS in cooperation with the American Jewish Committee, for many years the secular arm of the German III group, the very same people who were the powers behind the JTS.

The steerage group, not all totally religious, but generally repelled by the sycophancy of the rabbis for the uptowners, and imbued with the freedom permitted by America, resumed what had been developed in the Shtetl, the secular politics and enlightenment mentality program. They began to create in America a Yiddish world with theater, songs and literature, including a number of Yiddish newspapers and journals. They created organizations based on where they had come from, *Landsmanshaften,* workers from the same area, and they developed Yiddish schools at the primary and secondary level, as well as Yiddish speaking camps. Others formed Yiddish Zionist groups, such as the *Farband.* A whole milieu of Yiddishism was created without the power of the shtetl behind it. The power became the *Jewish Forward.* For generations this daily newspaper was the force behind the labor movement of Quadrant III.

In all of the coastal cities, the bankers, through their relatives whom they had just brought over, established factories, similar to the ones that had been the mainstays of the shtetl. Needle trades predominated, but there were also furriers, hat and cap makers, tobacconeers, leather-goods artisans and others who came with the skills honed in the Polish hinterland. Around each of the factories and home industries connected to the basic trade, the feeling of homelessness was replaced by the Yiddish groups, which provided friendship, insurance and loans to bring over other relatives. In addition, the group provided the necessary cultural milieu to make life worthwhile. So while there was an increasing division of the old parts of the shtetl society, there were now two separate sections operating without the shtetl, the religious and the secular.

These two groups came together only in emergencies, and usually under the auspices of the German III leaders; for example, when there were terrible events against the Jews on the international scene, or in the case of the Women's Strike against the Kosher Butchers for gouging the poor. Since most of the secular group still kept kosher and went to rabbis for their religious rites, even if the members had already broken with orthodox tenets, they would join in these protests. But the seculars side also began to develop socialist and communist groups, various Zionist organizations, which at the turn of the century were responding to Theodore Herzl's call for a Jewish state. Moreover, there was the founding of the Labor Zionist Organization to counter the Federation of American Zionists which, by 1902, was already holding its fifth convention, being what, today, one would call General Zionist.

By the end of the 19th century, the leadership had decided that there was a need for some sort of coordination and sharing of experience from the communities. They had already created a number of relief organizations in many communities, which together would become the Jewish Federations of Philanthropy. By 1902, the second biennial meeting of the National Conference of Jewish Charities in the United States was being held in Detroit, Michigan, Their concerns were the immigrants, free loans, children who were in jail for crimes or on probation, consumption (tuberculosis, very prevalent among immigrant workers) and moving immigrants from the big cities. Fifty-two community relief societies from San Francisco to Boston, and Butte, Montana to Galveston were represented, which indicates the vast ability of the Jewish community to communicate with each other, even before telephones and other forms of mass communication.

By the early 20th century there were almost one million Jews in the United States, with some 75% from Eastern Europe, mostly from Northern Poland, Lithuania, White Russia and Great Russia; most of the adults employed in some industry, and intellectually involved with the Jewish community. Quadrant III, through its two immigrations, overwhelmed the previous American population of Jews prior to 1881.

To recapitulate, there were by 1900 the following waves of immigration;

Sephardic	3,000
German I	3,000
German II	44,000
German III / Litvak I	180,000
Litvak II	607,800

Of course, these figures do not take cognizance of any natural growth, that is, children born to preceding groups. However, the importance is not in the total accuracy of these numbers, but rather the range of the amounts. For it is certainly true that each wave of immigration overwhelmed in numbers and problems the then indigenous Jews. How those earlier Jews superbly received and served this mass immigration has become the hallmark of the Jewish community in America. Cooperation and organization became key words. Every other ethnic and religious group, trying to become similarly organized, has turned to the Jewish community for guidance, styles and training. One can better understand this unique role of the community in the light of the waves of immigration, what those who were already here brought with them, and the structures which each wave brought to bear.

It is at this point that a major figure enters the American Jewish scene who embodied Quadrant III in all of its aspects, and dramatizes the impact of the American democracy on immigrants at the turn of the century. Although his contributions were all made in the 20th century, he was a product of Quadrant III in Europe. He was born in 1881 in a small town in Lithuania, and in 1890 his mother brought him to the United States, where it was expected that he would become a rabbi, as his father had been in Lithuania. He combined major studies at the Jewish Theological Seminary and at Columbia University, becoming a rabbi in 1902, as well as receiving the Master's of Arts from Columbia. He became the rabbi of an orthodox congregation in New York City. After a few years, he became the Principal and later Dean of the Teacher's Seminary at the JTS, and in 1911 he also became Professor of Homiletics. It was from that position that Dr. Mordecai M. Kaplan exercised the most major influence of any person in the American Jewish scene. He created the Reconstructionist Movement.

Dr. Kaplan, who lived to be 100, spent his whole career, developing and creating instruments to bring the Jewish community together and at the same time expand the definition of what being Jewish meant. Reconstructionism is certainly the most American of Jewish creations, and can best be explained, not only in philosophical terms, but also in historical logic. Most analysts of Kaplan have laid great stress on his dependence on Matthew Arnold, and on the beginning of the social science of Sociology, especially Durkheim, for his theoretical ideas.

Kaplan created a new definition of Judaism. He stated that, *"Judaism is the evolving religious civilization revolving around the Jewish people."* In one stroke, Kaplan was able to incorporate all the various facets of Jewish life that had existed in Quadrant III, from the most religious faction to the most atheistic, yet still Jewish. He was able to transpose the inclusive Kehillah, which had been part of the government to free, voluntary America, and

did it beautifully. With the above definition he was able to encourage so many Jews to feel a part of the American Jewish
life.

First, Kaplan affirmed that the Jews were a people
and that they shared some communal feeling in whatever way it was expressed. Further, he brought into the
Jewish community the idea that they had a civilization
that included art, literature and other legitimate forms of
group expression. When the word "evolving" was used,
Kaplan recognized the changing characters that have embraced the Jewish spirit. Calling it a religious civilization, he certifies, as he should have, the overwhelming
role that religion has and does play in the life of the Jew.

It is surely true, that only a Litvak brought up in
the milieu of the Kehillah and the excitement of the dia-
logues present in those communities, could have postulated the Reconstructionist definition and program.
Kaplan was among the first of the JTS rabbis to espouse
Zionism, political and cultural, when most orthodox were
hesitant to support Herzl's ideas. He certainly was among
the first orthodox rabbis who had the courage to question
commonly held ideas that the Torah was given on Mount
Sinai, that he did not believe in Resurrection, that modern thought and science had to be accepted and previous
religious thought should integrate this new knowledge
into its teaching and practices.

So Kaplan and some of his closest disciples, all
Litvaks, began to put Reconstructionism into practice.
For what is most obvious is that Kaplan had the wisdom
to see that the two movements, orthodox and reform, were
becoming divisive, as were the secularist and Zionists.
Some field theory of Judaism was needed, in much the
same way that in the physical and social sciences an attempt is always being made to share the macro vision
with the micro system. Kaplan's view was that the Jewish people have to organize themselves along democratic
lines in order to develop those positive parts of civilization, which Judaism had created. He propounded that Jewish Education in a modern world should be of the highest
quality and geared to community support. Hebrew was the

necessary facet of that education. Then he proposed that synagogues become Jewish Centers, where all facets of Jewish
life could take place, including swimming pools, dances, classes,
art – anything which would give meaning to Jews as Jews.

Kaplan also explored Jewish Theology with new attitudes, much of which came into use through the
Reconstructionist Prayer Books and Hagadah. What
Kaplan spoke and wrote was that he saw God as process
geared to the Good, and not the personal almost human
entity which is the traditional approach. Other Kaplan
ideas in theology are somewhat beyond the scope of this
book.

Kaplan, in his own way, was the American bridge
for those parts of the immigration wave that came from
Quadrant III, otherwise the various factions would have
diverged. So, he was the Litvak philosopher of the Jewish community. He was the one who suggested that Jewish centers become more "Jewishly" involved, and that
the federations should go beyond welfare. Most Jewish
social workers today operate on those premises, even
though they may never have heard of Kaplan. But it is
absolutely true that the field of Jewish Communal Service is predicated on the idea that a Jew is a Jew, and that
the appropriate adjective is no determinant for service,
the premise of Reconstructionism.

There is hardly a synagogue in the world today
that doesn't offer a gamut of activities beyond the religious services, thanks to Kaplan. In addition, Kaplan found
a way, philosophically, to keep the Kehillah idea alive,
without the onus of government sitting atop it.

To conclude this section about this wave of immigration, one must add the Jewish contribution early in
the 20th century to the formation of the labor unions in
the East. Most prominent were the Amalgamated Clothing Workers, the International Ladies Garment Workers,
the Hat and Cap Workers, the Furrier's Union and the Cigar
Makers Union. At almost the same time, the labor organizations within the Zionist movement came into existence.

With a million Jews, the American community be-
gins to take its place as one of the leading Jewish communities

in the world, surpassed in numbers only by Russia, with more than 5,000,000, and Austria Hungary with about 1,900,00. This was in 1900, when the estimated world Jewish population was thought to be in the neighborhood of 10,300,000. Thus, almost 10% of all the Jews in the world had entered the *Goldene Medina*, the State of Gold, as the century unfolds. On the world scene, American Jews, particularly those of German III, began to play a major role on the international level. Jewish ambassadors are appointed to a number of important capitals. An increasing number of Jewish congressmen are elected, as are a number of mayors and governors, generally a recognition of their intellectual skills and their participation in community affairs.

To paint a more complete picture of American Jewry at the close of the century, it is important to understand that not all the German III were top leaders. There were many middle class German Jews who were not included in the discussions of the elite group. They developed their own institutions such as B'nai Brith and lodges specifically for men. The women were involved in sewing circles and creating Sunday schools for the Reform Jews. But by and large, the impact of the leaders was immense.

They created a web of cultural and philanthropic institutions, both of the major seminaries, Hebrew Union College in 1875, and Jewish Theological Seminary in 1883. They had begun the federation movement, although the title was not yet so designated. The German leaders had made a major impact on the programs of Settlement Houses, and YM and YWHA's, the forerunners of today's Jewish Community Centers. And at the very same time they established themselves as the makers and patrons of many major cultural institutions from East to West. All of this took place in the short space of fifty odd years.

By 1900 the largest number of Jews in America were from Quadrant III, which has been designated as the Litvak area. Beginning about 1881 the total number tripled those who had been here prior to that date. They brought not only a culture different from the Germanic group, but also a variant on the idea of what the term, Jew, meant, To reiterate, the idea of a Jewish community was sharpened by the fact that in Russia-Poland, Jews were considered one of the many national groups, and not simply a religious grouping, as in Quadrant II. This multiplication of groups along ideological lines, created the same derivations as had been back in the old country. It was Mordecai M. Kaplan who endeavored to find a broad definition, which would include all Jews, regardless of predilection.

The reader must understand that there was no such thing as a Conservative Jewish Movement. That does not happen until the arrival of Dr. Solomon Schecter to head the Jewish Theological Seminary in 1912. So, religiously, there were the Sephardim, with their internal system, the Reform, built on an organization of congregations, and various Orthodox synagogues, who began a Union of Orthodox Jewish Congregations of America consisting mostly of synagogues on the east coast, including some Sephardic. It should be clear that most of the synagogues were "landsman" based, that is they were formed by people from the same general area in Europe. They even had nicknames such as the *Vilner Shul* or the *Kovner Shul.* It is very important also that these were *shuls* and not *shils* from the fourth quadrant.

By 1900 it is possible to observe the overwhelming wave of immigration that had moved to the United States and begun to shape a quite different kind of Jewish life and world than that which the Germanic group could ever had envisioned. But fate and faith had thrown these disparate groups together to face still another challenge, which would occur after the turn of the century,

Quadrant IV

To understand the impact of the fourth quadrant immigration it is necessary to once again turn to the American Jewish Yearbook which details the following information:

A summary of the Jewish immigration to the United States, 1881-1925.

1881-1898	533,478
1899-1907	829,244
1908-1925	966,293
Total	2,329,015

An analysis of these numbers, especially the last two periods, will be developed. Suffice it to say, the number of Jewish immigrants to the United States was almost ten times what had been here in 1880. Thus it fell upon the German III group to extend itself even further to help integrate all of these new Americans. It was doubly complicated by the fact that the German Jews who had some contact with the Jews of Quadrant III had almost no contact or understanding of the newer immigrants, who not only had a different style of orthodoxy, but they spoke a different dialect than those with whom they had dealt in the 19th century. They were not only poorer and superstitious, but also had no experience in working in factories and mills, for they were the product of areas which were essentially agricultural and rural. Even if they came from one of the larger towns, they were generally not as cultured as the preceding wave.

Russia which had become more oppressive now turned its attention to the area where a much larger part of the Jewish community lived and where they were more vulnerable. Russia had just lost a major war with China, the infamous Sino-Russian War. Looking for scapegoats, it turned on the Jews of the Ukraine and Podolia to the west. In 1903 a pogrom instigated by the Czarist government created a pogrom in Kishenev, where a number of Jews were killed, women raped and synagogues destroyed. The Jews of this area were so terrified that they began to find ways out of the country, some devious, where they had little money. Others bribed officials for exit visas. At the same time, a campaign to place Jewish boys in the army for thirty years was developed, and so many young men ran away to the west and Palestine, attempting to find refuge wherever they could.

At that time in the United States there was a great need for laborers, and the doors were wide open if people could get to a coastal town or to Detroit by way of Canada.

Some Jews established some of the early settlements in Palestine, or moved to that new town on the coast, Tel Aviv, but most of the Jews having heard about the gold in the streets of America headed for the West. The pressure of the decline of the Ottoman Empire, the *Sick Man of Europe*, as it was called, encouraged many of the Sephardim in that Muslim area to consider leaving. As a result the first major Sephardic group arrived in the United States since the pre-revolutionary times. They came from Bulgaria, Turkey, Greece and the Islands, including Rhodes. Some of them, however, particularly those who came from the almost entirely Jewish city of Salonika, helped to create the port city of Haifa. Probably no period in the history saw so much massive emigration as took place in the first quarter of this century. It was surely true for the Jews.

The reader should recall that Quadrant IV is the area approximately south of a line just north of the Carpathian Mountains and includes Galicia, Podolia, Bessarabia, Moldavia, Ukraine, Rumania, Hungary and all of the Balkans not previously mentioned; plus the European sections of the Ottoman Empire, the Hungarian part of the Austrian-Hungary Empire and Southern Russia.

The Sephardim from this Quadrant were mostly mystical as a result of the Inquisition in Spain and Portugal, and the poorest of the Ashkenazic Jews, the least educated and the least affected by the new thinking that came from the Renaissance. In short, they were the disinherited Jews. Through a cultural and religious exchange, the Sephardim below this line and Ashkenazim, there emerged the second Chassidic movement, created through the charisma of the Baal Shem Tov and his immediate successors.

They began a battle, community by community, against their opponents, the Mitnagdim, for control of the Kehillot of Russia and Poland, as well as parts of Rumania and Hungary. They eventually became the dominant religious force in Quadrant IV, although there were also reformers in Hungary, Austria and to a small extent in Rumania.

By the time of this immigration, the three movements had already been established, although the Jewish Theological Seminary contingent had not yet formulated into the official Conservative movement for another decade. Yet civility seems to have reigned among the movements, probably because of the strength of the German III leadership. But with the arrival of Quadrant IV into the major cities, a clash began to develop, particularly among the Orthodox, just as there had been in Europe. The religious groups hardly spoke to each other, and those who tried to enter the factories were faced with the new unions, all of which had been created by Litvaks, who insisted on their controlling the movement. The Galicianers simply had no understanding of any of the philosophical and ideological background of the old-timers. What happened in a number of unions was the development of two-level jobs with the Litvaks being piece-good workers, and the Galicianers having to work on an hourly level. Obviously, the older workers did better, and many of them became foremen, but still in the union. The union was meant for all who were not owners of the establishments.

It is out of the cultural differences, as well as the obvious religious levels, that initiated the jokes and calumny between the Litvaks and Galitzianers, even today among Yiddish speakers. The Quadrant IV people, by and large, had no experience with secularists and as far as they were concerned the others were *linkers* (leftists) who ate ham on Yom Kippur and went to the Yiddish theater on Shabbos.

The Jewish community, still basically run by German III, was beginning to create even more organizations to handle some complicated problems. For the first time, in response to the Kishenev pogroms and other unfortunate events affecting Jews, the American Jewish Committee was formed by "Our Crowd." The membership was limited to 50 and totally dominated by the wealthy German III of New York and Philadelphia. This took place in 1906. The same group had already created the *Jewish Publication Society* for the purpose of creating Jewish libraries in people's homes and public places, and they began the work of publishing the first major tome of American Jewry, the Jewish Encyclopedia, as well as an English translation of the Bible.

By this time, the Union Prayer Book for Reform temples had been produced, both for daily services and for the High Holy Days. Quite an accomplishment for these very busy men! Their women had themselves become involved in sewing circles and had formed the *Na-*

tional Council of Jewish Women and another group with a most unusual name, *United Order of True Sisters,* which was a direct translation, word for word, of the German name of a group of their sisters in Germany.

Shortly thereafter, in 1913, middle class German Jews based around the Midwest, especially in Chicago, decided to form an organization to combat the stereotypes of Jews being depicted on the stage, which was called vaudeville. The skits had Jews with long noses, heavy Yiddish accents, and who practiced shady businesses. This group called itself the *Anti-Defamation League.* Since most of the members of the ADL were members of the German speaking B'nai Brith, the ADL soon became an arm of that organization.

When World War I broke out in Europe in 1914, once again Jews were in the middle of the battleground, and relief for those Jews both in Europe and Palestine was necessary on both sides of the war. Palestine, then, was still part of the Ottoman Empire, which favored Germany, and many Jews in the United States had relatives fighting for Germany and Austria. Also, there were Jews serving with the British in the *Jewish Legion,* which helped the British General for the Middle East, Allenby, capture Palestine from the Turks.

During the war and especially after the United States became a participant in 1917, negotiations were begun with the Allies to insure that out of the collapsing Ottoman Empire, should states be created, one of them would be a Jewish state. Following the war, and the Allies victory, the League of Nations was formed, and when Britain was given a mandate for Palestine, she issued in 1922 the Balfour Declaration, indicating the British intention to help the development of a Jewish Homeland in Palestine.

(Because this book is geared to American Jews, not much space will be devoted to the development of the State of Israel, except its impact on the United States and on the structure or values of the Jewish community. It should not be construed as being for a lack of interest or commitment to Israel. In the same manner, the developments in Soviet Rus-

sia, South Africa, Ethiopia and Latin America will be hardly touched upon, except as the events have impact here.)
Turning again to the American Jewish Yearbook, this time to the fascinating statistics of the 1926-27 issue. A Survey of Jewish Immigration to the United States:1881-1925.

1881-1898	533,478
1899-1907	829,244
1908-1925	966,293
Total	2,329,015

During the year of 1924, a very restrictive immigration law was passed in the United States, which severely limited the number of Jews allowed into the country as immigrants. The law was particularly repressive against potential immigrants from southern and eastern Europe.

It is not necessary to give a year-by-year account of the number of Jews who arrived, but it is certainly obvious that the number of Jews who came from 1899-1925 far outnumbered all of the Jews who lived here before 1899. The horrendous quota act of 1924 was precisely what would keep a good number of Jews out of the country from Quadrant IV, where they were most numerous and most needy. What the law did was shift the impetus of immigration to England and other countries of Northern Europe who had sent their émigrés prior to 1890, for the quotas developed were 2% of the amount of the national background listed in the 1880 census, when such a question was asked. Thus the legislation effectively and with obvious prejudice acted against those who came the following year.

Dr. H. S. Linfield, the master statistician for the *Bureau of Jewish Social Research,* another of the fine organizations sponsored by "Our Crowd", estimated in 1925, the following statistics:

Europe	9,586,111
North and South America	3,966,780
Africa	573,670
Asia	473,346
Australia	24,645
Total	14,624,522

Of this total number, 3,600,800 were in Continental United States, making it the largest national population in the world. At this time, 1926, Poland had an estimated Jewish population of 2,854,000, and the Soviet Union had 2,662,139. In a sense, American Jewry had become the major force in the World Jewish Enterprise, simply on the basis of the vast numbers of immigrants who had arrived.

The group from Quadrant IV added their own type of synagogues, and moved into communities all over America and Canada, many of them becoming small businessmen, because they basically had few laboring skills or were not artisans who could work with their hands.

Their contributions to the organizations of the Jewish community were primarily in the area of other fraternal orders, burial societies and insurance organizations, such as the *Progressive Order of the West* or *The International Order of Abraham.* Most of these organizations went out of existence later in the history. However, two newspapers arose out of this immigration, both orthodox in orientation, the *Morgan Journal* (Morning Journal) and *Der Tag* (The Day). Other than those, the major contribution of this immigration was in the increase of synagogues throughout the country.

11 ✡ THE ORGANIZATION OF THE AMERICAN JEWISH COMMUNITY

Until 1933, when Hitler came to power in Germany with an agenda that the Jews had brought disgrace to the Reich and contributed to the country's downfall, Jewish immigration to the United States was very limited, and the total population of the Jews remained almost constant, except for the natural growth through child-bearing.

It is necessary to turn back to 1912, for by then the Jewish Theological Seminary had imported from England a scholar by the name of Solomon Schechter. He was a researcher who, on a visit to the old Cairo Synagogue, came across many ancient documents in a storage room for old Hebrew papers. The room was called in Hebrew, *Genizah,* or hiding place. The reason the documents were never destroyed was an ancient Jewish law which made it a sin to destroy any paper which might contain the name of God in it, and so all legal and religious papers were simply stored in this place.

Schechter, born in Galicia, but a student in Germany, came to Jew's College in England, the Jewish seminary in Great Britain, where he developed a magnificent reputation for his Jewish scholarship and scientific method. He was a natural selection for the German III to appoint as President, for what was soon to be the Conservative Movement. The officers of the Seminary were the same "Our Crowd," led by Cyrus Adler with a board that consisted of Guggenheim, Sulzberger, Marshall, Warburg, and Lehman, to name the most illustrious. Again the unusual connection was between the German III and Litvak religious groups.

Now it is necessary to highlight a significant difference between the Reform and the Conservative movements, which came together at the call of Schechter in 1913. The reader should recall that the Union of American Congregations, the organization of lay members of temples, started Hebrew Union College, whereas in the Conservative grouping, it was the Jewish Theological Seminary that was created by "Our Crowd," all Reform Jews. It was Schechter, who convened the United Synagogue of America, the synagogual group, patterned somewhat after the United Synagogue of Great Britain. Whereas HUC, by its by-laws, has more than 50% of its directors appointed by the UAHC, and is beholden to the congregations, the Seminary is independent of the United Synagogue.

The difference is not one of control, but of direction. With the Reform, the congregational leaders develop the goals of the seminary and the program of Reform, including the camps, whereas on the Conservative side, the seminary develops and staffs all of the important areas of concern for the movement – education, summer camps and public relations. The Seminary tends to be more conservative in theology and programs than the congregations, and so there tends to be a major gap between the seminary and the congregations. In the reform setting, the Union and the HUC share equally in the fundraising, whereas in the other movement, the United Synagogue barely participates in fundraising, which is done by the seminary.

The Union has an enormous physical position in New York, with a very large staff and regional offices all over the country, whereas the United Synagogue is scarcely visible as a professional force. For example, the Union runs the camps of the Reform, and therefore provides a direct service to congregations. In the Conservative side, the camps are run by the seminary, and therefore are part of the program of the faculty and administration; congregations do not participate, except to contribute.

(Note: *I have tried to be as fair as possible in de-*

scribing these movements, and to present this material as objectively as possible, but it may not come out that way. I would ask those active in the movements to check these observations.)

The Union of Orthodox Congregations of America was founded in 1900, and included both the Sephardic and Ashkenazic congregations. It might appear that the Orthodox Union was the second congregational movement in America, after UAHC since it precedes the United Synagogue. However, the OU played a minor role, until the large waves of immigration took place after 1907. Most of those who became active in OU were connected to Yeshiva Yitschak Elchanan, which is usually referred to as the Yeshiva, created in 1898.

Still many organizations, which have played a role in the structure of American Jewry, were founded in the first quarter of the century.

Probably in response to the exclusivity of the American Jewish Committee, the American Jewish Congress was founded in 1916, by Rabbi Stephen S. Wise and leaders of many of the Zionist groups and those which represented Jewish Labor movements. Wise saw the Committee as a very small and undemocratic, self-appointing group, with few roots in the Jewish community. The Congress went far to include everyone and every organization with a Jewish purpose. At first it really attempted to represent the whole Jewish community, but although many attempts were made to accommodate the Committee, the Congress tended to represent Quadrant III better.

Congress has remained the most militant of the Jewish mass groups. It certainly, among secular groups, was the most active with the Zionist movement and the Jewish Labor groups. In 1922, after World War I, Wise, who had resigned the Temple Emanuel pulpit in New York in a dispute over whether the rabbi was free to speak on whatever subject he desired or whether the Board of the Temple could intervene, founded the Free Synagogue of New York, and helped to found the Jewish Institute of Religion, a seminary aimed at serving the total Jewish community.

Dissatisfied with the direction that HUC was taking, in being Anti-Zionist and observing the control that "Our Crowd" had over the Seminary, Wise first asked Mordecai Kaplan to be the president of the JIR. Kaplan declined, for he was at that time involved with the creation of the ideas, formulations and structures of Reconstructionism. Finally, Wise himself, became the president, and until the late 1940's, JIR remained the Zionist force within the Reform movement. By 1948, when HUC and JIR were merged, just prior to Wise's death, the Reform grouping had largely ceased its anti-Zionism, although there were many rabbis and lay people who remained in that position. They founded another group called *The American Council for Judaism.*

Henceforth, the institution of Reform is called HUC-JIR, with the primary schools in Cincinnati, New York, and additional parts in Los Angeles and Jerusalem. The Seminary also expanded its base. Kaplan helped to develop after World War II what he hoped would be a Jewish Community University in Los Angeles, which was called the *University of Judaism.* This is now a part of the Seminary, although it is supported by many in the Reform Community.

Hadassah was another addition to the rainbow of membership organizations which arose in the first quarter century. Henrietta Szold, a member of a famous Baltimore rabbinical family, and a scholar in her own right, had been the secretary of the American Jewish Year Book. She was asked to visit the Jewish settlements in Palestine by the Year Book and report her findings. She was so appalled by the miserable conditions, the primitive medical facilities and the immense poverty, that she returned in 1912, and traveled throughout America, forming sewing circles which would make bandages and other materials for the support of the Hadassah Medical Organization which she had created. Chapters were formed in many of the cities and towns of the country in support of that institution. It eventually became the largest woman's membership organization in the United States.

One of the interesting organizations, which began in 1922, was the *American Pro-Falasha Committee,* again with mostly "Our Crowd" as leaders and with a director of Field Work, Jacques Faitlovich. He was the man who had found the Falashas, the Ethiopian Jews, on a field trip to Africa, and afterward determined that they were Jews, destined to be in time a lost generation. He found most response among the Reform and Conservative rabbis. It may be worthwhile to mention here the names some of the leaders of that movement, for they played major roles in the Jewish community at that time. Among them were Rabbi Edward Calisch of Richmond, Virginia; Rabbi Abraham Feldman of Hartford, Connecticut; Rabbi Solomon Foster, of Newark, New Jersey; Rabbi Samuel H. Goldenson, of Pittsburgh, Pennsylvania; Rabbi Israel Goldstein of New York City; Rabbi James Heller, of Cincinnati, Ohio; Rabbi Mordecai M. Kaplan; Rabbi Jacob Z. Lauterbach of Cincinnati; Rabbi Irving Reichert of New York City; Rabbi William Rosenau of Baltimore, Maryland, and Rabbi Louis Wolsey of Philadelphia, Pennsylvania. On the Advisory Council sat Rabbi Leo Jung and Rabbi Jacob Kohn of New York City. This organization was one which crossed denominational lines and which also was not unusual at that time. Currently, this happens far less often, because of pressure from the far-right Orthodox groups.

(I*s it not amazing that this was all taking place almost three-quarters of a century ago? We have been able to see the saving remnant of these Falashas, who could not have been salvaged without the establishment of the State of Israel.)*

Also about that same time, the *B'nai Brith Hillel Foundation* had been established in the midwest, primarily at the instigation of a non-Jewish professor at the University of Illinois, who was upset at the lack of basic Jewish knowledge and commitment of his Jewish students. The B'nai Brith of Chicago created the first Hillel there and by 1925, two others. Today, there is hardly a campus in the United States and Canada without a Hillel organization. The late Abram Sachar was the force behind the expansion of this program.

Still another organization which traced its formation back to 1893, and had shown amazing developments from that time on, especially among Reform women, was the *National Council of Jewish Women.* Many of their leaders came from college-trained mothers who used their intellectual and social skills to fight for women's rights and for the disinherited in the Jewish community as well as social welfare. It is still playing a vanguard role in its chosen area of concern.

Finally, almost as a footnote, in 1925, there were 84,477 members of the Workmen's Circle, a secular group, as announced at its 25th convention. This is mentioned in order to demonstrate the strength of the secular Jewish community at that time.

What was the mood in 1925 in the Jewish community? There was great concern about the future of Judaism. There was great worry about the number of intermarriages and public conversions to the Episcopal Church, Christian Science and the Ethical Culture Society, as well as a growing lack of interest in Jewish education.

At the same time, Hebrew University in Jerusalem was established. This was the period of the rise of the Ku Klux Klan and political anti-semitism was part and parcel of the terrible immigration law that seemed to be geared against the Jews. Politically, the United States entered a period of isolation from the world, and we had the calm of Harding and Coolidge. It happens that 1925 was also the year of my birth, which will make of the later history a more personal adventure.

12 ✡ THE PRESENT GENERATIONS

1925 becomes a sort of a watershed, because of the disastrous immigration law which prevented so many desperate people from emigrating to America. It was the period of accommodating the second and third generations of the last two quadrants who were born and bred Americans. They were, in general, poor, either as members of the labor movement or as owners of the many mom-and- pop stores, wherever they happen to have settled.

Yiddish in its many dialects was the main tool of conversation, whether one was on Blue Hill Avenue, South Bronx, the row houses of Baltimore, the West Side of Chicago or just off downtown in St. Louis. Even in small towns where Jews settled to make a living, Yiddish was their main culture.

It was these same people who developed, near each of the large cities, vacationlands. For New Yorkers, it was the Catskills. Others found the New Jersey shore their delight. Chicago had their Lake Michigan places. All towns had their favorite vacation spots.

This was the time of proving one's Americanism, so what better way than to support summer camps for the children at places with Native American names. Parents for whom ideology was important sent their children to Jewish camps so that their children would share the home culture.

There were also some Zionist camps, but these were primarily for those who were planning to go on aliyah to Palestine to live in the settlements there.

Again the American Jewish Yearbook offers some additional statistics:

American Zion Commonwealth	6,000 members
Hadassah	240 chapters and 700 Sewing Circles
Jewish Socialist Labor Party	5,000 members
Mizrachi Hatzair (Youth)	3,000 members
Mizrachi	20,000 members
Order of the Sons of Zion	7,000 members
Young Israel	900 Circles
Zeire Zion	2,000 members
Zionist Organization	40,000 members

It is certainly obvious that the total number of Zionist members in the United States in 1925 was not a very large part of the total population. Nevertheless, some of the major leaders in the community were identified with the Zionist movement, including Rabbi Stephen S. Wise, Rabbi Abba Hillel Silver, Henrietta Szold and Rabbi Emanuel Neuman. If one were to total the number in the statistics above, it should be clear that there were not more than 100,000 Zionists, Yet, with such figures and the support of Supreme Court Justice Louis Brandeis, the Zionists were beginning to have their weight felt in political life.

During this period the American Jewish Committee was slowly broadening its membership, but it still consisted mainly of the very wealthy German Reform group, very much concerned with the status of Jews in America. The AJCommittee became the voice of those who considered themselves non-Zionists.

The period between 1925 and 1933 was punctuated by two events that had a tremendous effect on the Jewish people. The first was the rise of public anti Semitism in Central Europe, particularly in Germany, with the rise of the National Socialist Party, the Nazi party. The other was the rise and decline of the American economy, which fell to its lowest ebb in American History with the October 1929 stock market crash, which plunged the country of Manifest Destiny into the depths of depression. That depression was the longest that this country has ever suffered, lasting until World War II.

It is not the purpose of this book to detail the horrors of the Holocaust that destroyed 40% of the living Jews of that time. That has been and will continue to be more appropriately covered in other forums, but we will attempt to trace the impact of these two events on the American Jewish Community.

As soon as Hitler took power in 1933, his party instituted the first of the outrageous attempts to deny any rights to German Jews because they were considered non-Aryans. Positions in universities, courts and official employment were taken away; shops were allowed to be destroyed by mobs and bank accounts were stripped. Jews could be lawfully incarcerated, tried and convicted for no reason other than that they were Jews. Jewish children were thrown out of schools; people who were only one-fourth Jewish were designated as Jewish.

To return to the discussion of the Quadrants, the records of the Jewish community were state property, under the Gemeinde system, and so it was very easy for the authorities to check up on the lineage of anyone who might be suspect. Those who were so designated were faced with the loss of position, livelihood or both.

Immediately, many German Jews began to realize that it would be impossible for them to stay in their beloved Deutchland. In particular, it was the most talented of the German Jews who were faced without support. It was the teachers, artists, writers and musicians, who prior to Hitler, had been the leavening agents to the growing culture with which the country had blossomed. Refugee committees all over the world were created by Jews and non-Jews to save, and in many cases to ransom, these illustrious giants. In Hollywood, there was a major effort to save writers, composers, movie producers and musical and artistic virtuosi.

At one time Los Angeles boasted the greatest colony of German artists, many of whom were brought out by the efforts of the leaders of the movie industry. Among them were Leon Feuchtwanger, Arnold Schoenberg, Bertold Brecht, Ernst Lubitch, William Klemperer, William Wilder, Kurt Weill, Otto Preminger, Stephen and Arnold Zweig and many others, all of whom helped to create in Los Angeles a cultural center, as well as some new directions in the cinema industry.

A number of the leading rabbis and Jewish professionals were also among the first to be saved. Two who became leaders of the Jewish and Zionist Communities were Rabbi Max Nussbaum and Rabbi Joachim Prinz. Later HUC helped in ransoming the leaders of the Reform Seminary in Berlin, some of whom became professors in Cincinnati and produced a number of the Reform rabbinate, who were the stimulators of the Reform Jewish-NFTY camps which are all across the country.

At this point the American Jewish Yearbook for 1933 indicated that the total immigration to the United States in 1932 was 35,576, only 2755 were Jews. In the same year, the number of emigrants from the U.S. was 103,295, and of these were 452 Jews. Obviously at this time the United States was not the *Goldene Medina,* the country of gold which the previous generations had perceived. The depression made it very difficult for Jews to be integrated. Those Jews leaving Europe went to Palestine, Australia, South Africa and to South and Central America. These places apparently offered more opportunity.

German IV

But with the rise of Hitler, America became another possibility. One begins to find in every large city and town, neighborhoods where German-Jewish solidarity could be shared by new Jewish immigrants. Washington Heights in New York, Douglas Park in Chicago, areas of Philadelphia and Boston, and of course the most German of towns, Cincinnati and St. Louis, had settlements of the new German refugees.

This new wave of 1933 added still another element to previous immigration. This group had more of those Jews who had rejoiced in the Weimar Republic of Germany after World War I and who were generally social democrats of the 20th century, as contrasted with those who had arrived after 1848. Many of this group were professionals, rather than bourgeois shopkeepers of the 19th century. A number were top scientists, scholars, writers, physicians and major creative artists, whose connections with the organized Jewish community were relatively tentative.

Quite a number were intermarried, or had declared themselves "confessions-los", that is, without a religious affiliation. If they had a relationship with the Gemeinde, it was primarily through a type of Jewish humanism, culturally expressed. Few connected themselves with a synagogue, although it remained that their close friends and business associates were of the same origin. It was certainly clear in Hollywood that the German intellectuals stuck together and most of them were Jews.

In these new German neighborhoods, the newest community began to create institutions which helped to create a feeling of belonging, retaining the mother tongue. They started a national German Jewish newspaper, *Aufbau*, which not only aided in their assimilation to the American scene, but also reported on the news of Germany, however bad. New synagogues were developed for those who wished them, and they were based on the old principle of being German temples, with much of the service and sermons in German. Some followed the German style of Reform, others followed the "Breslau" Conservative line and others were German Orthodox. In some cases, refugee rabbis recreated synagogues for their fellow refugees and operated as if they were back in the gemeindes of Germany.

Others, the more intellectually oriented, confined their activities to salon programs where people came together in friends' homes and sat around reading poetry, listening to other friends playing chamber music or composers trying out their ideas and writers reading their plays to the close critics These salons became the source for many discussions on universal and Jewish themes making a contribution to this German III wave of immigration.

When Hitler took over Austria and the Sudetenland of Czechoslovakia, still another group of immigrants began to come into the United States, although there was still much anti-immigration feeling here. Beginning in 1938, the immigration of these two communities began to arrive here as well as to other ports of refuge, such as Cuba, Dominican Republic, Venezuela, Brazil and Mexico.

Central Europe was being prepared by the Nazis for an area which should become *Judenrein,* that is free of Jews. The Jewish agencies (local, national and international), which had been relatively dormant in their refugee work, once more became the major focus of the Jewish community. The Zionist organizations were trying their best to fight the British Government, the mandated power of the League of Nations over Palestine, which was publicly demonstrating its pro-Arab bias by denying the immigration rights to those Jews who were trying to find asylum in Palestine. The *Yishuv,* the Jewish community of Palestine, began to organize an illegal immigration program which attempted to break through the British blockade of Palestine to Jews.

At the same time HIAS and the *Joint Distribution Committee,* an organization which had been developed by the German II group, reorganized to get food and medical supplies for those Jews in Europe suffering from deprivation during World War I. Local committees related to both of them were being recreated through the Federation network, which by the nineteen thirties were fixtures in most Jewish communities in America and Canada.

It was obvious that Hitler by 1938 was beginning his major campaign to destroy the Jews in his hegemony. Protests were organized and boycotts were called by major organizations, but the American government, still facing the major depression and a fairly isolationist attitude among the people and with an organized anti-Semitic campaign, actively led by local Bundists, Father Charles Coughlin of Royal Oak, Michigan and Gerald L.K. Smith, did not move to any extent to save the people who were able to leave the Hitlerian part of Europe.

Even President Franklin Delano Roosevelt, who had been elected in 1932 with the overwhelming support of the Jewish community, failed to support the results of a conference on Refugees from Germany. It is true that the story of his unwillingness to act did not come out until after the war, but it is also true that the United States in the 1930's was an incredibly weak nation economically, and even more so militarily.

(*My brother was an officer in the ROTC, a univer-*

sity military program. He was called to camp during the summer of 1940, and practiced shooting rifles by aiming broom sticks.)

It was only after Poland was invaded by Hitler in the fall of 1938, when England, France and Russia declared war on Germany and Italy, that Roosevelt ordered the development of a war machine, with tanks, airplanes and materiel for Lend-Lease for the Allies. In addition, he began the process of mobilizing the Reserves for the armed forces.

In a very few months, Poland was overcome by the German forces, and the large Polish Jewish community was taken into captivity. It was about this time that the *Final Solution for the Jewish People* was promulgated by the Nazi leadership. Concentration camps were created for the destruction of the great bulk of Jews who were captured by the German army, as well as those Jews from Holland, Belgium and France, which had also been overrun by the Nazis. Italian Jews were also subjects of the Nazis as Germany forced Italy, its ally, to put the Jews into concentration camps.

There is no need to go into details into the horrible Holocaust story; our intent here is to demonstrate the impact on American Jews by this unforgivable act of the murder of 40% of the total Jewish population in the world at that time.

The facts are evident that the number of Jews who were put to death was in the neighborhood of 6,000,000. It certainly is beyond belief that such a number and such a percentage of our people were destroyed; that figure has become part and parcel of the mood and liturgy of American Jews. The Holocaust sits on the conscience of almost every Jew.

To turn back to the pre-World War II period, it is true that many Jews in America watched the news daily about Hitler and the growing cruelty of anti-Semitism. There was no television, so most people got their news from the radio, and it was on radio that Hitler and his home-grown Nazis and allies played their bigotry on the American and world scene. Hundreds of anti-Semitic groups arose, many with the funding coming directly from the German government. Their purpose was to create splits in the American community by blaming all the ills of the society on Jews.

Father Coughlin had a regular network radio program

on which he pushed a particularly virulent anti-Jewish propaganda. His newspaper, Social Justice, was distributed at many Catholic churches on Sunday mornings.

There were many non-Catholic forces. Reverend Gerald L.K. Smith, who also spoke on the radio, went on regular tours of fundamental churches, holding "Americanism" rallies, at which he ranted about the Jewish bankers and their control of "President Rosenfeld." There were so many other groups and leaders of this group of bigots, that this subject would take up volumes. But it was this native anti-Semitism that woke up many Jews to the dangers of American bigotry.

During the 1930's, the fight against anti-Semitism expanded three community relations organizations: the American Jewish Committee, the American Jewish Congress and the Anti-Defamation League of B'nai Brith. Other organizations with special interests also became larger in importance, such as the Jewish Labor Committee, whose basic responsibility was to save Jewish labor leaders in Europe from Nazi onslaught, and the Jewish War Veterans, which was a much older group, but became more prominent in the veterans' community.

Each of these organizations made a bid for the resources of the Jewish community; efforts were made to coordinate their programs and fundraising, for each claimed that it was *the* major group fighting bigotry. During the same period, many communities, especially in the larger cities, combatted local bigotry and attacks on Jews, by organizing their own counterattack structures.

These committees or councils hired staff to work with its burgeoning membership and to coordinate with allies in other groups. They soon created effective and active inter-group organizations which banded together to fight bigotry.

Eventually, in 1938 a coordinating group of the four major Jewish organizations, AJ Committee, AJ Congress, Anti-Defamation League and the Jewish Labor Committee was formed under the *General Jewish Council* banner. Basically again, it was developed through the efforts of the same German II grouping, although it was a later generation. In order to keep the balance of the three major organizations, the director was selected from the Jewish Labor Committee, Isaiah

Minkoff, an escapee from Soviet Russia, who was active with the secular Socialist Movement.

But by 1939, with the beginning of the war in Poland, the focus of the agencies was forced to change. The truth began coming out about the concentration camps, which the Nazis claimed were only work camps. The major efforts of the American Jewish community necessarily turned to the war programs, with vast attempts to extricate the Jews out of Europe. Much of the work was also expended to open the doors of Palestine, but the British were playing their own game for the benefit of the Arabs, by making it very difficult for Jews to escape to the Holy Land. Nevertheless, the population of Jews in Palestine grew perceptively, so that by 1948, the Jewish population had risen to about 600,000.

Beginning in 1939, a number of Jewish men and women volunteered into the British and Canadian military. The United States already had begun a program of Lend-Lease to aid the British and the Free Forces of France, Holland, Belgium and Poland, and when Germany attacked the Soviet Union, the U.S. government added the USSR to the list. We had begun to transform our factories into military producers. Such industries as Douglas, Boeing and McDonell grew from minor airplane manufacturers to major suppliers to the Allies. Automobile manufacturers became major defense plants, turning out tanks, jeeps and other vehicles.

With many of the young people of the Jewish community from the age of 18-36 beginning to be drafted into the Armed Services, an old organization, the *National Jewish Welfare Board,* which had been the bailiwick of the "Our Crowd," and which coordinated the Young Men's and Women's Hebrew Associations around the country, joined five Christian groups to form the United Service Organization. The JWB created local committees and USO Clubs in Jewish communities all over the United States and overseas where Jewish servicemen and women might be stationed. It was also the JWB which took responsibility for the Jewish Chaplaincy.

The USO, with its JWB component, played an immense role in the development of post-war American Jewry. Many Jews, being primarily from the larger cities, found that they were alone and ill at ease when they were far from their neighborhoods. The Jewish USO, with its wonderful abilities at organization, created local committees, which greatly helped these Jewish warriors to find a "home away from home."

Young and not-so-young ladies were invited to be hostesses and junior hostesses on a regular basis, and as a result, many permanent relationships evolved in such far away places as Casper, Wyoming; Gulfport, Mississippi; Bremerton, Washington; Pensacola, Florida and so many others. Many Jewish service people, who might have never gone to religious services in their own home town, suddenly appeared at the services on the military bases and found warmth and friendship, especially if there were junior hostesses from the USO,.

Many marriages took place as a result, which encouraged the men and women to consider a life in some other place than the old home town. In addition, the American government for many reasons created a *GI Bill of Rights,* which allowed the returnees to attend college, in many cases far away from their family. Some took up residences in their spouses' home towns, and many more decided to try their luck and fortune in far-ranging communities and newly founded suburbs.

One of the first items on the agenda was the creation of Jewish institutions, mostly synagogues, which would give their children some of the warm feelings that so many had for the Jewish community during the war. Couple this with the information that the Jewish service men and women had about the Holocaust, a number still trying to leave the concentration camps, and the soon to be State of Israel. A new sense of pride and dedication to the future of Jewry developed.

Thus, after 1945, one saw the burgeoning of new Jewish communities through the expansion of the synagogues and temples, Federations and Centers and all of the rest of the Jewish agencies. It was fortuitous that all of this was going on at the same time when the concentration camps were being opened and the organized needs of the world Jewish community became so urgent.

It was also a very exciting time for the State of Israel was now being created through the new United Nations. These simultaneous occurrences created the milieu for all sort of programs and priorities for the organized Jewish Community.

Jewish Education, which had been in such miserable shape in the twenties and thirties, now begins to impinge on the minds of the leadership. Many programs were developed for teacher training in almost every Jewish community, with an eye towards professionalism in the field.

The same revisions were taking place in other fields of communal service, such as fund-raising, research, family services and programs for the aged. Heretofore, many Jewish professionals had been co-opted into the work, now one began to seek ways to have specifically trained professionals with advanced degrees.

It is since World War II that the rise of the organized Jewish community came to a level of maturity. During the war, the beginnings of further coordination in the field of fighting anti-Semitism again took place. Under the auspices of the Council of Jewish Federations and Welfare Funds (CJFWF), a special study of the entire field was initiated in 1950.

The National Community Relations Advisory Council had already begun, in 1944, to pick up the pieces of the original General Jewish Council. By 1950, the Union of American Hebrew Congregations and the Jewish War Veterans had joined the original four national bodies, and some 27 local community relations agencies were together in the NCRAC. For the next several years, conflicts arose among the national agencies as to which one would handle certain projects. As a result, a comprehensive study was commissioned and led by Dr. R.M. MacIver, a well known sociology professor at Columbia University.

It took over a year for the MacIver Report, to be completed and placed before the Federations. Among the recommendations were that religious organizations, UAHC, USA (Conservative), and UOJCA (Orthodox) should have responsibility for inter-religious work. In addition, he assigned various areas to each of the national agencies – each one responsible for the area in which it had specialized. For example, the ADL was assigned mass media, AJCommittee to be responsible for negotiations, AJCongress for law and legislation, Jewish Labor Committee for the labor movement and the Jewish War

Veterans for veteran organizations.

MacIver stressed the importance of the local community and that the local CRC should have prime responsibility for the work there and to coordinate its work with the national organizations. NCRAC was assigned the task of helping to organize more CRCs in those local communities where there was none, and to encourage them to join NCRAC.

A major battle took place when the report was issued in 1951, with the AJCommittee and ADL on one side, and the NCRAC, the other national agencies plus the local communities, on the other.

The issue was basically whether a national organization, such as these two, had the right to work in all fields of fighting anti-Semitism, or whether some coordinating group could ask them to give up some of their autonomy. In 1951, the two organizations broke away from the NCRAC, formed a joint fund-raising group, leaving the NCRAC with the AJCongress, Jewish Labor Committee, Jewish War Veterans, the UAHC, and more than a score of local CRCs. Attempts to bring them back to the fold failed, until the 1960's when continuing efforts and the fact that the total number of CRCs was increasing, as well as the power of the Federations, convinced the two groups to rejoin the NCRAC.

In the interim, all sorts of *ad hoc* committees were formed, in cooperation with the NCRAC, but never under its own auspices. For example, when there was a major effort to change the previous immigration laws, in order to have a unified Jewish position, a "no auspices" immigration committee was formed with all national groups as members. When there was a need for a joint position on certain church-state legislation, as well as several court cases on this issue, the convened committee was called "non auspices" church-state committee, and finally in 1956, a major attack on Kosher slaughtering in Congress, called together another across-the-board committee.

(I served as the secretary of all three committees while working at the NCRAC.)

In 1951, another most important organization was created, which is still having a major effect in the Jewish community. Abba Eban, then ambassador from Israel to the United

States, came to the conclusion that there was a need for a pro-Israel lobbying arm in Washington. At the time, much foreign aid was being distributed, and Eban wished that there be a group of American Jews, who would be able to talk to Congress and the President in a way that an Ambassador could not. He called on a long-time associate in the Zionist movement, I. L. Kenen, a former newspaper man and one who had been the major coordinator for a conference in 1944, the *American Jewish Conference*, whose object was to pull together the work of the world Jewish community when the war would end.

In 1951, the American Israel Public Affairs Committee was formed to represent American Jews in Washington on Israel matters.

All of this growth took place as the Jewish community was spreading all over the country, in much greater numbers than ever before. New communities were blossoming in almost every state, and there was hardly a small town where some Jewish presence was not felt. The United Jewish Appeal during the war had developed a structure so that in almost every single town and village there was a campaign for the UJA, itself a coordinating arm for three other groups. A remarkable achievement of this field operation was that almost anywhere in the United States and Canada, many Jews could feel a part of the rescue effort for saving the remnant of the European Jews, and the development of Israel.

Much of this information is given to enable the reader to understand the tremendous expansion of the Jewish activities during and after the war. All national agencies and organizations expanded. Membership groups, such as B'nai Brith and Hadassah, grew to enormous proportions compared to pre-war times.

Hillel Foundation, which had only a handful of campuses before1939, began a major expansion during the war, and soon had hundreds of foundations and counselorships to serve Jewish students on many more campuses than ever. It should be noted that whereas prior to the war, the majority of the adult Jews were part of the labor movement or were small business owners, the war and the subsequent GI Bill of Rights encouraged the veterans to attend college and prepare for professional positions.

Very shortly, there was a tremendous increase of Jewish doctors, lawyers, scientists, psychologists and even college professors, areas which had barely been available to Jews previously. Many universities,such as Harvard and Yale, had quotas for the number of Jews who could be admitted, especially in the professional departments.

As the number of professionals grew in the community, more demands were made for fighting anti-semitism. All of the community relations groups expanded as concern for the rights of Jews and others, who were discriminated against, became a major force. As the Jewish community became a more middle class group and more affluent, the Federations raised even more money, which was granted to these organizations.

It soon became clear that Jews would have to create alliances with other groups if they were to have any effect on the role of the Jew in this society. In terms of inter-religious work, after the war, Judaism became the third major religion on the scene, and no major program on the country's agenda could be without a priest, minister or rabbi. At another level, Jews were considered one of the racial and ethnic groups here. In fact, in the fifties, major discussions were rampant on the subject of "What are the Jews, a religion, a race or a people?" – a subject scarcely discussed today.

In 1956, another event changed the face of American Jewry. In the Middle East, the first Sinai campaign took place, in which Israel, in conjunction with England and France, attacked Egypt, under Nassar, who had threatened to close the Suez Canal. England and France still had major colonial lands in the Orient and East Africa, and closing the canal was seen as a major attack on these two powers. It also obviously was an attack on Israel, Egypt's enemy.

Israel, led by the famous one-eyed general, Moshe Dayan, won the war, but the Soviet Union, anxious to throw its weight as a major force in the Middle East, threatened to enter the war on the side of the Egyptians. The United States, under President Dwight Eisenhower, forced the victors to retreat. In the Jewish community, Israel began to make an impression on the masses, far more than previously. No longer was Israel only the refuge of the concentration camps, but was now a military force in the Middle East.

The Jewish Community Relations agencies, which had scarcely been involved in matters of Israel, now began to see that Israel had something to do with the relationships of the Jews and the rest of the American people. Some of this had to do with the pro-Arab position of many of the mainstream Christian denominations, but also because many of the anti-Semites made common cause with the Arab propagandists. It was no accident that the Arabs began circulating one of the most virulent anti-Jewish pieces, *The Protocols of the Elders of Zion,* which warns that Jews were plotting to take over the world.

The NCRAC convened a meeting of all of the community relations agencies at that time to discuss *Community Relations Implications of Events in the Middle East.* It was obvious to those present that some distance had to be noted, that this was not a Zionist meeting, for several of the groups were certainly non-Zionist and at least one was almost anti-Israel. Nevertheless, the fact that the meeting was held with such a title indicated how Israel was impinging on the consciousness of all Jews. Programs were developed on how to interpret these events, who should carry such programs and which alliances needed to be developed.

Obviously, on this level, some relationship between the agencies, the NCRAC and Zionist organizations was needed in order to develop a unified effort, for each was doing public relations on behalf of Israel. Out of this came the *Conference of Presidents of Major Jewish Organizations,* with the assent of the almost a score of organizations to represent the efforts and concerns of the organized community about Israel. The chair of the Conference has rotated among the organizations and, in general, it has done a remarkable job in its role. There have been times that the Conference has seemed to be an arm of the Israel government; at other times, it has taken Israel to task for certain actions.

Sometimes ad-hoc organizations have been created which were essentially one-issue oriented. In 1963, after many years of Jewish organizations not being able or willing to tackle the politically difficult problem of the treatment of the Jewish population of the Soviet Union, an organized program was initiated, which first was aimed at urging the Soviets to grant rights to the Jews, which were spelled out in the USSR constitution. Primarily, what was demanded was that Jews be allowed to practice their own religion and to foster their culture. The call was for granting the right to bake matzos for Passover and for the printing of religious books. Furthermore, there was the request to allow Soviet Jews to train their own religious leaders, and the demand for the Soviet government to permit Jews to leave Russia.

In 1967, the Six Day War in Israel changed the whole campaign, for the Soviets tied themselves totally to the Arabs. They broke diplomatic relations with Israel, closed the Israel Embassy, where Golda Meir had served as Ambassador to Moscow. Her embassy had been a focus of great strength for the Jews there, and had been the center of Jewish educational efforts and cultural programs in the whole Soviet Union.

After the Israelis defeated the Arabs in that campaign, the focus turned to "Let My People Go," with the intent of convincing the Soviets to allow Jews to leave. Tremendous efforts had been made to arrange to move Jews to Israel, and to other free countries. Among the efforts that were made and seemed to have some effect on the Russian mentality was the political effort to have the United States government endorse the Jackson-Vanik act, which denied to the Soviets Favored Nation status, until there was a significant change in their emigration policy. Favored Nation Status improves trade arrangements with the United States.

In time, with the Soviet Union faced with major economic devastation and the breakdown of control over Eastern Europe since the end of World War II, the flow of Jews out of Russia has been at a pace unheard of in history.

During this same period, another extraordinary grouping was organized, which had as its purpose the saving of the remnants of the Ethiopian Jews, "Falashas." It may be recalled that in the second decade of the twentieth century, "Our Crowd" had organized the American Pro-Falasha Committee around the pioneering work of Dr. Jacques Faitlovitch. The program of that committee was dedicated to the *"educational and religious rehabilitation of the Falasha Jews of Abyssinia."* Immense amount of efforts, some with almost fatal bravery, was finally able in the 1980's to redeem most of these Jews, who had been lost for so many years, to be brought to Israel, and to work for their rehabilitation. These Black Jews, whose traditions precede the whole rabbinical times, had some difficulties, because some Orthodox rabbis refused to accept them as Jews under the Law of Return of Israel, a rule which permits any Jew to come to Israel and receive automatic citizenship. The growth and health of this group in Israel is one of the remarkable achievements of the Jewish community of the world and in Israel. There are still many Falashas left in Ethiopia at the present writing, but it appears that Israel and the Ethiopian authorities are cooperating to allow them to emigrate.

AL MELLMAN

13 ✡ THE AMERICAN SCENE
IN THE 1990'S

Almost 4,000 years of history and some three thousand years of Jewish life have been covered. My primary purpose was to indicate to American Jews how vast and significant were the changes in each step along the way; what being a Jew meant. At this time in American Jewish history, it is obvious that there are so many varieties of Jews and Judaism, that it is scientifically impossible to define what a Jew is anymore. It may never again be possible – we will have to rely on a different measure or system to define a Jew.

Quite possibly, one would have to turn to physics and to derivations of the Einstein system, What has proceeded from that great genius was the *Heisenberg Uncertainty Theory.* Basically, what Heisenberg proposed was the following: if a high speed physical body is in motion, it is not possible to measure its speed or its position, for the speed changes the position and the position is affected by the speed. For example, one cannot accurately measure the speed of an electron which is moving near the speed of light, nor can the actual mass be extracted. It is necessary to stop the electron to measure its mass, and the speed can only be approximated.

The inference here is that the members of the Jewish community are moving so fast in America that one has great difficulty in precisely defining what being a Jew is. Had this history been written immediately after World War II, the definition and direction would not be the same as it is today. They have been quite altered. Nevertheless, it is important to draw a picture of the present Jewish community.

To help us in this discussion, I will draw from a book by Vance Packard, *The Status Seekers.* Packard defined the American national community as being built in the style of a pyramid. His analysis created seven levels of society, with the largest category at the very bottom, the lower-lower class. Each level above it was smaller, until one reached the smallest, the upper-upper class.

Packard provided characteristics of style and values of each class. Of course, there are anecdotal exceptions to every one, but these are relative terms. The following were his breakdown of the seven categories, starting from the highest:

Class I. Upper-Upper class. They have inherited wealth, are members of both town and country clubs, which are exclusive, so that Class I people never use them. They never work, but tend to be gentlemen or lady farmers, travel in private planes, or on the most restrictive yachts, engage in various philanthropies, but never attend the functions, allowing those whom they have elevated to Class II to represent them at these social activities. Conspicuously inconspicuous, one never sees these people. Generally very conservative politically, they make sure that their children and grandchildren attend only the most appropriate schools and functions. They are very High Church, either Catholic or Episcopalian, although the religion may be modified by regional considerations.

Class II. Lower-Upper Class. These are the guardians of the first class, and are dependent on the Class I people for their connections. They are the board members of the right charities, country clubs, symphonies, museums, etc. They are placed on the boards, not only for their own contributions, financially, but also because they are direct connections to the Class I and their contributions. The more intellectual, the more high toned the institution, the more it depends on the Class II individual. It is the Class II persons who have created the boundaries of the Upper Class. They may do so through discrimination or by political means. They believe that they are following the values of Class I, setting up criteria in employment, college entrances, membership in town and country clubs, loan criteria at a bank, or by invoking traditional values.

Class II tend to be executives of firms owned by Class I, or reasonably controlled by them. They may be their lawyers, their financial advisors or their political advisors. They are members of the same churches as Class I, but they attend and insure the finances of the church.

Class III. Upper Middle Class. This class is larger than Class II. There are a number of ways to enter this class. These are people who are unable to enter Class II, but have a leadership at a lower level. A person would be able to enter this category if he or she had access to Class II, and could call upon it for help in support of Class III values – traditional American values, such as Family, Motherhood, Church, the Flag, Religious Holidays, the Military and Education. The list could continue indefinitely, but certainly the values are easily identifiable. Those who are qualified to be in this group would be doctors, lawyers, professors, ministers, and others who provide services to the community. Of course, the higher the church, or the more important the specialty, the higher in Class III one becomes.

It is possible for a Class III person to "make it" into Class II, but one has to be so exceptional and financially able to march with the rest of that group. The leaders of this group tend to be the national leaders of service clubs. They love mass programs, because the more people who support or attend, gives impetus to that group as an important part of Class III, and possibly may be noticed by those above.

Class IV. Middle Class. These people are the great middle class, who make up the followers in the programs of the Class III group. They will march on call, attend baseball games, support the local charities, send their children to public schools and are the major support of movies and other mass media, fast-food eateries, shopping malls, public beaches. Disneyland is geared to Class IV. These are the lower executives of businesses, self-employed entrepreneurs, insurance salesmen, teachers, public employees in general and very skilled laborers.

Their greatest hope is to reach Class III, but few can make it, for once again that class has guardians who prevent the wrong people from rising. Encouraged by the discrimination at the top, they are ripe at appropriate times to operate on their own prejudices. Class IV people tend to be insecure financially, since their income tends to be eaten up by middle class needs, and seldom permits the luxury of much savings. Since they are also dependent, to a great extent, on those above them for their livelihood, they can not be too independent.

Class V. Lower-Middle Class. In this class we find the unskilled laborers, or immigrants who work when they can. In addition, we have here those who have fallen out of Class IV, for any number of reasons. These are people who have little or no savings, and the only thing that keeps them from falling into the lower class is the fact that they desperately wish to keep trying to move up. They are the ones who try to take academic class after class, with the hope that will bring them up to Class IV. These are the retirees who barely make it on their last funds, and one major illness or disaster leaves them destitute.

Class VI. Upper-Lower Class. This is the category with very little education, frequently recent immigrants, whose vision of America is to live a little bit above subsistence. They are destined to work at the most menial jobs, at the lowest ends of the working class. Their positions are those with the least security, and therefore with the least hope for any more than keeping that position, or pure poverty will result. The perfect examples are the immigrants who stand on corners seeking day work. Yet these people dream of moving into Class V.

Class VII. Lower-Lower Class. This class has been called the "Permanent Under Class." Included in this group are the generational poor, the mountaineers, the aged who have given up, waiting for death, the permanent homeless. They really have no hope of ever moving out of this class. They are the perpetual indigent, the mentally ill, with no place to go, those whose whole existence is involved with liquor and drugs.

Having drawn these seven classes, Packard postulates that except for the first and the seventh classes, members of the other five are driven in one way or another to strive for at least one class above the one they are presently in. Thus the title of his book, *The Status Seekers*. In a broad generalization, one might determine the class of a person by possession or association: automobile, art, membership, etc. In fact, one might also say that products and advertisements are predicated by the public or class which the sponsor wishes to reach. Packard also emphasized that the whole American system is dependent on the issue that each class is proud of the exclusivity of its group – simply that there are more people in the lower classes!

Now it is necessary to apply the Packard classification to the Jewish community so that we can better understand the sociology of the current Jewish community.

If the American total community can be described in terms of a pyramid, then the Jewish community might best be pictured as a diamond shaped figure. It is possible to develop a similar seven class characterization about the American Jews to enable the reader to comprehend the present developments and structures within it; it is most evident in Jewish organizations. People generally associate along class lines, although obviously there are no absolutes. Caution must be advised that we should not personally identify too closely to any particular class, for the structure is a general one.

The Jewish Community – Packard Style

Class I-J. Upper-Upper Class. The same basic determinants of Packard's Class I for the general community applies with some Jewish differences. The persons in this class have inherited money, do not work, never attend meetings, are politically conservative on both Jewish issues as well as general and political items. They do not flaunt their wealth by conspicuous consumption, yet they are members of the right Jewish clubs, but never, never, go. They may, if invited by the Class

I people, be permitted to attend the local non-Jewish town and country club, but only with the approval of other Class I personages. They support the arts in the general community at a far greater rate and amount than their counterparts in the non-Jewish area, not wishing to be considered parasites. The same is true in charity giving, where it is quite well known that contributions by the Jewish leaders are far more than their non-Jewish associates.

In the Jewish community, Class I-J persons seldom attend dinners for charity and the arts, but do make major gifts, although a number see Jewish giving as parochial. Their contributions are generally to the Higher Arts, important and intellectual parts of the academic life, specialty hospitals, and institutions of research – the more obtuse the better. So, in the Jewish community, Class I-J would support the major hospital and a local hospital, a major university in Israel, and to balance, one of the major universities locally or Ivy League, especially in one of the medical or high scientific areas. He or she might support a major museum in Israel and, of course, to the local museum, or symphony. Their names will appear on the walls as major contributors, but they seldom attend functions, unless it is an intimate Class I or I-J affair.

Class I-J is a member of the most auspicious Reform Temple, the most important country club, lends his or her name to the American Jewish Committee, which traditionally has been the elite of the community. However, the family does not attend, unless the organization is honoring him or her, or a close associate of theirs. He or she supports inter-group relations, but has few friends, other than his or her own I-J associates.

Until recently, members of this class were predominately from the German-Jewish extraction, with those at the very top of multi-generational German background. However, in time, a certain number of Eastern Europeans entered, provided that they accepted the values of those already in. One of the ways to enter was to join the Reform Temple, make an unusual community contribution, be a Noble Prize winner, be a conductor of the local symphony, possibly a noted psychiatrist, or a prize winning writer on the national scene.

Class II-J. Lower-Upper Class. This is a growing category, primarily made up of higher levels of professionals, major entrepreneurs, major real estate developers, some rabbis who have access to Class I-J, some writers and politicians. It is very possible that members of this class may have more money, larger homes than the previous class, but inasmuch as they earn their money and do not have the distinction of a second generation of leisure, they are not in the top class, and they know it. They are the *Nouveau Riche* of the Jewish community, who have many of the appurtenances of Class I-J, but not enough to be in. Yet, they are well known in the community, for not only do they accept the leadership, many actively seek it. (Their children or grandchildren may one day be elevated to that other class.)

The higher members are in Class II-J, it is because they are able to represent those who are in Class I-J. II-J is the fastest growing group, largely because of the increasing number of Jews who have attended college and professional schools. In fact, studies have shown that almost 90% of all Jews eligible for college, do attend. This is some 20% more than any comparable ethnic or religious group in the United States.

These people are world travelers, many having been to Israel a number of times. They are generally members of the Reform Movement; some, however, belong to the larger Conservative congregations. A few are Orthodox, except in New York City, where they are usually immigrants, who arrived after World War II. They will associate themselves with the universities in Israel, preferring to support the high-tech medical and scientific departments, or possibly the Fine Arts. In the local community, they support similar institutions. Their living in two civilizations makes this mandatory. Their children attend private schools, are geared to attend Ivy League colleges and to prepare for professional and artistic endeavors. Their pictures and names appear regularly in both print and broadcast media as they support their organizations,

In fact, this is one of the ways that members of this

class are able to demonstrate their position. Persons in Class I-J seldom have their picture taken for the mass media, although it might happen if another member of the Class was there as well.

The important factor in this grouping is that they are, and consider themselves, the arbiters and guardians of the Jewish Upper Class. They do this through their gifts, their homes, their temples, their rabbis, art, and other accouterments of culture. They tend to set the standards for clothing, hairstyles and travel. Of course, this may vary from community to community. This group travels with people of their class wherever they live, producing a leveling and merging of styles.

Class III-J Upper-Middle Class. This is the most representative, as well as the largest, of the Jewish community. Because of their increased education and upward mobility, the upper middle class is where the points of the diamond should be the broadest. It is in this grouping that most Jews see themselves, and this is a most important part of this analysis. It is in Class III-J that we find the individual entrepreneurs, the salespersons, teachers, professors, scientists, social workers, psychologists, lawyers, doctors and the middle level executives in corporations and their spouses. *In no way is income or estate the determining factor in this class – it encompasses millionaires as well as individuals whose income is barely above subsistence.*

The actual components are more a matter of style and values than income. If these people join a Jewish group, it may be a smaller Reform temple or one of the larger Conservative synagogues. More likely, they will join an intellectual or study group and will attend cultural classes and events which represent values of their class.

Many of this group take up music and art as an avocation, or possibly teach as part of their attempt to share their values. They tend to be more liberal in religious and political life than the previous class. In many ways they show some contempt for that class, by not adopting the II-J activities, as being snobbish, conserva-

AL MELLMAN

tive or some other response to indicate their differences (or indifferences). The leaders of the Middle Class love to set the rules of the class. They often become the presiding officers of mass organizations. It is through these mass associations that Jewish group values are played out; for example, marches on behalf of Soviet Jews – Federation telephone sessions are organized, and other mass functions are promulgated. They also make up the leadership of synagogues and temples.

The leadership of III-J generally has access to the leadership of Class II-J, although few of them actually become members of the upper class. Nevertheless, because the Jewish community is much closer and better organized than the general community, the association of classes is a natural and workable reality.

To parallel the other groups, Class III-J is primarily made up either of successful Eastern European who arrived after 1933, or the children and grandchildren of the 1881-1925 immigrations. In a few cases, they might even be new immigrants from Iran, South or Central America and even Israel. It is these for whom the mass events, such as Israel days or Holy Days celebrations, are so important.

Again, let it be emphasized that income or holdings are not the qualifications for membership in a group, similar cultural and societal values are the keys to entre. In some cases this group will also include the vast majority of the aging population, who have the income to maintain their standard of living.

Class IV-J. Middle-Middle Class. This category contains the joiners of the mass organizations in the Jewish community, the temples and synagogues, B'nai Brith, sisterhoods, brotherhoods and Jewish or almost all-Jewish fraternities, such as Eastern Star, Knights of Pythias, Masonic Temples, etc. Much of the Jewish community is involved with services and programs for the Class IV-J. As a now obvious standard the leaders IV-J have access to the leaders in the adjacent higher class; but the balance of the middle-middle class neither care nor want to know more than the society to which they belong. The same is true of the synagogue and temple members.

The great bulk of the members are almost unaware of temple policies, or national and regional operations. They are the self-employed small business owners, lower level laborers, secretaries, teacher's aids, all of whom have minimum income, but almost all of it is spent on necessities. In many cases both spouses work in order to meet ongoing bills. This is the true center of the Jewish community.

Class V-J. Lower Middle Class. This division is growing smaller. It consists of those who are tied to a lower level manual job. The labor movement as it developed in the early part of the century was greatly populated by those in the garment and millinary industries, or meat packing and tobacco factories, or were printers and deliverers of newspapers. They were, at least in the big cities, really laborers.

But as the Jewish community took advantage of the educational benefits in the United States, their children progressed to entrepreneurships and professions, almost none of which were organized in unions. As a result the number of Jews who are currently in the labor movement has tremendously declined, except in two major areas, government service and teaching.

Today, at the beginning of a new century, professionals have progressed to the higher classes. Nevertheless, one still finds Jews, particularly new immigrants, who work with their hands for someone else, and live just beyond subsistence level. These are the hourly wage employees, who have neither the money or the inclination to really participate in Jewish communal life. As the divorce rate rises in Jewish life, there are more and more single parents and families in this group.

More attention is being provided to this group by federations and temples, offering Jewish education and activities for the children, and special counseling for divorced and widowed parents. The problems are even more aggravated when more and more Jews move to distant cities, away from family, relatives and their extended family, which at one time was so important in Jewish life.

Yet these V-J people are upward-striving, hoping

to somehow, either through marriage, education or luck, claim a role in IV-J. This factor is a major morale creator, which enables them to keep from falling into the next lower class.

However, it should be noted that many homeless, a tragically new phenomenon in the Jewish community, are drawn from this group. How to rebuild these people back to normalcy will be a major problem for the organized community. This is particularly true where housing costs are high, and where welfare is not sufficient. This occurs mostly in large urban areas where so many members of this class fall through the cracks of society.

Class VI-J. Upper-Lower Class. In a strange, unexpected development, this is a growing category in the Jewish community. Here we find many of the aged and aging, some who once had sizable or median incomes, but find that the cost of growing old is draining them of their resources.

Many of these people have never needed the help of the Jewish organized community and may not know how to draw on the programs and activities available. Often, they are too geographically distant from their close relatives, and in many situations, psychologically distant, and are left to their own devices. Medical costs are rising for them, and at a higher rate than for the rest of the community. Many have to chose between eating and medical services, and because in America people are now living longer, the force is to push such people further into poverty. Many live in what is euphemistically called a changing neighborhood. Crime dogs them where they live. Moreover, many of the centers have moved into the suburbs to serve the young. Few young Jews live in the same neighborhood and the seniors have a sense of being abandoned. (Society, in general, has really not prepared for the burgeoning senior population, although many programs in major cities are now directed to them.)

Included in this group are recent immigrants, who are still not able to provide for themselves. The difference for many of these new Americans is that they come with a future orientation and hopes for improvement, whereas the aged know that their life can only be extended, not regenerated.

Nonetheless, many of these people try to find some activities through whatever local or Jewish functions enter their lives. Those who do participate seem to want to be a part of what they remembered or what they feel is expected. A few even make contributions to the annual federation campaigns. They do look up to Class VJ for their ideas and programs.

Class VII-J. Lower-Lower Class. This is the one group that does not strive to be in the group above it. These people have given up. And, unfortunately, the numbers there are increasing. They include the infirmed, aging, anyone who has no chance for life outside their home or nursing home. No activity can include them, for they have no resources, neither financial nor physical, and of course, their mental outlook is clouded by medical circumstances. There is no future existence for them.

We must include in this class a growing number of Jewish men and women who have become part of the welfare network. Circumstances beyond their control have overtaken them, and they are destined to remain on the public dole without hope or inclination to improve.

This has been an attempt to detail the sociology of the Jewish community in America through these seven classes. It should be stated as sharply as possible that these arbitrary divisions are not iron-clad nor as hard-bound delineation as the general community. It is quite possible for someone brought up in class V or VI, through education, character, a contribution to the world in some esthetic or scientific way, to find himself or herself in Class II. But for most Jews, the largest possible move might be two upward classes. It is also possible for someone, regardless of background, whose contribution to Israel or the Jewish community, or to the political scene, is significant, to be accepted in a higher class. Writers, composers, teachers, professors, artists and politicians, are typical of such movers.

To return to the general community and to compare it with the Jewish community on a national level, (for each city will have some variation) Vance Packard describes the structure as a pyramid, with the number in each descending class larger than the one above. In the Jewish community, the diagram is different. It can best be charted as an off-center diamond, with the largest group in the third or fourth class depending on the city. The widest part of the diamond would be above the center of the figure.

The Jewish community thus plays a different tune in the symphony of America. Its values tend to be more upper-middle class, not pure middle-class. This certainly reflects the high level of education and culture. In the 21st Century the Jewish community is the most successful in our history, and barring a catastrophe, should continue to be so.

14 ✡ SUMMARY AND RECOMMENDATIONS

If history is to teach, authors must conclude. What is foreseen for the future and what needs to be done to have some impact on the future? Jewish history has been described horizontally (history) and vertically (sociology); now we must attempt to project what the future holds for American Jews.

There are currently some 6,000,000 Jews in the United States and several hundred thousand more in Canada. This is the largest number of Jews ever to exist in one area since the beginning of history. These Jews are for the most part affluent and the most influential community in the 4,000 year span. Never has there been such an explosion of culture and creativity than what has eminated from this community, which has flowered in the American milieu. Jews have made significant contributions in most facets of American life: music, literature, theater, science, politics, jurisprudence, social work, business and academia.

This is not meant as an encomium for all Jews, but rather to indicate how Jews have been able, in a relatively free and open society, to play a role far beyond the numbers in the two countries. Certainly, the emphasis on education and the drive for excellence that the immigrant families imbued into their children had much to do with this. But there is also the fact that since the founding of the republic, the economy has been relatively an open-ended one, with excess capital available to allow newcomers to join the parade. Of course, there have been recessions and depressions, and Jews have suffered as much as the general public, and yet the thrust of America has always been to expand the economy.

This may explain why there has been limited Anti-Semitism in the United States; anti-semitism rises or deflates in the same manner as the economy.

In general, America has been good for the Jewish community, as it has been good for almost every other immigrant group, with the exception of the Blacks, who originally were not really immigrants, and the Asians on the West Coast, both Chinese and Japanese. Yet, even these groups are sharing in the openness of the society.

Some statistics are needed at this point, some real and some extrapolated. Studies have shown that over 90% of all Jewish children eligible to attend college, do so. These numbers are astounding, for the numbers before World War II were about 28%, with men in the majority. 40% receive a second degree, and some 15% a third, usually the Doctor of Philosophy.

It is common understanding that major cultural events in music, theater and fine arts depend on the general support of the Jewish community. It makes little difference whether this takes place in New York City or Los Angeles, or in smaller towns such as Nashville, Portland or even Oshkosh. Almost everywhere, the Jewish community is expected to support and participate in the arts.

One should expect that Jews attend adult education classes and lectures far in excess of its numbers. This is an extremely important when the literacy of things Jewish is brought to account. For it is certain that the average Jew, unfortunately, knows very little of his or her heritage.

Nevertheless, more Jews are involved in Jewish activities than ever before; more Jews have attended religious schools, including day schools, than at any time in the past. There are more professionals and rabbis who have been trained in America than at any previous time. Many American Jews have visited Israel, often repeatedly, indicating major interest in the new State. However, surprisingly, the numbers have not been overwhelming. Thousands of children and college students have spent summers and university years there. A similar number have volunteered for public service and have even joined the military when Israel was in danger. In a period of Middle East conflict, the eyes and ears of Jewry are constantly directed to the print and broadcast media for the latest news. Compare it to the period between both world wars when there was a severe disinterest in any conflict beyond our borders.

What else is found? There is an abysmal ignorance of Jewish knowledge and understanding, not only among the children, but also among the adults, their parents, who read the Wall Street Journal as their Bible.

How is it possible that the very people who are so talented and bright in secular matters, who can split an atom, or write symphonies, analyze the most complex problems, cannot read, or want to read, a simple prayer in Hebrew, nor speak with any authority on a matter of Jewish history, nor can they handle ideas of Jewish philosophy or ideology?

Add to this the increase of intermarriage, which has created extremely difficult interpersonal problems for many Jews. Moreover, the divorce rate is approaching that of the general community, where there is almost one divorce for every marriage. And children, upon graduating college, frequently find new residences in communities at a distance from their parents. It is not unusual for Jewish parents to have each of their children living thousands of miles from home, but also separated from each other. This makes family relationships more tenuous and difficult to maintain, although the Jewish Holy Days are lovely times for a gathering of the clan, where ceremonies are secondary to the meal. Still another observation: when a child moves away from home, he or she seldom is as involved with the temple or synagogue as the parents.

The marrying generation today shows less inclination for formal association with synagogues, organizations and lodges than the preceding one. However, since many of the new generation are schooled and successful, the ideas that appeal to their implied class will have to touch them. The old institutions either have to change or fade into the past. Rabbis will no longer be able to invoke the same words which fit the immigrant population and previous generations. Most members of temples and synagogues have had more education, read more, travel more than the great bulk of rabbis. Is their membership social or religious? What will entice non-members to join?

So, an exploration as what these past 4,000 years have placed on the American Jew is offered here. First of all, it is impossible for a modern Jew, trained with the scientific analysis and method, to accept the Bible as "The Truth." There are too many contradictions and errors, which biology, astronomy, paleontology, physics, and so many other ologies have been able to disprove. But in no way does this mean that we throw out the Torah. Quite the contrary. We must do what the Maccabees and the Pharisees did over 2,000 years ago – *expand the meaning of the word Torah.*

Torah should include all of God's creation and wisdom which becomes a part and parcel of Jewish life. Too often, Judaism is thought to happen at the sanctuary of the temple or around the dinner table. Torah is practiced when a doctor saves a life through the creative means of the new medical technology. A Jew is religious when she teaches in a public school and helps a minority child climb his or her way out of desperation through education. Judaism is practiced at a glorious concert, even if no Jewish music is played, nor a Jewish musician visible. It is providing housing for those who do not have it. There are thousands of ways of practicing Judaism, including keeping kosher, for those for whom it means the world. It also means that at community functions, no Jew should be excluded because non-kosher food is served. Better no food, than that one should be discriminated against.

What seems to be necessary at this time is to first rethink a definition of what is Jewish, just as Mordecai Kaplan did some 70 years ago. Those who speak in the name of Judaism must know that, for most Jews, it matters not whether a person wears a Yarmulke or Tallit, keeps kosher or not, but rather whether he speaks and acts morally and ethically, both at the same time. Ritual and service must make sense to most young Jews. *This is the challenge.*

The Pharisees developed an ethical life, because of a philosophy that if one is good, says the right prayers at the right time and gives charity, that God would reward that person with eternal life in heaven. No matter what happened to the body, the soul of a good person would be saved at the final Yom Kippur. Today, most thinking Jews have given up that idea, yet all of the rituals of life and death are punctuated by these ideas. No wonder that our young people, and many of the older generation, are either confused or turned off. It is almost as if the Copernican Revolution never took place, never mind, the Einstein Theory, the transistor, world-wide television and telephone, the computer, democracy and all the massive changes since the Industrial Revolution.

What changes are called for? First of all, the role of the American Rabbi has become primarily that of the ritual master. He is called on more often for the *"rites de passage,"* especially marriage and death, than to help explore deep ideas for the community. He and she must come off the pulpit and become more of a democratic teacher, helping his group to explore the deeper problems of life and death. It is not enough to know how to deliver a eulogy, but much more important to find ways to discuss the implications of death, long before the gravesite is opened. The rabbi has to learn to become the professional who in many cases is more qualified to help the grieving family.

A more modern ritual needs to be made available, which does not strain the credibility of the living. What occurs after life? Using the phrases of poetry written millennia before is a one-shot program, because this seems to be the lowest common denominator in the Jewish community. Persons whose connections to a Jewish community are nil, or almost so, are entitled to the same burial ceremony as any devoted member who has participated fully. Even murderers and embezzlers are given the same treatment. Somehow, our young should know what is correct behavior and what is not.

A total revamping of our Jewish educational system is absolutely necessary. Far too much time is devoted to children in Hebrew and Sunday Schools, which seems to end precipitously at the age of thirteen with the Bar and Bat Mitzvah.

The author once proposed that all religious schools for children be closed and that Jewish education take a radically different role. We must start the Jewish education with adults, who would then have the responsibility of teaching their children at home, not in just the prescribed hours in a restricted environment. If children attend religious schools, the emphasis should be on learning to read and speak one, two, or even three of the Jewish languages: Hebrew, Yiddish and Ladino.

Teachers have always said that a language learned early in childhood stays with that child all through life as long as it is used. It is much more difficult to teach adults a new language. It makes no sense to spend so much time on Jewish holidays, when the parents do not celebrate them, and they are not a regular part of the family life.

Children should not be permitted into a religious school, unless the parents also are attending their religious classes, and be ahead (if not abreast) of their children.

Were it up to the author, no family would be allowed to join a synagogue, temple or center, unless they attend a certain number of adult classes, while being considered for membership. In fact, it would be a wonderful idea for prospective members to register for the very courses that a convert to Judaism must take to enter the fold. As it is, any Jew can walk in off the street and join any organization, knowing nothing, caring nothing, and believing in nothing. But a non-Jew who wishes to share the Jewish destiny must go through a whole ritual and study.

No wonder so many converts are more aware and concerned than those who are born to the people. The problem is more aggravated when one sees the procession of Bar Mitzvah and Bat Mitzvahs who are able to read their blessings and from the Torah as well, but the parents can only badly stumble through their Hebrew transliterated prayers. The community must move away from the child-centeredness of our institution and make Judaism or Jewishness an adult occupation.

Adult Education also must become the first priority in the Jewish community. It must be massive and critical, for while more Jewish children are attending Jewish school for some part of their life, there are fewer and fewer adults willing to discipline themselves in their past and present. Jews can no longer live off the European experience, whether religious or secular. They must use the great and vaunted intellectualism that has made the American Jew what he is today. Will the Jews accept such a discipline? One empirical example of what is possible occurred in Los Angeles in a major synagogue. Rabbi Harold Schulweis of Temple Valley Beth Shalom of

Encino, California has been able, week after week, to elevate the lives of his members, by speaking to and with them at a remarkably high intellectual level.

It is no accident that he is one of the most prominent disciples of Mordecai Kaplan. Rabbi Schulweis has inspired most of his congregation to join in Chavurot, small intimate groups of adults who study, sing, have holidays together, and who are constantly encouraged to upgrade their intellectual life through study. Most impressive was the full house of more than a thousand at the temple, when Schulweis gave a series of immensely profound lectures on Baruch Spinoza. This was Torah at the highest level.

The most difficult problem facing the Jewish community is that the present level of adult education and adult information is too little and inappropriate. A cursory overview of many bulletins of temples and organizations holding adult courses would show a surprising number of programs in Mysticism, Meditation, Kabbalah and the Zohar, while the intellectual and non-mystic courses of philosophy are hardly proscribed. When such courses are offered, the titles are so muffled that one must strain to find an intellectual approach. Obviously, the author has more than a little interest in Jews learning history. It is probably true that more Jews have a better understanding of French history or of the Renaissance in Italy than the basic facts of their own people's chronology.

How are we to overcome this Jewish illiteracy? There are *No Easy Answers,* the aptly titled book by Philip Klutznick, the past president of International B'nai Brith. But a start must be made. What is proposed is community-wide adult education programs primarily geared to answering adult questions with adult responses, or at least methods of finding some answers. Nothing is absolutely certain, and yet even scientists, who base their professional lives on the basis of more accurate estimations, still are able to operate, within recognizable bounds, without having assurance of total truth. Jews who are humanistically intellectual should be able to frame their lives in a Jewish style, without the need of surrogates advising how to say a prayer, what to do at a wedding, what are the appropriate rites at death, and know the "why" of these.

Frankly, as we have indicated previously, and to repeat, it would be better for many children not to attend religious school. My preference would be "Home Schooling," not
unlike the practice by a number of parents for general education. This would require the parents to assume some responsibility for the Jewish upbringing, which presently consists of
depositing the child at the right time at some institution, and
occasionally bringing him or her to a holiday program, hoping
the child will retain what the parent might have forgotten or
ignored or never learned. Until we get the kind of parental
support that is really meaningful, religious schools will continue
to fail.

This leads to still another subject, the whole area of
audio-visual. Quite a number of Jews get up very early in the
morning to take advantage of educational courses offered on
public television. These courses are sometimes extremely esoteric, such as "The Customs of Polynesia" or " Practical Eco-
nomics for Singles." In some cases, the local community colleges give credit for the course, upon receipt of a test taken or
a written paper.

The Jewish community has absolutely failed to take
advantage of cable television, which must offer public service
time under their contracts. What has taken place under Jewish
auspices are programs parallel to standard television broad-
casts, talk shows, news from Israel, and musical entertainment. Occasionally, there will be a program on some exotic
group such as the Kurdistani or Indian Jews. Though the programs may be conceived professionally, they add very little to
the body politic or education of the members of the Jewish
community.

Were it only possible, via closed circuit television and
radio, to develop and offer programs, to enhance the knowledge of the average intellectual Jew, courses in Jewish philosophy, liturgy, organization, identity and history should be
scheduled, using the most skilled and articulate teachers. Hebrew could easily be taught, as well as Yiddish and Ladino.
Instead of listening to Yoga lessons or Body Building, a Jewish
businessman could relax to a reading from Abraham Joshua
Heschel, followed by a discussion by an informed intellectual.
Two-way telephone, e-mail, and faxes would allow for ques-

tions and answers and even discussion. What teacher would not be excited and stimulated by receiving a call or answering on mass media a question on Spinoza? There should be talk shows totally geared to Jewish subjects and questions, and not limited to political matters.

Another possibility could come from a new phenomenon, the "Books on Tape." Yes, there have been sales of tapes of major addresses and discussions at conventions, but some teacher or rabbi should experiment with the idea of sending a tape or lecture out to the congregation, with the idea that the subject would be the basis of a discussion at a later date. The speech could be easily be prepared by some expert in his field, which may not be the particular field of the rabbi or teacher. Copies could be sent to college students, most of whom have a tape recorder and could be, if parents are alert and aware to the times, vehicles across generations. Wouldn't it be thrilling if parents could discuss with their children in a dialogue beyond, the subjects of classes, grades, expenses, and dates?

Still another new program in the Jewish community has been the increasing interest in the search for family records and genealogy. Those who have become involved with searching their own family roots have found an unusual tree, for they have also touched a good part of Jewish history. It is now very possible to learn more about our great-grandparents and with the lengthening of the span of life, it is probable that many of us will be great-grandparents. Thus many of the present generation will have shared a part of seven generations. Since there have been approximately 100 generations since David, some of us will have touched 7% of Jewish history, and it will not seem too distant to young Jews.

There has been a tremendous increase of intermarriages, with many of those not born Jewish choosing to join their fate with ours. Although we have in some communities, especially the larger ones, organized programs for these situations, they depend on the leadership of Reform and Conservative leaders. In all cases heretofore, the question of faith has become a necessity for the one coming into the fold. Seldom has there been the same requirement for the Jewish member. Mordecai Kaplan suggested years ago that there ought to be a registry of Jews, where anyone wishing to remain a Jew in a

free society would have the choice to sign the registry or simply leave. Although this seems almost dream-like, there is a
kernel of truth. As long as Jews can be Jews by not being
something else, there is no call to find a definition, personal or
communal.

It is time for Jewish organizations to make more than
a financial demand on their members. What is proposed here
is that some sort of commitment be made by those wishing to
be a part of the Jewish future. For example, we might require,
as the Mormons do for two years, a term of service to the
Jewish community. Or an agreement by adults to follow a long-
term program of study, aiming at some sort of certification,
such as a credential to teach other adults or serve in religious
schools in communities where there simply are not enough Jewish teachers.

Another possibility would be hands-on social action in
areas of poorer Jewish neighborhoods. Possibly there is a need
for something similar to what former President Jimmy Carter
created, the Habitat program, for building housing for young
married Jews. These should be placed near enough to Jewish
temples, so that there would be a natural affinity, and if the
young couple helped in the building, they would share the excitement.

Other programs could be developed in which support
could be given to young married couples, before they have
children, to spend time in Israel, learn Hebrew, develop a feeling for the breadth of Jewish life, and have a warm relationship to world Jewry.

There must be hundreds of projects that could be developed, depending on the physical area, the resources, and
the willingness to experiment. The important kernel is that whatever is done, the adult education facets must be inherent. This
is not simply social welfare, with the rich supporting the needy.
The whole Jewish community is needy. This time the need is
for education, justification, and stimulation.

In Los Angeles, the center of the entertainment industry, hundreds of brilliant and creative Jews can hardly find their
role in the future of Jewish life. True, there are three synagogues of the arts here, but, mostly, the programs are looking
back to New York or Chicago, not to the future. If someone

could only embrace these massive talents, direct their minds, hearts and energies to develop a new vision of American Jewry, based on a comprehensive knowledge of the past, we would soar! It would not be created by the many self-hating Jews who appear on comedy shows, trying to recreate the Catskills, but rather by sensitive, progressive and socially concerned positive Jews who can apply their talents to this area.

Think what great writers might do to plot the way, or fine musicians who might follow up what Leonard Bernstein did in a number of instances with Jewish texts. Certainly, there are thousands of means to add to the future, and thus make the present more meaningful.

Since this final chapter is being written during a very special time in Israel, where the concept of peace is being actively and publicly pursued, a word about the relationship between American Jews and Israel should be added. Since World War II and the Holocaust, the Jewish community has been involved naturally with the saving of remnants of our people. First it was those who were in the camps, then it was Israel itself, in its attempt to deal both with wars and the absorption of the many who had to or wanted to be a part of that miracle of the twentieth century. Then it was the Jews of the western Arab countries, those of the eastern Arab sphere, as well as the Yemenite Jews, the Russian Jews, and then the Falasha Jews, all brought back to the homeland. Without massive help from American Jews, plus the great support, financially and politically of the American people, Israel would not be in as favorable position as it is now.

Great institutions have developed there, with worldwide reputations. The universities, and scientific organizations rank well with their peers around the world. The aid that Israel has given to countries in Africa, Asia, and Central and South America is remarkable, a story that essentially has not been told properly, or at all. Israel, while on the road to peace, must budget much of its taxes for the military, as long as armed conflicts are still possible.

In the United States and Canada, billions have been raised to lend, give and invest in Israel, again properly so. However, the time has come to devote more energies to the American communities, which are all in desperate shape structurally.

The number of people entering the Jewish education field is decreasing. The Federations are not able to raise the sort of money that they did in the past. Temples are having difficulties as the war generation is reduced each day, either by inevitable death or simply by moving to retirement communities, and quite frankly. because there is not the same sense or vigor that was available after the war with Hitler. On the other hand, there has been a revitalization of the Orthodox community, at the very same time that science has reached more and more advancements.

If one can be foolish enough to predict about the American Jewish community, there will be three main groups, each less and less in communication with the others. The Orthodox will remain a separate and separatist group, who have the righteous attitude of "True Believers." Funded now almost totally by refugees and later immigrants, their financial base will decline.

The Conservative movement will eventually split on ideological grounds. It has done so already on the rabbinical level, with forward-looking rabbis proposing new ideas on ritual, laws and other matters, which the Reform movement, by and large, had already accepted long before. As more women join the rabbinate in the Conservative movement, they still will not be universally accepted, whether they have been ordained at the seminary or not. (Seminarian leadership has not completely favored women rabbis.)

Except in a few unusual cases, the children of Conservative Temples are not coming back to their "shul." They are voting with their feet, either by joining Reform temples, or returning to one or another form of Orthodoxy. Indeed, many of the most talented are making "aliyah" to Israel, feeling that only there can they practice authentic Judaism.

Reform Judaism is also suffering pains, for it, too, is having great difficulty holding onto its young people. It suffers because so many of its adherents today are not the shopkeepers, bankers, and other self-employed entrepreneurs who built a business or practice to which children could join, when they were old enough. Today, it is unusual for the children of members of temples to join their parents' synagogue, for they truly are the "Wandering Jews." Because Reform children are usually from the more affluent, the probability is that children of members will attend college for two or three degrees and finally reside in a city a distance from their family.

Under such circumstances, the future for individual temples in the Reform orbit is not too favorable. As the author is and has been involved with the Reform movement for over forty years, he obviously is more concerned with its future. Many of the major temples hold onto their base of membership by creating satellite temples and schools. Others have and are creating day schools, including high schools. Nevertheless, it seems obvious that the Reform Movement will have to move into some new areas which will encourage their members' children, attaching themselves as liberal or progressive Jews. Were the author clairvoyant and had the power, his suggestion would be that a class of membership be established on the national level, with the temples being connected in a looser federation, serving areas, rather than a particular membership group.

The last suggestion was meant to allow Jews of liberal persuasion to identify with the movement, rather than to the institution where their children attend. It might also encourage some of the almost 50% of American Jews who do not affiliate with a religious institution to do so. Of course, there are Jews who are anti-religious, or who really do not care one way or another. The Jewish community must find ways and means to bring them closer.

If any group will touch the information-highway in a Jewish way, it will be the Reform grouping. The movement is still the most creative of the three branches and the least bound to tradition. As more and more of the following generation become computer friendly, they will turn to the internet for basic information. If many people turn to websites for all sort of esoteric news and other programs, does it not make sense that some group in the Jewish community try to expand its arena through the same source?

If the chavurot program, such as Rabbi Schulweis has fostered so beautifully in his congregation, were to use e-mail and faxes to join other chavurot all over the world, it would help to create the sense of unity that is more needed today than ever before.

So, having placed this panoply of history for those who have taken the time and energy to read through this book, it is necessary to do what all scientists do well, if they are success-ful. The author has placed a field of hypotheses and theories to explain the causes for what has occurred, and to build on these facts an explanation of the past and the present, and to offer thoughts and suggestions for the future.

The singular purpose was to stimulate and view Jew-ish history in a new light. This book represents more than a generation of searching, teaching and working *in* and *for* the Jewish community.